The Ecology of the Soul

A Manual of Peace, Power and Personal Growth for Real People in the Real World

The Ecology of the Soul

A Manual of Peace, Power and Personal Growth for Real People in the Real World

Aidan Walker

BOOKS

Winchester, UK
Washington, USA

First published by O-Books, 2016
O-Books is an imprint of John Hunt Publishing Ltd., Laurel House, Station Approach,
Alresford, Hants, SO24 9JH, UK
office1@jhpbooks.net
www.johnhuntpublishing.com

For distributor details and how to order please visit the 'Ordering' section on our website.

ISBN: 978 1 78279 850 7
Library of Congress Control Number: 2015946137

A CIP catalogue record for this book is available from the British Library.

Design: Stuart Davies

Printed and bound by CPI Group (UK) Ltd, Croydon, CR0 4YY, UK

CONTENTS

To Baba

Part I

Introduction

About this book

This book draws a parallel between the outer ecology of the earth and the inner ecology of the human spirit, seeing the 'balance of Nature' in a spiritual as well as a physical sense. *The Ecology of the Soul* is about self transformation. You're here because you want to change yourself for the better, to achieve that inner peace and power that you know to be your natural state of being, but which right now feels very far away.

There are already a myriad of books telling you how to become the person you want to be, how to have whatever you want – how to become happier, richer, thinner, how to gain love, wealth, success, profound and lasting contentment – how, in short, to overcome your personal circumstances and short-comings and turn yourself into a peaceful, powerful, prosperous, highly-evolved human being. Generally, their message boils down to gaining control of your mind. Some of them talk about a global awakening of consciousness and humanity's readiness for that evolutionary change, and most of them address the spiritual dimension, in that to change yourself for the better you have to understand yourself, by which I mean, your 'Self', your true, essential nature. And to do that you have to pay attention to what's going on inside your head, to spend time in 'intro-spection', which leads very quickly to an awareness that there is much more to your essential Self than just what's happening at the mind level. Call it spirit, call it Soul. You can't embark on a journey of self change without awakening to the relationship between the physical and the non-physical – the spiritual – and indeed accepting the existence of the non-physical.

One of the basic facts of human existence is that there is always a dissatisfaction, an awareness that things – we ourselves and our circumstances – could be better. No one on this earth at this time can rightly say that they are completely fulfilled because that means perfection, and perfection is impossible in an imperfect world. You wouldn't disagree that the world is imperfect, right? Could be better, right?

So if we have at least established that 'most people' feel there is something lacking, somewhere in their lives, either in their own personal makeup or in their situation (usually both), then we have established that there is a need to fix it. Whether you personally accept the existence of that need and choose to do something about it is entirely up to you. If you do, you are not alone. There are millions out there like you, which explains why self-help, self-transformation and self-improvement books sell in their millions, why religion is still powerful and meaningful, and why there are so many courses and classes teaching yoga, meditation, t'ai chi ch'uan – a vast range of self-transformational or semi-spiritual, or even properly spiritual, knowledge and practices that demand you focus on your inner space.

Why Ecology?

Yes, but what does this have to do with Ecology? The imperative for sustainability, going green, the environment, saving the pandas, the rainforests, the oceans, the whales, the planet? Why is the book called *The Ecology of the Soul*?

Because ecology is an inner as well as an outer phenomenon. The word is made up of two Greek words – 'eco' means 'home,' and 'logos' means wisdom, knowledge or words. The Wisdom of Home. If our inner ecology is in balance and harmony, our behavior and hence outer ecology become balanced and harmonious. We can't change our behavior without changing our thoughts, because thought creates action. It's that crucial link that 'most people' miss, and that this book concentrates on: how to change our thinking to make the practical change in behavior by which we become the inhabitants of the new world.

For make no mistake, the new world is definitely coming. We

aren't all going to die out. It's our very instinct for survival that ultimately makes us embrace the idea of the new world; if we don't make the profound and powerful changes in ourselves – for that is really all we have power over – then we're part of the outgoing system, which is doomed. No question.

Understanding the Ecology of the Soul – the balance of our inner ecosystem of mental and spiritual powers – gives us a set of principles for thought and action that help prepare us for what's coming. It empowers us to change into the kind of people we need to be, both to make our way through the last stages of the old world, and to help make the new.

The fact that there are people – and companies – working on new socioeconomic models such as the 'Triple Bottom Line' and 'Eco-Capitalism' gives us hope; and with that hope, we can turn to the only thing that we do know for sure we have power to change – ourselves. A socioeconomic system, after all, is made up of the people that created it, that live in it and by it, and once those people change and start demanding things that the old system can't supply, then that system changes. We ourselves are the drivers, the building blocks. We're at the beginning of the change process, not the end. Can't change the outward world unless and until we change our inner selves.

A bit about me

Who am I, and why should you be interested in what I have to say, specifically? My own personal journey has taken me through a number of phases in my life, each one of which has added to previous experience and all of which are now contributing to the creation of this psycho-spiritual system, and to the writing of this book.

I was born in the grimy, depressed and war-ravaged industrial northeast of post-World War II England, the son of a Church of England priest, a clever and thoughtful but withdrawn and deeply unhappy man. His beliefs and spiritual desires were so at odds with his own abilities and the institution to which he had devoted them that he was driven into profound clinical depression. He identified with the Church, the Church was moribund and my father was in pain. His marriage too was miserable. My mother succumbed to what was then known as a 'breakdown', partly because of the strain on their marriage and partly because both my parents were brought up in the pre-Second World War English middle class, where a 'stiff upper lip' and a willful ignorance, a refusal to acknowledge structural problems of personality and relationships, were the norm, if not an actual requirement. It was all about keeping up appearances. The conflict between what she thought ought to be happening and what was actually happening, and her efforts to fool herself, to pretend that all was as it should be, drove her to become a patient in the same mental hospital where she worked, and where my father was also a patient.

It so happened that it was that same mental hospital, in Powick in Worcestershire, UK, in which two pioneering psychiatrists, Ronald Sandison and Arthur Spencer, had set up an experimental psychiatric treatment program based on the use of lysergic acid diethylamide (LSD) in the early 1950s. I was very alive to my father's debates and discussions with his friends and colleagues about how new thinking about the nature of God, mind and spirit could be accommodated in the Church (they were threatened and enthralled by the Bishop of Woolwich John Robinson's *Honest to God*, published in 1963). Also, literally as soon as I was confirmed into the Church of England at the age of 16 I began to question its tenets and its relevance. I was already aware that there were other ways of understanding the workings of the spirit and the psyche than those with which I had been brought up. The Christian way, as administered by the Church of England, just didn't cut it for me.

One school vacation that same year I was confirmed, I spent a week in Powick looking at what was going on. I was interested in the work of another pioneering psychiatrist, RD Laing, whose book *The Divided Self* (1960) was at the time provoking a whole new understanding of schizophrenia, and whose *Sanity, Madness and the Family* (1964) had acute relevance to my own later experience. It is also significant that by the time he reached *The Politics of Experience and The Bird of Paradise* in 1967, Laing's work – to me, anyway, a 16 year old on the brink of the New Age revolution – seemed to demonstrate a clear connection between 'altered' mental states and spirituality. Hence my interest in LSD as a medicine, just at the time it was entering popular culture as a recreational or 'creational' drug. Let's just say that in the day I spent on the Powick LSD ward I saw more humane healing than I did anywhere else in that godforsaken place.

This is not an autobiography. Suffice it to say that whatever sort of 'awakening' that began at Powick led me to travel, both to the US and India, fast becoming more and more aware of the importance of the spiritual dimension in my life. I went up to Cambridge University to study History, and there I took up a lifelong practice of Hatha Yoga, which I later taught. In the mid-1970s I spent six years of intense meditation and spiritual practice – 4am meditation every day of the year, radical vegetarianism, celibacy, renunciation of the material trappings of 'normal' life, commitment to service – as member of an institution rejoicing in the Hindi name 'Brahma Kumaris Ishwariya Vishwa Vidyalaya', literally translated as 'The World Spiritual University of the Virgin Daughters of Brahma'. Their teaching is Raja Yoga, the single most influential and seminal philosophy that defines this book's understanding and experience of the Soul.

Parallel with this, after taking my history degree from Cambridge, I did what was then much more common than it is now, and became a carpenter and cabinetmaker. That taught me the nature and the value of craftsmanship and led me to an awareness of design, and eventually to writing and editing magazines about it. That has been my profession for more than 20 years. The 'full circle' part of it is that the design process can be applied to our path of self transformation, our journey to enlightenment. We design ourselves, create ourselves. Or in this case, re-create ourselves.

A question of habit

You will probably have gathered by now that this book is not an academic project. I haven't studied learned text after learned text, though part of the reason why I talk about myself is to persuade you that my experience and study, such as they have been, have brought me to a comparatively coherent synthesis of the concepts of mind and Soul, and of the ramifications of action, of power, peace and inner stillness. It's an understanding I've been working on all my adult life.

Not to be academic, but I will quote you a paper written as long ago as 1994 by a very dear friend of mine called Guy Claxton, an educational psychologist and cognitive scientist, for the academic journal *Environmental Values*. Entitled "Involuntary Simplicity: Changing Dysfunctional Habits of Consumption," it suggests that "some methodologies of self-transformation associated with spiritual traditions such as Buddhism may have much to offer the environmental movement."

'Voluntary simplicity' is an idea that goes back to 1936 and is the subject of Duane Elgin's book of the same name from 1981,[1] saying essentially that we can't change habits of consumption without changing our belief systems. But where Guy's proposition did it for me is the concept of habit as *involuntary* action. It's a strange idea that much of our action is involuntary, ie performed in a state of unknowing, or at least, unthinking. But think about it. That's what habit is, right? Things that you do without having to think. To change, you have to get inside, change your mental habits, your spiritual processes; and then our habitat changes as a matter of course. That's what this book is about.

The Seven Powers, Power Seeds and the Magic Minute

The following chapters lay out the Seven Powers on which the Ecology of the Soul is based. Each power comes with seven Meditations, frameworks to transform your consciousness for new thinking, new awareness and new actions. By focusing on these separate aspects of the power, you gain a deep understanding of how it works within and outside you, and as your awareness reawakens, you find yourself going deeper and deeper through layers of insight. These are powerful concepts, and you can't expect to plumb their depths all at once. We are creating a way of life here, after all. Discover that these powers are already within you. The way to reconnect to them and bring them into your daily life is blindingly simple. All you have to do is think about them.

One: The Power of Nature
Silence
Centeredness
Self organization
Inwardness
Aggression
Resilience
Dispassion – Detachment

Two: The Power of Creativity
Reproduction
Joy
Enthusiasm
Imagination
Transformation
Self Creation
World Creation

Three: The Power of Endurance

Acceptance

Persistence

Faith

Hope

Optimism

Serenity

Stillness

Four: The Power of Love

Commitment

Excitement

Ownership

Passion

Spirit

Energy

Responsibility

Five: The Power of Communication

Listening

Speaking

Open mindedness

Seeing others

Seeing your Self

Seeing the Beauty

Vision, Purpose, Goals

Six: The Power of Focus

Accuracy

Compartmentalization

Concentration

Craftsmanship

Determination

Clarity

The practical stuff comes at the end of each Chapter, in the form of mini-meditations or 'Power Seeds' of thought that you plant in your mind. (We also go through the yoga poses of Salute to the Sun and the Chakras.) All it needs to start is a single minute in your day. I'm calling it your 'Magic Minute', because it's 60 silent and powerful seconds you devote entirely and exclusively to transforming yourself – your Self. Those 60 seconds will probably turn into 120, for the simple reason that as soon as you start trying to control your mind and make it do what you want, it refuses to lie down and be quiet and jumps up and runs about like a naughty child. You have to find a minute of silence, in a state of mind that is entirely inward looking. What you don't have to do is lock yourself away from the world in a specially prepared meditation room, with a cushioned floor, low lights, joss sticks and sound recordings of whales or waves.

See your mind as a garden, or at least a patch of fertile soil. Thoughts and feelings grow in it, like plants. Currently it's a riot of tangled and intertwined mental vegetation; much of it good and useful – and most of it neither good nor useful.

Plant Power Seeds to grow a new garden of consciousness – Soul Consciousness – and change your actions. They are a bit like the Zen 'kōan' (eg 'the sound of one hand clapping') that kick your mind out of gear and raise the level of your awareness. You can't be – or act – greedy, angry, jealous, anxious, depressed or hostile when you're Soul Conscious – alive to the knowledge of your Self as an infinitesimal pinpoint of conscient light and life, burning steadily without consuming itself, giving off the vibration, the spiritual energy, of peace, power and love.

When you drive your activity from that Soul Conscious level, your actions and perceptions are more aligned with your true Self. As you become more and more aware of the true nature of that true Self, it becomes clear which thoughts and attitudes arise from the mistaken sense of Self – the 'body consciousness' that identifies your Self with your physical body, appearance, roles, relationships and material circumstances. You are not your body. You live in the center of your body's forehead and use your brain to drive your body.

The task, then, seems to be to identify negative and counter-productive thoughts and weed them out as if you were preparing your plot to plant a new crop – which, in a way, is exactly what you are doing. But you'll find that, like the most persistent of weeds, those thoughts tend to stay, or spring back; they are deep-rooted. Without noticing it, your mind is back on that familiar track of struggle: anxiety, depression, frustration, anger, whatever negative state it might be. Same with actions, habits. So it comes as a pleasant surprise that you don't have to struggle with the weeds. All you have to do is plant your mental plot with new seeds – Power Seeds – which grow into thought, attitude and feeling, which grow into action. Which feeds back to you and creates new thought and feeling; and lo and behold, you have created a new mental and spiritual garden. And a new framework for your behavior.

The Technique

You need an undisturbed space and an undisturbed 60 seconds or more – go on, go wild, make it two minutes. It's better to be sitting. You mustn't be doing things; you can't do this while you're driving, but you can do it in a traffic block (as long as you can see you won't be moving for at least a minute. Or two.). Or on the bus or train, or waiting for the bus, or at your desk (as long as you have turned off your phone), or even in the bathroom. In fact, the bathroom might be quite a good place, because it's a retreat. You're allowed to lock the door. Just make yourself that space and time.

Leave action behind. Settle. Close your eyes. Turn your attention inside. Listen to your breathing. Make it sound inside your head, right where the nasal passage connects to the windpipe. It's at the top/back of your nose/throat, the patch where snoring or snorting happens. You don't want to be sounding like a warthog, though; it's a little trick of focusing on the spot where the moving air makes contact with the sides of the airway. You can hear it inside your head, a hollow sound, a bit like the operating theatre scene in a movie when all you can hear is the in-out of the breathing apparatus. You listen to your breathing.

Turn your attention, which is constantly focusing on all the things outside you that you are doing or that need doing, on your Self. Pay attention to your own mind (that idea in itself is a Power Seed), and detach from the activity in it. It is not You. Watch the thoughts float through it. Listen to your chatter, then relinquish it. Introduce a Power Seed and contemplate it, in the mental quiet you have created. Here are some samples:

Sample Power Seeds

You the Soul are conscient, self-aware. You are an indivisible, unique unit of consciousness.
You are a pinpoint of light.

Energy is power.
You are energy, but energy is not you.
Are you breathing? Then you are making and using energy.

Are you thinking? Feeling? Dreaming? It's energy.
Our personal energy crisis is that we are disconnected from our internal power.
To connect, go inside.

You the Soul, being no more nor less than energy, are incapable of being destroyed and therefore of being created. But self exploration, acquiring self knowledge, is the ultimate creative act.
Create your Self.

A good meditation is a perfect balance.
You sit on a wellspring, a source of power.
You balance on top of it, like a ping pong ball on a jet of water.
But in that balance is stillness, silence, peace.
You aren't bobbing about like the ping pong ball; you are floating on a cushion of glow.
Perfect balance.

Create a beautiful mind.

Design yourself.
Redesign your Self.

Light. You are light.
When you experience yourself as light, you are enlightened.
You enter delight.
This is enlightenment.

Saluting the Sun, Asanas and Chakras

Although you don't *have* to practice yoga as part of the study of the Ecology of the Soul, each chapter includes a detailed explanation of one of the seven asanas or positions of Surya Namaskar, the 'Salute to the Sun'. Use it to explore one aspect of the practice of hatha yoga, which is useful and relevant to the process of balancing your internal ecology. Sooner or later we see the link between spiritual and physical health – balance – and realize the need to treat mind, body and spirit as a single interlinked system – an ecosystem. But you don't need to commit to hours a day to benefit from these notes; in fact it's not mandatory that you practice at all.

The reason why we are looking through yoga eyes at this point is because it gives you direct experience of mind, body and spirit, or Soul, at work interacting and affecting each other. It will help you kick-start your awareness of the energy that is your silent, powerful Self. By merely physical action, you still your mind. If you do practice yoga but only as physical exercise for health and flexibility, now's the time to make the connection to its mental and spiritual realm and use it as a way of uplifting your consciousness. That, after all, is what it is meant for. If you study T'ai chi ch'uan, meditation or any other discipline that focuses your inner awareness, demanding and creating inner stillness, then you will already know what you are trying to do. They all have the mental/spiritual element because most of them are based on the same understanding of the subtle energy flow in the body; the same understanding which underpins Chinese medicine, the chakras and a host of other esoteric knowledge systems.

Practice one of them to know and love the difference between your physical and spiritual self, and to allow them to work in harmony with each other. Yoga happens to be the one I know, and the one from which I have learned the value of letting go. Just as you can't force your muscles to stretch, you can only let them go, so you can't force your mind to relax, to be still. You can only let it go.

'Surya Namaskar', the 'Salute to the Sun', is the template for a basic yoga experience, a beginner's course if you like. Something you can do every day without completely rewriting your life.

There are of course numerous versions. The one we work on here is my individual take, the result of many years of study and practice of the BKS Iyengar system of Hatha Yoga, including working with the Master himself. His *Light on Yoga* (HarperCollins, 2001), originally published in the 60s, is still the preeminent text for serious students. This version has seven asanas, the practice of each one of which is explained in detail at the end of each one of the 'Power' chapters. But some of them repeat as you go through the sequence, so there are actually twelve 'position moments', periods (ideally of seven deep breaths) when you are holding each asana. And when it is holding you.

As with your Magic Minute, you need to make yourself a personal, private space in the day. Unlike your Magic Minute, it needs a minimum of about five minutes. Best to try and stitch them together, steal six or seven minutes for yourself and make the two contemplative practices feed each other.

Obviously, since it's Salute to the Sun, that five minutes ought to be first thing in the morning. You are greeting and celebrating the new day from the consciousness of your powerful, peaceful, inner Self, and it's a great way of setting yourself up for the day, especially if you have managed to get your Magic Minute in too – but that may not be possible. Even if you get up five, ten or 15 minutes earlier it might not work. Too much rush, too many things to think about, you can't give it the slow, contemplative attitude it needs. No matter. Find a time in the day that you can make for yourself, and do it then. Just before bed when everyone else is asleep can work very well, as long as you haven't been partying wildly; if that's the case, leave it out for tonight. If you do manage to fit it into your morning routine, don't launch straight into it as you literally put your feet on the floor; go to the bathroom, brush your teeth, drink a glass of water, shake your arms and legs to warm up a bit, get yourself generally ready while keeping the quiet, inward focused state of mind.

The asanas in the 12 steps are:

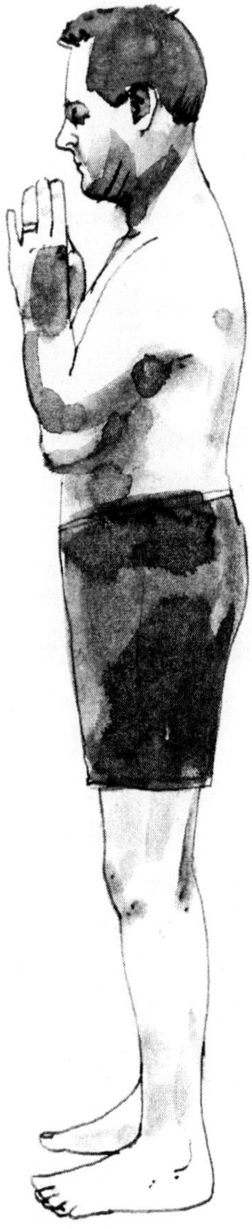

1 Standing Prayer (Tadasana 1): The Power of Nature

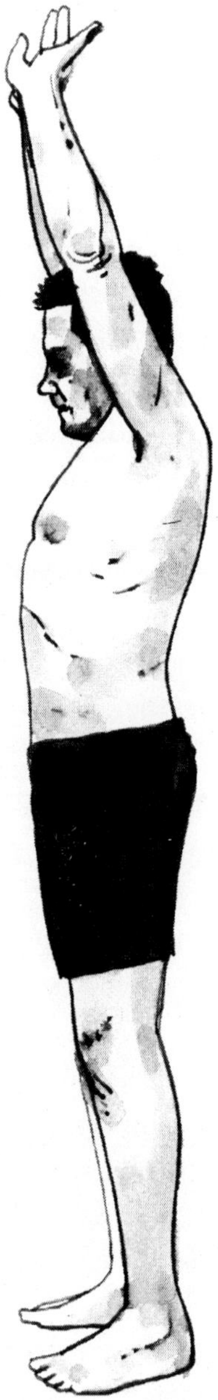

2 Extended Mountain (Tadasana 2): also The Power of Nature

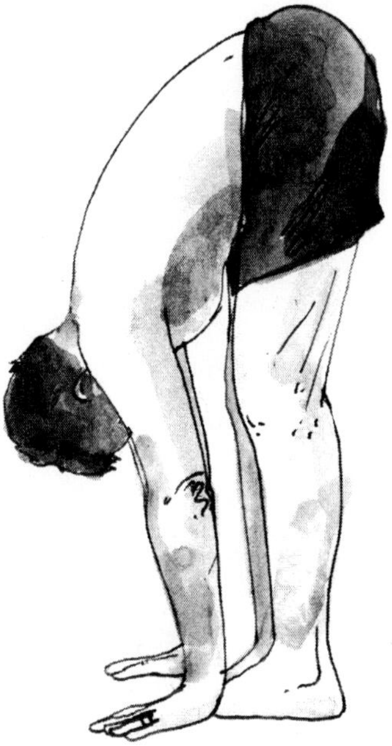

3 Forward Bend (Uttanasana): The Power of Creativity

4 Lunge (right leg forward. I can't find the Sanskrit name for this one. It may not be a traditional yoga position at all): The Power of Endurance

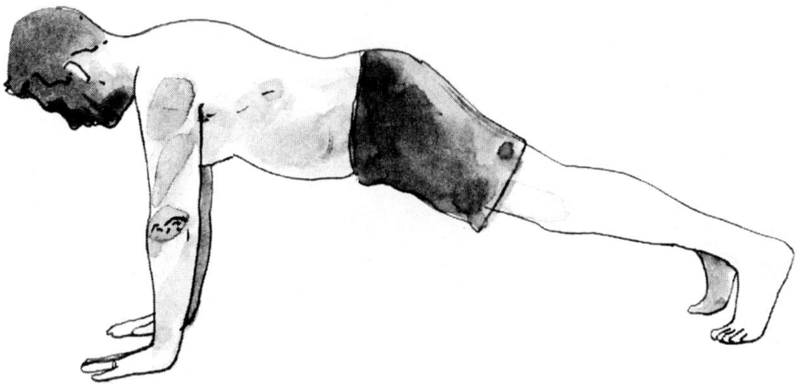

5 Plank (Chaturanga Dandasana): The Power of Love

6 Dog (Adho Mukha Svanasana): The Power of Communication

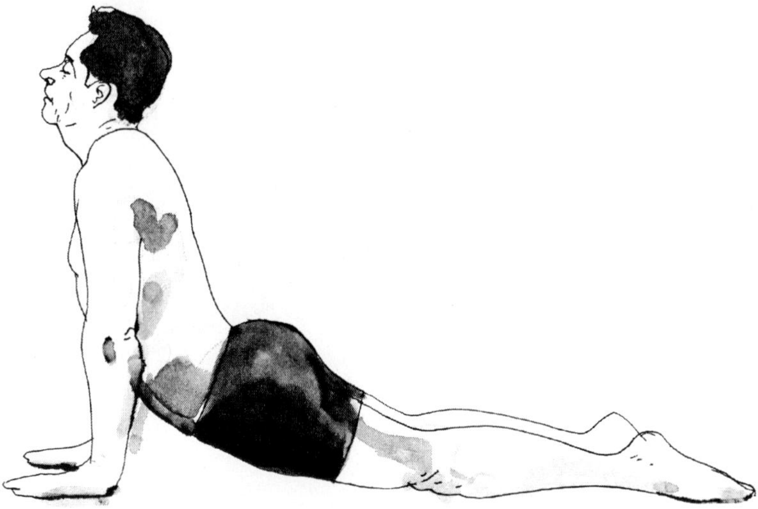

7 Cobra (Bhujangasana): The Power of Focus

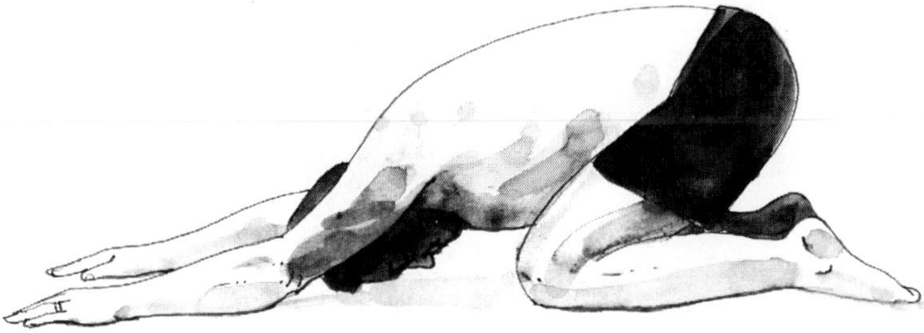

8 Child (Balasana): The Power of Connection

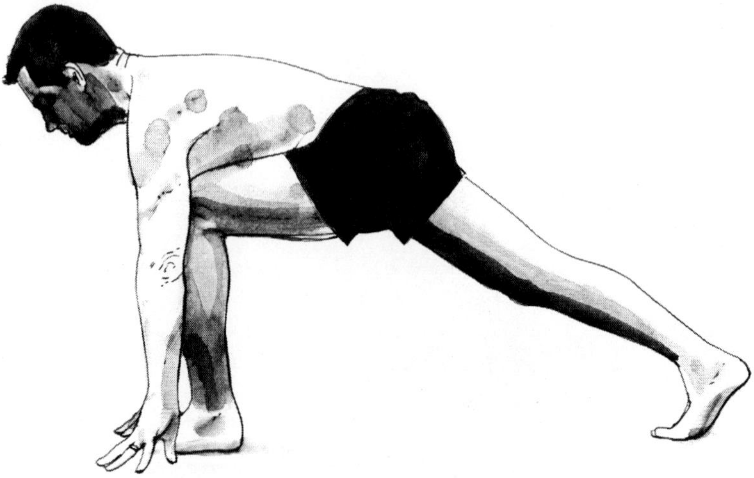

9 Lunge (left leg forward): as above

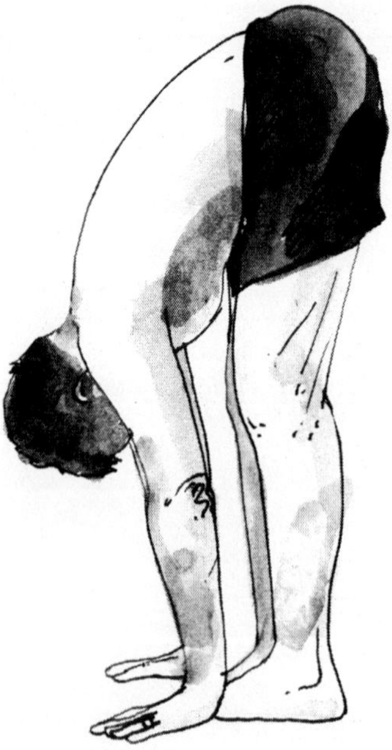

10 Forward Bend (Uttanasana): as above

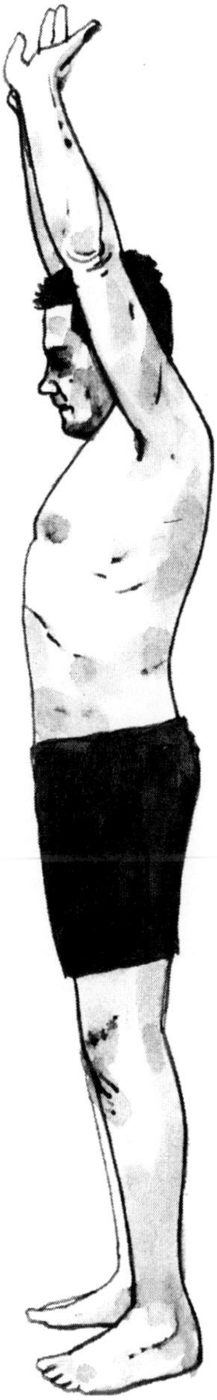

11 Extended Mountain (Tadasana 2): as above

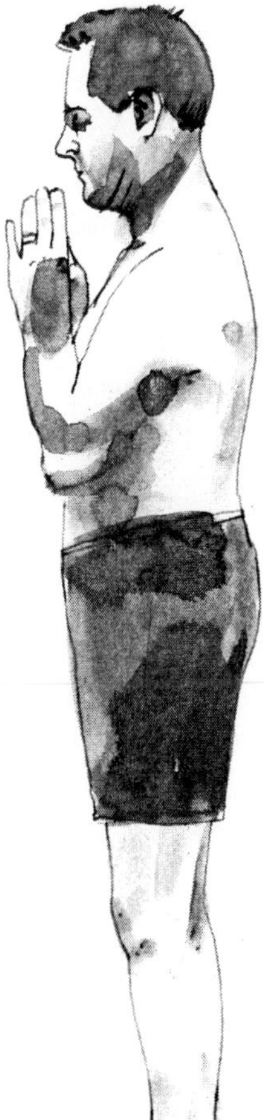

12 Standing Prayer (Tadasana 1): as above

A Note on the Chakras

My yoga practice has been given a notional shot in the arm by concentrating on the chakra centers of 'subtle' energy (in between physical and spiritual) while holding each asana, an additional source of inner focus and a definite help in keeping the attention on the channels of Prān or Ch'i in the body – which feed back directly to the mind and spirit. They also fit uncannily neatly into the Ecology of the Soul's seven spiritual powers.

I spent about two years thinking about the Powers, how many there are and what they are. It came down to seven – you know, days of the week – maybe I should structure the book as a 'mental/spiritual breakfast', a food-for-thought manual to dip into every day. Seven is also a beautiful number, lucky for many, and with many resonances. Of course I was familiar with the chakras, but I swear, honest to God, I didn't research them again until long after I had settled on the seven powers. When I did look at them, I was astonished and uplifted to find that the seven powers of this spiritual ecology are more or less directly equivalent to each of the seven chakras.

You probably know the chakras, or at least know about them. Essentially they are understood as 'hubs', nodes of subtle energy in the body that have an effect on, and are affected by, specific areas of your physical, mental, emotional and spiritual being. Having at least a passing acquaintance with them really helps you make the leap from physical to non-physical experience, because you start right there at a specific part of your physical body, focus on it and very soon become aware of its subtle link to spiritual energy. The image of the meditator with all seven of his or her chakras lit up and glowing is a powerful and profoundly compelling one. Kundalini yoga is a kind of meditation which focuses on the power of the chakras, awakening the 'energy snake' inside you. But we don't have to go there – not yet, anyway.

This is how the chakras and the seven spiritual powers work together:

1. The Power of Nature
Muladhara, the base or root chakra, governs sexuality, stability, sensuality, and courage, stamina and spiritual security.

2. The Power of Creativity
Svadhisthana is either the sacral or the spleen chakra, depending on where you look. It governs sexual desire, reproduction, creativity, joy, harmony and spiritual enthusiasm.

3. The Power of Endurance
Manipura, the solar plexus chakra, 'honors the life force', the Ch'i. It governs digestion, personal power, expansiveness, and spiritual growth.

4. The Power of Love
Anahata, the heart chakra, governs circulation, unconditional love for the self and others, passion and devotion.

5. The Power of Communication

Vishuddha, the throat chakra, governs communication, independence, fluent thought, and a spiritual sense of security.

6. The Power of Focus

Ajna, the brow chakra, or 'third eye', 'honors the psychic'. It governs the balance of the higher and lower selves, trusting inner guidance, intuition, visual consciousness and clarity.

7. The Power of Connection

Sahasrara, the crown chakra, 'honors spiritual connectedness'. It deals with the release of karma, meditation, universal consciousness and unity, 'beingness'. 'Connection' in this case means linking your consciousness to a higher one, which many call God. Right now all you need to do for a start is link your consciousness to your own higher consciousness – to see, understand and experience yourself as a Soul. Connection and connectedness also refer to community and communality, our sense of interdependence, of belonging to one organic whole.

An understanding of the chakras, like the practice of yoga, isn't necessary. But it helps. How you can reawaken your own personal powers is the subject of this book, and, I hope, the inspiration for a new way of life based on mental and spiritual harmony, inner peace and profound fulfilment. The payoff is very practical. It's about doing. But we can't fix the doing until we fix the being (no do-be-do-be-do jokes, please). So that's where we start. Enjoy.

---

1 *Voluntary Simplicity: Toward a way of life that is outwardly simple, inwardly rich,* by Duane Elgin. Quill (William Morrow), 1981, revised 1998. ISBN-10: 9780688129; ISBN-13: 978-9780688127

Part II:

The Seven Spiritual Powers

Chapter 1

The Power of Nature

Muladhara, the base or root Chakra

In this chapter:
Introduction
Silence
'Centered-ness' – 'Is-ness'
Self organization
Inwardness
Aggression
Resilience
Dispassion – Detachment
Power Seeds for Thought
The Salute to the Sun: Standing Prayer and Extended Mountain (Tadasana 1 and 2)

> Adopt the pace of nature: her secret is patience.
> *Ralph Waldo Emerson*

> If you wish to know the divine, feel the wind on your face and the warm sun on your hand.
> *Buddha*

Introduction

The seven powers arrange themselves in the same bottom-to-top order as the chakras, the nodes of subtle energy in the body that represent, among other things, gateways or transition points to higher consciousness. We are starting, therefore, at the bottom and working our way to the top, which is how the kundalini energy does it, up from the base of the spine and out through the crown of the head. The progression, in most of the traditional understanding of the chakras, is from matter to non-matter, entirely physical to entirely spiritual.

Which is why the Power of Nature is associated with the root chakra, the one that keeps you grounded. But as you'd expect, and as we shall see, the Power of Nature is in no way a simply and exclusively physical power. Not when it comes to the Ecology of the Soul, anyway. One of the traditional ways in which the chakras are understood maintains that Muladhara at the base is concerned exclusively with matter, seen as 'condensed or gross consciousness'. Which is a common vision of creation, maintaining that every single physical thing, right down to atoms (quarks and neutrinos, even?), is consciousness in some form, leading to the prevalent belief in the omnipresence of God, or spiritual energy, call it what you will. Chakras are called 'nodes of subtle energy in the body', or, more significantly, 'energy points or nodes in the subtle body', which gives us a clue: gurus, teachers, thinkers, philosophers and meditators through the ages have blurred the lines between spiritual and physical, or even claim that there is no such line. Although that conjunction has power and endurance, it doesn't work for the Ecology of the Soul. Soul is soul, Soul is spirit, each and every single Soul is individual, indivisible, indestructible, eternal. Matter is also eternal and indestructible, but it changes form. It is energy, but it is not spiritual energy. It is not consciousness, however gross or subtle, condensed or expanded.

But we do 'feel the flow'. So the physical energy of which we speak graduates to subtle energy when we experience it as Prān, Ch'i, the life force. It is the energy that is life, not directly felt in a piece of wood or other inert but living things (until you set them on fire, for instance), but definitely felt passing up and down our body's energy channels, or meridians, in yoga, t'ai chi, meditation or any one of the host of other physical/spiritual disciplines. The progression from physical to spiritual passes through subtle; but subtle is as far as it goes when we 'feel the flow'. We are indeed feeling subtle energy, but it is not conscious energy, aware of itself. That is the exclusive reserve of the Soul.

The first thing our minds go to when we consider the Power of Nature is its apparent indifference, even cruelty, capriciousness and downright destructiveness. 'Red in tooth and claw' goes the cliché, conjuring up pictures of the lion tearing its terrified prey limb from limb, or, on a giant scale, the power and fury of a hurricane, a volcano or a tidal wave. All that turmoil notwithstanding, right down at the root here, at the foundation of our rising edifice of energy, with matter at one end and Soul-, even God-consciousness at the other, we start with the firm and certain knowledge that the essence of the Power of Nature is balance. At the same time as it is laying waste and causing death and destruction, nature's creative power is hard at work generating new life. However much havoc it has wreaked, nature organizes itself, heals itself and restores its own complex equilibrium. The very nature of nature, we might say, is balance. And our whole Ecology of the Soul project is about finding balance. Finding, rediscovering, nurturing and cultivating our natural, innate powers, and finding and establishing the balance between them.

That's why the Power of Nature is the first power we deal with, because being physical beings – or at least, spiritual beings in a physical body, in a physical environment – we have to grapple with the physical/spiritual relationship right from the get go. That's also why each Power chapter includes a section on yoga. You don't have to practice yoga, but the Salute to the Sun is a perfect platform from which to drive your understanding and experience from the physical through the subtle to the spiritual.

Being at the start and the root and the foundation of this edifice, we climb up from nature's base position, heading for enlightenment and non-physicality. Does this mean we separate ourselves entirely from the physical domain? Not a bit of it, if the quote from the Buddha at the top of the chapter is anything to go by. Being at one with our surroundings and environment, knowing deep in our hearts where we belong, where we come from, is a quality of enlightenment. We are spiritual beings in a physical body, which makes a whole human. Without knowing our roots, we can't understand ourselves enough to elevate ourselves, to climb to the top of the consciousness tree. Are we at one with nature, consciously unconscious, a part of it, or are we detached, undisturbed, indifferent? If we're Soul Conscious enough, that is, sure and certain enough in the experience of our essential non-physical being, then we have no need to apply for a begging bowl and a mountaintop to permanently detach, dissociate from the physical. That's not a path of balance. Yes, we detach completely in meditation, to bask in the ocean of light, bathe in the ocean of peace. The body and all experience of and through it drop away. But, perversely, when it comes to action, it's that very detachment that makes us effective. We observe ourselves, right there in the center of it, engaged, efficient, focused, unstressed. Like a force of nature.

The seven sections that follow are meditations on particular aspects of the Power of Nature. Each chapter works like this. As you ponder them they create an atmosphere for the mind, calling its attention to matters deeper than itself and diverting it from its everyday, ceaseless inner chatter. They are meditations in the sense of active thinking. Read, contemplate and apply them to your own experience, with the full awareness that you are working on the building blocks of your power. At the end of the chapter you will find some suggested 'Power Seeds' which are designed as thought triggers to kick-start your daily Magic Minute. That is the tiny slice of time you allocate daily to yourself, your Self, a 60-second silent meditation in which you still the mind, go deeper than active thought and plant your Power Seed to grow your new and beautiful mental and spiritual garden, your new consciousness and new thought patterns. Its effect lasts and comes back to you throughout the day. So it's much more than a minute, really. But a minute is all you need to start.

The Power of Nature Meditation 1: Silence

Silence is a true friend who never betrays.
Confucius

Silence is a source of great strength.
Lao Tzu

Silence is so freaking loud.
Sarah Dessen, Just Listen

"Fools," said I, "You do not know –
Silence like a cancer grows.
Hear my words that I might teach you.
Take my arms that I might reach you."
But my words like silent raindrops fell
And echoed in the wells of silence.
Paul Simon, The Sound of Silence

We need to find God, and he cannot be found in noise and restlessness. God is the friend of silence. See how nature – trees, flowers, grass – grows in silence; see the stars, the moon and the sun, how they move in silence...
We need silence to be able to touch souls.
Mother Teresa

Silence is tangible, silence is powerful. Silence, above all, is peaceful. For some, like Paul Simon perhaps, it is alienating, dark and inimical; for some it is merely uncomfortable. 'Go away and leave me in peace' doesn't usually mean 'leave me in silence' though, because many people fear silence and avoid it, protecting themselves from themselves with the constant background noise of music or news on the radio or TV. A lack of external stimuli forces one to engage with one's own inner being, and if you're not seeking that, it's upsetting and disturbing. This is powerful stuff, strong meat (or its vegetarian equivalent). Too strong for those who aren't already on a spiritual path, or at least taking the first steps with books like this one.

To know silence you have to go inside, become introverted. As you move forward, leave the ever-present soundtrack behind. Let others turn it back up, waking to the chatter and remaining firmly in sound till they go to sleep again.

Silence is power, silence is peace, silence is a place. Paramdham, the non-physical dimension of unborn souls, is a place of silence. As with stillness (see Chapter 3: The Power of Endurance, Meditation 7, Stillness), it's not a place that *has* that quality; it's a place that *is* that quality. And as we discuss with stillness, it's not a place in the sense of somewhere you can physically go. The only route is through your own Soul Consciousness.

That silence is just as much Your home, from which You came and to which You will return, as Mother Nature is to your body. Ashes to ashes, dust to dust, and the body melts away to transform into a myriad of other particles. Not you the Soul though, the smallest particle of all. You are an indivisible, indestructible, integral whole whose attributes or characteristics can be separately understood, but which can never be dismantled into component parts. The fact that the number of humans continues to grow demonstrates that Souls are coming from somewhere. Once You're here in the physical domain, You're not going anywhere except into another physical body, but that dimension of light and peace is at the beginning and end of Your cycle of births and deaths. It's your non-physical nature, if you like. You are silence. You are light. You are peace.

Silence, as we see in the Stillness meditation in The Power of Endurance, is so closely related to stillness that you can't have one without the other. Not the same thing; not merely an absence of sound, or in the case of stillness, an absence of movement.

Each is on the way to the other; through stillness you reach silence, through silence you reach stillness. Not a negative property, the silence we are looking for is something you enter, something almost tangible. Which of course it isn't, but it's worth giving meditative thought to the sense of silence as a thing, an entity, something you can feel. It's inside You, it is You, but it's also outside You. Something you can access, tap into to draw on unlimited reserves of power, of peace. Of Silence.

And as we all know, when it comes right down to it, in the physical world there is no such thing as silence, because the silence we seek is complete and perfect, and nothing in the physical world is complete and perfect. Nothing in nature, in fact, which is a bit of a hard one to swallow, because we are much given to making unfavorable comparisons between the heedless beauty and majesty of nature and humankind's perishable constructions and activities. Head to the vastnesses of nature for your silence and you will be disappointed. Momentary peace and stillness, yes; enough to catch the compelling power and perfection of complete silence. But random creatures are rustling, the breeze is whispering, and the foliage is creaking. And even if you're below ground in a cave somewhere with no sound, no light and no living thing, your ears are still whistling. Perfect silence is not a physical thing. The only way you can enter it is by silencing your mind, and that, in the first stages anyway, is difficult to achieve and likely to be momentary.

So you cease the mental chatter, let it fade away, bring your mind to silence. You get a tantalizing glimpse and move forward for more. This too, you realize, is also an activity of the mind. It must shut itself down, or be shut down, maneuvered into a place where a wave of Soul Consciousness overwhelms it. There is also occasionally the sense of outside help, of being taken into silence almost without effort, which I myself have experienced more than once (see Chapter 3: The Power of Endurance, Meditation 3, Faith). Now that you have firmly established the thought: "I am a Soul, a pinpoint of non-physical, conscient light in the forehead of this physical body", and the thought has taken root and flipped you into the bloom and glow of pure experience, you are there. In Silence. The silence which is you, the same silence from which you came and to which you will return. Your home, or Ōm. Everyone has to go home once in a while – the more often the better, in fact. I recommend a visit at least once a day, ideally twice.

The Power of Nature Meditation 2: 'Centered-ness' – 'Is-ness'

A mind at peace, a mind centered and not focused on harming others, is stronger than any physical force in the universe.
Wayne Dyer

Flow with whatever may happen and let your mind be free. Stay centered by accepting whatever you are doing. This is the ultimate.
Zhuangzi

At the center of your being
you have the answer;
you know who you are
and you know what you want.
Lao Tzu

To be Self centered is not such a bad thing.
Center on your Self.
Know yourself.
To know your Self, stay centered.
Your Self is at your center.
But your center is not your Self.
If you're centered, you're rock solid.
Balanced.
The Ecology of the Soul

Each one of the meditations in this chapter sets up resonances or tensions in your mental state, your perceptions of yourself and your Self, because we are engaging with the Power of Nature, and nature is physical, non-conscient and non-self aware (though many, especially followers of Gaia, would dispute this).

Nature doesn't do: it just is. Of course a lot happens, but nature follows its own course with indifference, without human logic, rhyme or reason. In fact it's not even really right to say that it is indifferent, because that implies a choice to engage or ignore. Nature doesn't meditate or pray, it doesn't ask questions about the meaning of life or choose to investigate itself. It is neither introverted nor extroverted. It just *is*.

You and I have done, are doing, and continue to do all that seeking, questioning, practicing and learning. So why are we here, equating ourselves with nature and drawing from it, making parallels in our own lives with it? Are we part of nature, in it but (in consciousness terms at least) not of it? Well, clearly identification with nature is unavoidable: a) because the physical bodies we non-physical beings inhabit are of course part of nature; and b) because our consciousness has become degraded to such an extent that we experience ourselves as our bodies, identifying completely with the physical container. We need to lift ourselves out of that mistake, especially because action (karma) carried out in that mistaken sense of self – body consciousness – leads to pain. We need to understand our Selves as non-physical, but also come to terms with our existence in the physical. No point in trying to exist as an entirely non-physical being at all times; we have to get on with our daily doings in the world.

Starting at the bottom, in both the physical and subtle sense, the chakras are the key to understanding and experiencing this material/spiritual relationship, and this power. Nature itself, in its mindless, heedless, consciousness-less way, is perfectly, powerfully and purely on center; its 'is-ness', if I may coin a phrase, is quintessentially nature's nature. From spectacular beauty to raging havoc and destruction, the range of nature's effects never shakes its abiding inner truths of resilience, recovery and self healing. Self righting, we might say. Our conscious parallel is reached through the chakras, each one of which is a center located in our physical body, and each one of which, through the experience of the subtle energy of Prān, Ch'i, the 'force of life', is notionally a graduated step from matter to pure consciousness. Sahasrara at the very top, the crown of the head, is in fact the connector of our consciousness to a higher one, but that is for the last chapter. Right now we are with Muladhara, at the root and base of the spine, where the flow begins, or rather, where it enters from the earth. From nature, in other words, the force at the center.

It's not straightforward Kundalini meditation (if Kundalini could be called straightforward, for which may I be forgiven), because the Ecology of the Soul is crystal clear about the nature of the Self and the nature of its surroundings. You can't sort of slide from one to the other. Focusing on each center of subtle energy as you go upwards will help you towards full consciousness of your spiritual Self, but 100% Soul Consciousness demands that you leap the gap between physical and spiritual, or even start at the spiritual right away with 'I am a Soul'. The chakras, as centers of subtle energy on the way from physical to spiritual, are the elevator on which you rise from body consciousness, but they can only take you so far. Remain centered, using any or all of them; they are your two-way link to nature below, and super-nature above.

'Centered-ness' and 'Is-ness' are both kind of clumsy coinages, intended to convey the quality of perfect, unquestioning being, of pure existence, that we see in nature and that we ourselves can experience in our Selves. Without knowing itself, nature is always in touch with itself, with its truth. But taking the analogy further, it's not to say that nature has one and only one center of energy akin to our simple, single Self, the Soul. It has a million billion squillion centers, each and every one of which is existing thoughtlessly, without self awareness, but within what we might call the bliss of being. It's unknowing, but it's centered the whole time. Everything that is, everything that exists in nature, is centered. Look far and wide enough, or close and narrow enough, and you'll see it. And if what you're seeing isn't somehow centered, then something's wrong with it. Even the most raging, destructive storm has an eye.

So for us Souls in bodies, it sounds complicated when set out in words, but in straightforward experience terms it's very simple. And it's also why this book carries yoga exercises and refers to the chakras, as part of our discipline of reawakening our Soul Consciousness. Walking, talking, doing, running, sitting, standing, driving, working, cooking, playing, eating, drinking – doing, in other words, whatever it is we do from minute to minute, hour to hour – we can remain in touch with our center. It might be a strictly physical experience – your attention on the pit of the stomach, the bowl of the pelvis, where Ch'i resides; it might be more subtle, or perhaps more emotional, where you go inside the heart or mind; it might be entirely spiritual, the 100% pure, unadulterated experience of your Self as a non-physical Soul. That is the center to which you constantly refer, and constantly turn. The center of your being is your being itself. You the Soul.

The Power of Nature Meditation 3: Self organization

> The Law of Divine Compensation posits that this is a self-organizing and self-correcting universe: the embryo becomes a baby, the bud becomes a blossom, the acorn becomes an oak tree. Clearly, there is some invisible force that is moving every aspect of reality to its next best expression.
> *Marianne Williamson*

> The reason that Google was such a success is because they were the first ones to take advantage of the self-organizing properties of the web. It's in ecological sustainability. It's in the developmental power of entrepreneurship, the ethical power of democracy.
> *Ron Eglash*

Self organizing is self managing, self healing, self helping and self righting. It is self discovering and self rediscovering, self creating and self re-creating. None of which you can do without knowing yourself. Your Self.

Nature is a 'smart system' that wrongs itself, then rights itself. Anything upsetting the 'balance of nature' is ultimately brought back into its dynamic equilibrium.

We non-physical beings can't do self management, self organization (and self healing?) without being self aware. But nature is entirely un-self aware, hence our attempts to anthropomorphize it, or at least impose some form of intelligible consciousness on it. We've put spirits of the earth, water, air and fire into it, we've battled with ghastly, ghostly mythical monsters, trolls, ghouls and harpies, we've been enchanted by the fairies, sprites and elves. We've been injecting nature with recognizable forms of life and personality, in other words, to help us understand what we can't explain.

But from here we'd better leave nature's power of self organization, self healing and self righting alone, because it is unconscious power, and although we share that power, being – in physical form at least – of and from nature, our own power of self management depends entirely on self awareness. Nature's defining characteristic is balance, to which it will always automatically return, however much havoc has been wreaked in the upset. Our own ability to regain our natural, innate balance of powers is clearly much more compromised, and in fact the process by which we return to it is the whole point of this book. Having followed the wrong road for near enough half our existence on this planet (arguable, but we'll come to that in this or another book), it's now our task to strip our Selves down and give our Selves an overhaul, re-calibrate our priorities and adopt the truth of Soul Consciousness. There's plenty of instruction (of varying efficacy) available on how to do that, but there's one thing clear, whichever path you follow – no one and nothing will do it for you. You're on your own.

Hence self organization and self management – which, when you come to think of it, and when Self or Soul consciousness is applied, are not exactly the same thing. The management part comes first, because it requires decisions based on knowledge. Any successful athlete or competitor, in sport, in battle or in business, knows when it's better and wiser to back off or rest, and when it's time to put in maximum effort for the desired result. My own meagre experience of running, which I have taken up for some bizarre reason during the time I've been writing this book, is enough to show me that longer distance, better pace, better technique, overall lightness and less likelihood of injury are all products of knowing when to push and when to ease off. They are all also products of listening very carefully to one's body, learning its warning signs, keeping inner focus on posture and balance, and letting your Ch'i drive you from the bowl of your pelvis,[1] somewhere between Muladhara, the chakra at the very base of the spine, and Swadisthana, centered on your navel.

It's one form of body consciousness, which, like hatha yoga, could probably be called 'good' or 'positive'. You're paying attention, you're in a state of mindfulness. You're actually Soul-consciously body conscious, because you're very aware of being the aware being, controlling its physical apparatus. Exactly the same thing happens at a mental and spiritual level; the Soul is looking after itself, choosing activity (we hope) that supports and enhances self awareness, checking itself for indications of its state of mind, remaining focused on the experience of non-physicality in a physical body. Or even, in meditation, in no body at all, when the power of said experience takes you completely away from the physical and you spend time awash in the ocean of bliss.

So managing yourself (and your Self) is the first step to organizing your Self, which in this context is a process of rediscovering and returning to the experience of your true nature, and making thoughts, feelings and actions from that consciousness. Self organization, for a conscient, self-aware being, is self creation – or re-creation, renewal, making your eternal, indestructible Self all over again. Very recreational (see Chapter 2: The Power of Creativity, Meditation 6, Self Creation).

We're down in the basement for this whole chapter, starting at the bottom with Muladhara, notionally the crossover point between 'gross' matter and subtle. Although the Ecology of the Soul doesn't subscribe to the idea of matter as 'gross consciousness', it is from here that we engage, as non-physical conscient beings, with the physical world of matter and of action. Thoughts create feelings, or feelings create thoughts, and either

1 *ChiRunning: A Revolutionary Approach to Effortless, Injury-Free Running*, by Danny Dreyer, Pocket Books, 2008. ISBN-10: 1847392784; ISBN-13: 978-1847392787

or both, often in conflict, create action. Which is the key point for Self awareness, Self organization and Self creation: once you come into action, you the non-physical have made your irreversible mark on the physical. You're engaged. The Law of Karma has kicked in, and for that action you will get an equal and opposite reaction, in both the physical and the spiritual sense. If you push, an equal force pushes back; when you act, whether by decision or habit, the non-physical reaction is to record it in the Soul as a sanskar, a character trait that will return to and reinforce that action.

Thus are habits born. You create, or reinforce the already created, 'track of probability'. The more you do something, the more likely you are to do it again. Hence habit, the idea of involuntary action, which can be dangerous and destructive or uplifting and creative, depending on your initial input.

Here is the nub of self organization: with enough self awareness, you have the power to choose the actions that make you. Remake you. It's in circular, or rather spiral, fashion, but you have to make the choice that leads upwards to the light and lightness. It's not always an easy choice, but it's one that you've already made, as a general principle. Otherwise you wouldn't be here. Plant your Power Seeds, give yourself your Magic Minutes, and your self-organized spiritual garden will bring forth amazing flowers and fruit.

The Power of Nature Meditation 4: Inwardness

> A man who as a physical being is always turned toward the outside, thinking that his happiness lies outside him, finally turns inward and discovers that the source is within him.
> *Soren Kierkegaard*

Most of the meditations in this chapter focus on one or another aspect of the direct experience of the Self, in the self-discovering, self-exploratory, self-examining sense. Of course Soul Consciousness is the point of every meditation in the entire book, but right here right now we're setting the scene, laying the ground; turning our attention inwards.

From the point of view of nature, as with self organization and self management, the lesson to learn about inwardness comes, not from nature's own activity as an exemplar, but from the steps we take to lift our own consciousness from the physical. When we contemplate the 'isness' of nature, the raw power of creation and destruction, the beauty, caprice or apparent cruelty, our breath is taken away by its 'unconsciousness'. As we've said, nature doesn't think, ponder, look inside or meditate. It doesn't question itself, it doesn't have to go inside itself. It just is. Inwardness as a meditation is here in this chapter, drawing on the power of nature, because in physical terms we're at Muladhara, the root chakra through which we connect to the earth – to nature, in other words – and draw energy upwards towards an ever higher consciousness, from physical to subtle to spiritual. We are taking it, feeling it climb up the spine, but it is also firing up our own innate energy. And none of that is possible without turning our focus inwards.

Sounds so obvious as to be not really necessary to say at all, right? Of course we have to turn our attention inwards. But remember that many, many, if not most, people don't. They don't have this habit, and often they don't understand it and are uncomfortable with it. Every little thing they think, do and be is outward. Don't feel smug about it, but you have a massive advantage going through life if you have the power of inward consciousness – that is, looking inside. Your peace and your power (two sides of the same thing) are here in unlimited abundance.

You the Soul are a non-physical (super-natural) being in a physical (natural) body. While we concentrate on this truth to achieve Soul Consciousness, it also helps us see ourselves as physical/subtle/spiritual organisms. This is ourselves with a small 's', right, not a capital 'S', which we reserve for our actual, essential, spiritual Selves. It's also why the book includes sections on yoga and constantly refers to the chakras; we have to make sense of ourselves as beings coming from and connected to the physical, even as our awareness of our true non-physical being gains traction.

Inwardness starts with turning your awareness inside at the physical level, the first point of focus being the breath. Amazing. It's right there inside you (your body, actually), inlet and exhaust, in-out, all day and night. Never stops until you die. And it's the perfect carrier of your mind from the physical to the subtle, and possibly beyond.

You're sitting comfortably, cross-legged or however. Your back is straight, supported if you need to. Let your head tip slightly forward by letting your chin fall a little so your neck vertebrae have some space between them – not so far as to squish up your neck muscles and bunch up your throat. Let your shoulders drop, and move the point of 'friction' in your airways to the top back of your nasal passage, where it turns the top corner to go down your throat. You can hear and feel the air moving up there, right up inside your head, the place where you make the sound when you (if you) snore. Just adjusting this sensation demands your very specific attention, and I absolutely 100% guarantee that as you get it, and start hearing and feeling the passage of air in that place – it makes a kind of hollow sound – that your mind will quieten. Your thoughts will slow down to a point where you genuinely believe you can let them stop. You can never make them stop, of course; only let them go. No one's claiming it's easy. And if you get to a point where you can watch your thoughts drift slowly through your mind, with a palpable lag between one and the next, you're doing extremely well. It might come as a surprise to discover you don't actually *have* to have thoughts. Your mind isn't going to disappear somehow or suffer irreparable damage if it's kicked out of gear and turned off for a while. The reverse is true, in fact; you will return to it refreshed and revitalized.

The other straightforward physical technique to secure the inwardness we need to move our consciousness ever upwards is to relax the throat and tongue. We cover this in the yoga section of the introduction, another cast-iron guaranteed trick to quieten the mind. Somehow – the biology and psychology escape me – the daily activity of your mind keeps your tongue engorged, swollen, charged with fluid. It's what you automatically, involuntarily do when you think, and it's certainly what you need when you talk. So as your breath starts touching that upper back nasal passage and your head tips slightly, shoulders dropped (not pushed – never push), turn your attention to the muscles in your neck and throat. Let them go soft, see how your head settles a little more. And as those muscles relax – worth repeating over and over again, it only happens when you let them go, you absolutely cannot push them to stretch or relax – the softness and looseness spreads inside, to your tongue. Which is after all a muscle, and a very active one. Just let it go. Don't send any signals that will make it perk up and engorge again. Lo and behold, it shrinks. As it gets smaller, the space it occupies in your mouth gets bigger. And your mind gets quieter. And quieter.

And with your breathing very slow and quite audible in your head, your neck slightly extended and your throat and tongue relaxed, there you go. You're inside. Now turn your attention to your Self, the impossibly tiny and inexpressibly powerful pinpoint of conscient light in your forehead that is You. The Soul.

The Power of Nature Meditation 5: Aggression

To control aggression without inflicting injury is the Art of Peace.
Morihei Ueshiba

My passions were all gathered together like fingers that made a fist. Drive is considered aggression today; I knew it then as purpose.
Bette Davis

Seems inappropriate to even mention aggression, let alone devote a whole meditation to it, wouldn't you say? This is the territory of peace and love, where anger is one of the enemies we are determined to eradicate, right? How can aggression be the focus of a meditation?

Well, for a start, anger and aggression are not the same thing. Aggression suggests – at least in this meditational, spiritual, self-examining context – the kind of control you don't normally associate with anger. Anger is an emotion. Aggression is a force.

As we've seen in some of the earlier meditations in this chapter, nature's nature is 'unknowingness'. It is self organizing and self managing, for instance, but it doesn't know itself as such. It's our habit to ascribe emotions, motivations and human qualities to it – nature is cruel, nature is fickle, nature is kind, nature is soft – as a way of coping with it, handling whatever it doles out. But, working with an organic, physical/subtle/spiritual understanding of our ordinary everyday selves, as distinct from the strictly non-physical Self or Soul, and our connection to nature through Muladhara, the root chakra, we draw on the qualities of nature that we can use in our spiritual project, and indeed in our ordinary everyday lives as well.

Any successful competitor has aggression. Whether it's the world's fastest human over 5000 meters, or the world's most enlightened human on a mountaintop somewhere, the drive to succeed has been dominant, feeding and forcing, pushing and pulling their efforts. Because make no mistake, that sadhu on top of the mountain didn't get there without pushing herself. It's a bit of a conceptual jump to associate aggression with the path of a spiritual seeker, but no one achieves any goal without pushing him or herself, even in the paradoxical world of Zen where the most effective effort is no effort at all.

In this context, your aggression needs to be a kind of compassionate determination. Grit your teeth and drive yourself, find that extra pace, lengthen your stride for the last 100 meters, or haul yourself out of bed 15 minutes earlier than your normal crack of dawn wake time, just to give yourself that extra impetus. You push, but you treat yourself with love at the same time. If you don't come in with a better time over your 5K or 50 miles, or lose concentration and maybe doze away most of those extra 15 minutes' meditation, don't turn the aggression on yourself, feeding it through into beating yourself up. Let it strengthen your determination, yes; but it's controlled. You know when to apply it and when to give yourself a break. There has to be love inside the aggression, compassion for yourself, your Self and all living beings. Otherwise it's just destructive.

It's the force that you take from nature, not the intent. If nature is unknowing, then it has no intent anyway. It's our job as beings at whatever stage of enlightenment to take what we need from nature and not what we don't. For our spiritual purposes, aggression is applied when it comes to a struggle or battle. And we shouldn't be in any doubt that this path needs a fighting spirit. Courage, stamina and determination to win are essential: to conquer the vagaries and waywardness of our own minds, the self-destructive behaviors, the attractions and seductions that pull us into body consciousness, the weaknesses and the lazinesses. Remembering of course that the Ecology of the Soul is for real people in the real world; we aren't promoting or proposing full-blown renunciation. Of course you want to watch the game, gossip with your girlfriends, have a drink, eat ice cream, enjoy yourself, make love to your husband, wife or lover; succeed in business, get that better job, house, car. We aren't saying throw all that away. We are saying, understand and recognize where it fits into your life and karma, and knowing that these physical things are not the source of peace, power and happiness, pay attention to the non-physical realm, where all that engagement with and attachment to the physical just fades away.

You have to battle with your own demons, actions, habits – involuntary, or at least, unknowing, oblivious action. Even action that you don't really want to do, know very well that you shouldn't do for whatever reason, but go ahead and do it anyway. Of the weapons you need, courage is, after all, nothing more nor less than conquering fear (not that it's easy, by any manner of means). Stamina, determination and aggression need to be correctly tuned and correctly focused. Gritting your teeth is not a great habit for meditation; you'll bunch up your tongue, neck and throat, tighten your brain stem and tie yourself down. If you want to rise, to fly, you'll need to master the trick of gritting your mental and spiritual teeth, screwing your courage to the sticking point, and then letting your physical body go. You are a conqueror of unwelcome, unnecessary and destructive forces. No conqueror ever conquered without aggression. It's just a question of knowing when to fight, and when to let go.

The Power of Nature Meditation 6: Resilience

Nature works with five polymers. Only five polymers. In the natural world, life builds from the bottom up, and it builds in resilience and multiple uses.
Janine Benyus

It turns out that there are many powers of the heart – among them intuition, intention, gratitude, forgiveness, resilience, and, of course, love.
Baptist de Pape, The Power of the Heart: Finding Your True Purpose in Life

If your heart is broken, make art with the pieces.
Shane Koyczan, "Blueprint for a Breakthrough"

Life ain't all you want but it's all you got.
Stick a flower in yer 'at and be 'appy.
Cockney saying

To 'resile' is to draw back from an agreement, contract or statement, says the *Shorter Oxford English Dictionary*: to shrink, to retreat from something with aversion or non-acceptance. In the language of materials, it is to recoil or rebound after contact, and when it comes to elastic bodies, to return to their original position after being stretched or compressed. Resilience is defined as the act of rebounding or springing back – rebound, recoil. Also, as a quality of elasticity, the power of resuming the original shape or position after compression, extension, bending and so on.

Notice the use of the word 'power'. Resilience is bouncing back. Resilience is bounce, it is strength, it is balance. Strength with flexibility; the old story of the oak and the rushes. The rushes bend with the wind. The oak resists, firm and strong, until… cra-a-a-a-a-a-ck. Here and now, you have the flex of the rushes *and* the strength of the oak. You are unbreakable.

Nature's resilience is inbuilt. It is another facet of the same phenomenon as self organization or self management. However big the hole that appears in nature's fabric – self made or man-made, natural disaster or destructive human intervention – it has the wherewithal and the capacity to fix it. Unconsciously. Over time, the weeds, creepers, plants and trees grow back and take hold; the birds and the beasts return. Nature folds in on herself and renews; but she doesn't know herself, and she doesn't know she's doing it.

For us, resilience is a daily life thing rather than a silent, internal, meditative thing. It is born in the power of silence and Self-awareness, but applying it in everyday terms is simply a matter of getting bent out of shape and then bouncing back (as if that were easy). It also has the sense of durability, longevity, indestructibility. And in nature's case, since we know that matter can only change, it can never be completely destroyed as in cease to exist, we know for sure that that's what resilience means. Indestructible. Shape shifting and form changing, but ultimately it's always there.

Resilience is limitless, therefore timeless, therefore eternal. The more you bounce back, the more you keep on bouncing back, the more you keep on keeping on. It's an inherent quality in you the Soul precisely because you are eternal, indestructible. At the Soul World, silent, glowing, ocean of peace level of consciousness, you don't need resilience because nothing happens. There is no action. Once you come into the physical world of action, you have reaction to deal with, the results of your own actions, the actions of others and indeed of the physical world itself – of nature. Which is where your inherent resilience comes in. Simply and straightforwardly drawing on your knowledge and experience of your Self the eternal Soul, you tap into the peace and power that is your true nature. Yes, there will be tough obstacles, disasters, crises and setbacks – often appearing insurmountable. You might as well give up. But they're not, and you can't. An eternal being can't give up, right? Now that you're Soul Conscious, nothing can stop you.

In inner space, there is one and only one form, and ever more shall be so. Unlike matter – nature – the shapes do not shift, and there are no material components, broken down into atoms and sub-atoms, that pick themselves up, dust themselves off and become incorporated into a new and different form. There is only the Soul, itself – your Self – already a pinpoint smaller than an atom, a quark or a neutrino, and made of light, of spiritual energy, of consciousness. Keep your mind, your awareness in that state of being and you will have no problem with resilience.

Resilience is strength, resilience is bounce, and there is no bounce without balance. All your bounce, all your balance, come from inside. Meeting and interacting with all sorts of people in all sorts of circumstances, it pays to remember that 'most people' don't have this option of going inside, tapping into the inner source. Exasperation, frustration, impatience, sadness, disappointment and despair jostle in the consciousness of 'most people' with optimism, satisfaction and contentment – all of them fleeting, changeable, unreliable and impermanent. Based on a material view of the world, such states of mind can be nothing but unreliable and impermanent. Because: a) matter itself is constantly changing; and b) we Souls, being 'not matter', are automatically separate from it. We're not made of the same stuff. How can our fulfilment and contentment depend on it?

It's inside. This whole book could probably be boiled down into those two words. The strength, the presence of mind, the patience, tolerance, endurance or stamina you need to bounce back: all come from your close connection to, understanding and experience of, yourself as a Soul. A pinpoint of metaphysical light. Your Self is eternal, indestructible; the energy that is You is eternal, indestructible. Limitless, an inexhaustible source. Now tell me you can't bounce back.

The Power of Nature Meditation 7: Dispassion – Detachment

Dispassionate objectivity is itself a passion, for the real and for the truth.
Abraham Maslow

It is the higher self that becomes dispassionate or unattached as self-awakening occurs. The ego mind can remain passionate and engaged while it fulfills its life purpose or dharma. As long as the silent witness is the dominant reference for the self, and not the ego, spiritual evolution can flourish even while one remains passionate about life.
Deepak Chopra

Attachment is the great fabricator of illusions; reality can be obtained only by someone who is detached.
Simone Weil

The essence of the Way is detachment.
Bodhidharma

A tricky one, this. Might be the biggest challenge of all 49 meditations, in fact, because it is so crucially important for a meditative, spiritual experience – but on the face of it, it looks as if we are encouraging people to disengage. Throughout the book we focus on the necessity of doing the exact opposite – compassion, engagement, commitment, responsibility, community, the search for enlightenment on behalf of all sentient beings. None of that makes any sense in the context of dispassion or detachment. Am I really asking you to disengage, not to feel, not to get involved? And aren't they one and the same thing, anyway, dispassion and detachment?

No, they're not, but they're considered here as component parts of one meditation, or meditative state, because they're inextricably intertwined. You can't have one without the other; but there is a sequence. In the strictly meditative context, detachment from the body is the first lesson of Soul Consciousness. You leave your physical senses behind. In the 'action in the world' context, dispassion comes before detachment and is an essential prerequisite. But dispassion also requires more emotional subtlety to understand and practice; not that detachment doesn't itself have layers of experience and wisdom to uncover, but its opposite – attachment – is easier to reject. (Non-attachment is something else again.)

One way of understanding them is through their opposites. Detachment vs attachment is easy enough; but if the opposite of dispassion is compassion, then we need to do some defining.

Nature is dispassionate. It doesn't care. It doesn't feel. For us human beings, dispassion will never be a matter of not caring or not feeling, but it is very definitely a matter of not getting involved. Which is hard enough anyway, if we see ourselves as devoted to our own enlightenment for the sake of all living beings. We need to avoid becoming so deeply involved that we start to share or trade karma with other souls. Our close friends and family, work colleagues, even enemies, are enough, thank you very much. Plenty of karmic credit and debit there. Do all you can at a subtle level for every soul, and more indeed for the ones that you come into random contact with, but don't engage at the level of action. If you give money, for instance, it just intertwines your karma with that of the recipient. The creation of an 'account' of debt and credit. No way of knowing if this is a new karmic bond you're tying, or the final payment in the closure of a karmic account. Better not go there in the first place.

It's the emotional – actually, the non-emotional – element of dispassion that puts us off. We don't want to not feel or not care; but here is the subtlety. Care, yes. Feel, yes. Engage as in be drawn in, dragged down, diverted from your own spiritual path, no. The Buddha's search for enlightenment for the sake of all sentient beings didn't require him to have direct dealings with all sentient beings aforesaid; in fact, if he'd have tried he would certainly have failed, and so would his project. We can probably say that failed anyway, because demonstrably not all human beings are enlightened, never mind all the rest of the sentient universe. But we can at least agree that it got farther, to the tune of the world's 370 million Buddhists, than it would have done if he'd started giving meditation lessons to the local grasshoppers.

So, perversely, it is actually dispassion and detachment that demonstrate your caring nature. In fact they are prerequisites for your caring nature to be expressed and acted upon. You feel compassion, but dispassionately. Got it? I said it was tricky. You separate your Self out from your feelings and emotions – you're used to doing this by now, it's basic meditation technique – observe them, watch them at work, and come into action where your higher, analytical, discerning intellect says it's OK.

Which is to say, that it's when thinking and feeling come into action in the real world that all this detachment and apparent disengagement count. You can't be attached to your actions or their results; that will forever tie you to the physical plane at the expense of your subtle and spiritual consciousness. No more can you be attached to your body-conscious idea of yourself; train driver, call center worker, mother, father, butcher, baker, candlestick maker, tennis player, gambler, fat, thin, medium sized. All these and all the other myriad of ways in which you define yourself in the world mean nothing to the eternal truth of your Self. Equally, and this we all know to be true, attachment to your status in the world, your dignity or public position, to other people (you can love without dependence, can't you?) and to material possessions will lead inevitably to dysfunction, disappointment and discontent.

With your intellect you are discerning, analyzing, making

judgements, arriving at insights. You are using the clarity, determination, mindfulness – even compartmentalization – that we meditate on in Chapter 6: The Power of Focus. At the intellect level, dispassion is not hard to come by; you simply (simply? Ha!) have to remove or rise above emotion to be able to make clear judgements. It's the same with both sides of this particular coin, whose understanding comes via an understanding of its obverse. Dispassion is understood through compassion, in contrast with it as an intellectual process, whereas compassion can arise from straightforward emotion but, much more powerfully, from detachment itself. Detachment is understood through the perils of attachment, dramatically illustrating Deepak Chopra's point quoted above that you can be all these things and have all this stuff without undermining your spiritual progress – as long as you don't make the mistake of identifying with it. Dealing with the *desire* for status, position, self definition and material wealth is another matter entirely.

The Power of Nature Practice 1: Plant a Power Seed Every Day

Power Seeds are mental devices, thought triggers to generate Soul Consciousness, and hence change your actions. They are a bit like the Zen 'kōan' (for instance the idea of the sound of one hand clapping) that kick your mind out of gear and raise the level of your awareness.

Using Power Seeds, you grow a new garden of consciousness. See your mind as a garden, or at least a patch of fertile soil. Thoughts and feelings grow in it, like plants. Your mind is a riot of tangled and intertwined mental vegetation, much of it good and useful and most of it neither good nor useful. So it's a pleasant surprise that you don't have to struggle with the weeds. All you have to do is plant your mental plot with new seeds – 'Power Seeds' – which grow into thought, attitude, feeling, and action. Which feeds back and creates new thought and feeling. You have created a new mental and spiritual garden – and a new framework for your behavior.

If you really focus all the innate power of your calmed, stilled mind on the Power Seed you choose for 60 full seconds, that thought pattern will repeat and recur throughout the day, accumulating much more than a single minute of your mental activity. It's meditation in action, because the meditation is about action.

Plant one of the mental Power Seeds that appear on the following pages. The Power Seeds section in the Introduction gives the full explanation of how to prepare the mental and spiritual ground for your new garden; Part III gives you a whole range of Power Seeds to suit your circumstances. Ultimately, as your Self knowledge increases, you will be creating and planting your own.

Soul is soul, Soul is spirit. Each and every single Soul is individual, indivisible, indestructible, eternal.

Matter is eternal and indestructible, but it changes form. It is energy, but it is not spiritual energy. It is not consciousness, however gross or subtle, condensed or expanded.

The progression from physical to spiritual energy passes through the subtle, but subtle energy is not conscious energy, aware of itself.
That is the exclusive reserve of the Soul.

The very nature of Nature is balance.
The very nature of the Ecology of the Soul is balance.

We are spiritual beings in a physical body, which makes a whole human.

Without knowing our roots, we can't understand ourselves enough to climb to the top of the consciousness tree.

Silence is tangible.
Silence is power.
Silence is peace.

Silence is a place.
The only route there is through your own Soul consciousness.

It's your non-physical nature.
You are silence.
You are light.
You are peace.

Silence is a thing, an entity, something you can feel.

It's inside You, it is You, but it's also outside You.
You can draw on unlimited reserves of power, of peace.
Of silence.

Silence is You, in the way a person relates to his or her home. Self defining. It is where you came from and where you will return.
Your home.
Or Ōm.

100% Soul Consciousness demands that you leap the gap between physical and spiritual with 'I am a Soul'. The chakras, as centers of subtle energy on the way from physical to spiritual, are the elevator on which you rise from body consciousness. But they can only take you so far.

Everything that exists in nature is centered. Look far and wide enough, or close and narrow enough, and you'll see it. Seeing your Self is seeing your center.

Once you come into action, you the non-physical have made your irreversible mark on the physical. You're engaged. The Law of Karma has kicked in, and for that action you will get an equal and opposite reaction, both physical and spiritual.

Center on your Self.
To be Self centered is not such
a bad thing.
If you're centered, you're rock solid.
Balanced.
Your Self is at your Center,
But your Center is not your Self.

Inwardness starts with turning your awareness inside, to the

breath.
Amazing.
It's right there inside your body, inlet and exhaust,
in-out, all day and night.
Never stops until you die.

You don't actually *have* to have thoughts. Your mind isn't going to suffer irreparable damage if it's turned off for a while.

Your aggression needs to be compassionate determination. You push, but you treat yourself with love.

If you want to fly, grit your mental and spiritual teeth, screw your courage to the sticking point, and let your body go. You are a conqueror of unwelcome, unnecessary and destructive forces. No conqueror ever conquered without aggression.
Know when to fight, and when to let go.

You have the flex of the rushes *and* the strength of the oak.
You are unbreakable.

Resilience is limitless, therefore timeless, therefore eternal. The more you bounce back, the more you keep on bouncing back, the more you keep on keeping on.

Resilience is strength, resilience is bounce, and there is no bounce without balance.
All your bounce, all your balance, come from inside.

Dispassion and detachment demonstrate your caring nature.
You feel compassion, but dispassionately.

Compassion can arise from straightforward emotion but, much more powerfully, from detachment itself.

The Power of Nature Practice 2: Yoga Seeds – Salute to the Sun (Surya Namaskar)

Positions Tadasana 1 and 2: Standing Prayer/Mountain

The Salute to the Sun, like most things in yoga, has many variations. The one we use here consists of seven 'asanas', to use the Sanskrit name for positions, done in a 12-step sequence: Prayer, Mountain, Forward Bend, Forward Lunge (one leg forward), Plank, Dog, Cobra, Child, Forward Lunge (other leg forward), Forward Bend, Mountain, Prayer. Aim to hold each pose for seven in-out breaths. You can do less if it hurts!

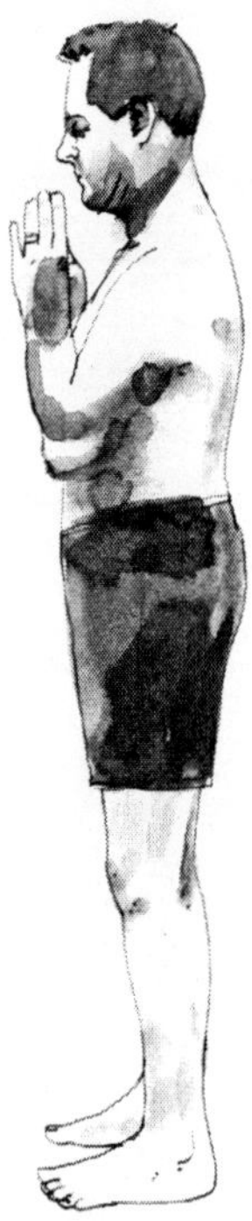

Tadasana 1

Tadasana 2: Urdhva Baddha Hastasana

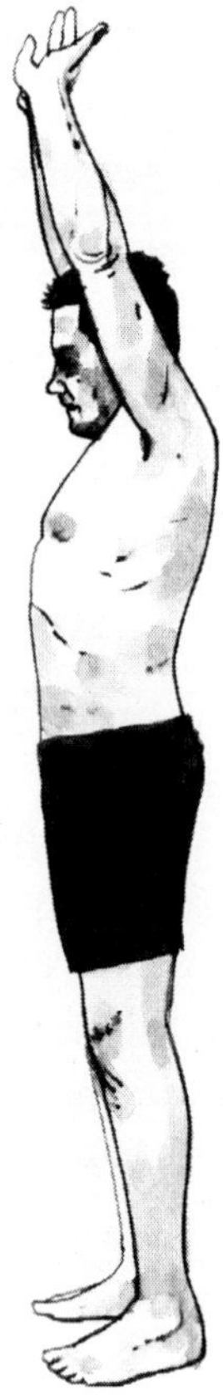

"People do not pay attention to the correct method of standing,"[1] says BKS Iyengar in his comments on this basic, initial pose, from which everything else emanates. May not come as a surprise to learn that the entire focus is on inner balance, and that that inner balance expresses itself outwardly through practice of all the other asanas, and indeed in your daily life as well. Standing waiting for the green man crossing light, the train, the bus, the plane, the elevator, the post office, the morning coffee; anywhere and anyhow you have to be on your feet for more than a few minutes, bring this habit of body to mind and then apply it. Stretch, relax. To stretch, you have to relax.

First things first: the feet. For proper practice of course you need to be barefoot; tadasana in shoes in the bus queue comes later. Plant them the same width apart as your shoulders, in a direct line, and rock a little back and forth on them to get them settled and spread. Stretch your toes, energize the soles of your feet, spread them out in all directions as far as you can, feel the edges, feel them tingle, feel them make live and living contact with your mat. Then all the energy can rise up from that contact.

Second thing first: your breathing. All yoga asanas are driven by the breath. Every move you make should always be on the outbreath. Your breath is your most direct route possible to a calm, still, quiet mind, which is exactly what you want in all yoga and meditation. Always breathe through your nose. Focus your attention on the inner airway, way back in your head, at the back of your nasal cavity, right towards your throat. Feel the air touching the sides of the passage. Hear it inside your head, the hollow sound that could be a snore if you let it catch. (This is the section of your airway where snores come from, if they come at all.) Let it slow right down. Aim for one complete in-out cycle to take about four seconds, with at least a second's rest before you breathe in again. Don't force it; let it happen automatically.

Once you have got a hold of this and can hear your breath coming and going, you can start to let go your tongue. Take a look at some Google images of the throat and larynx area, and it all comes clear. The tongue is actually a huge lump of muscle, of which the long, mobile 'tonguey' bit is only the very top. As your breath sounds inside your head, let your tongue go and you realize how tense and active it normally is. It will take a few tries to really let go. As you crack it, you realize it is shrinking inside your mouth, taking up less space and making less saliva so you

---

1 BKS Iyengar, *Light on Yoga*, paperback revised edition, 1979. ISBN: 0-8052-1031-8

have to swallow less often. It is the simplest and best trick for quieting the mind; let go your tongue.

Your legs should be solid as a rock, but sensitive, unlike a rock. I think of them as a pair of pipes, up through which the Prān or Ch'i energy can rise. Your knees must be locked, your kneecaps pulled up at all four corners to make those legs a solid foundation, but as they settle, strong and firm, they give you such a strong base that it's comparatively easy to tuck in your tailbone (your coccyx, if we're being anatomical), pushing your hips slightly forward and tipping the bottom of your pelvis forward so your stomach can relax. This is crucial. It's a very strong learned response to keep your stomach tucked in and tense. Although with the right pelvis position it isn't going to stick out, you are nevertheless relaxing your stomach muscles and this may not chime with your idea of elegant posture. Forget about that; no one is looking at you for the moment. Let go.

Your legs are solid; your pelvis is tipped. Automatically this will open your chest, as if it were being pulled up by a string attached to your sternum, and your shoulders relax, let go and drop back. Your arms hang loose down by your sides. Your chin drops, your neck lengthens. Remember not to let your tongue tense up. Make space between the vertebrae in your neck, then up and down your spine, which is being kept straighter than normal because it's tucked in at the very bottom, flattening out the 'lordosis', the natural inward curve of your spine above your hips into the small of your back (it is an area of weakness, actually). As you gain greater and greater awareness of what your spine is doing you can extend it, gain extra space between each vertebra. Bring your hands to your chest, palms together, fingers up, in the traditional prayer gesture, let your chin drop again and take seven long, slow breaths, quieting your mind the whole time.

And go straight into the Mountain version, which is basically exactly the same only with your arms up, as straight and as high as you can get them. Raise them, and as they pass your face interlace your fingers. Bring them over your head, your palms facing up, your elbows locked inwards. Try to get your palms as flat as they will go, turning the insides of your arms outwards and stretching up (gently! – don't push!) so you can feel the stretch all the way round your arms, not just at the front. The muscles in between your shoulder blades will be shrieking. Focus on them, let them go, return the focus to your hands and palms, stretch up. It's almost as if you are pulling yourself up with your own hands. Make yourself taller; but you have to know where to let go to be able to stretch. It's an intense listening experience; you are listening to your body with 100 percent more attention than you normally give it. And, surprise, surprise, that attention feeds directly into your state of mind, and your consciousness.

Bring your arms down gently after your seven breaths, and get ready to go straight into Uttanasana, forward bend. The detail of which comes at the end of the next chapter.

Chapter 2

The Power of Creativity

Swadisthana, the Spleen or Sacral Chakra

In this chapter:
Introduction
Reproduction
Joy
Enthusiasm
Imagination
Transformation
Self Creation
World Creation
Power Seeds for Thought
The Salute to the Sun: Forward Bend (Uttanasana)

But unless we are creators we are not fully alive... Creativity is a way of living life, no matter our vocation or how we earn our living.
Madeleine L'Engle, Walking on Water

Creativity is the natural order of life. Life is energy: pure creative energy. We are, ourselves, creations.
Julia Cameron, The Artist's Way: A Spiritual Path to Higher Creativity

Introduction

Every personal Power, each one of the seven that you are reawakening, is interconnected and overlapping, and they are all already within you, waiting to be experienced and expressed. You are creating the new You – or, as we are getting used to saying, *reawakening* the original You, the true You the Soul.

But interconnected and interdependent though they are, each power also has its dominance. Creativity is dominant because without it there is nothing. In many religions God is called the Creator, and when we speak of heaven and earth and all things, living or inert, in them, we speak of Creation. You are using the ideas in this book as you set out on the path of self-transformation, and in that sense you are creating yourself. Your Self. Nothing more directly, essentially creative than that.

This path is a journey inside to discover the hidden treasure, the truth of this pure, powerful, peaceful Soul that you already are and always have been – your natural state of being. But most people's mental and spiritual state is so far removed from this essential truth that it feels like embarking on a creation process, making something entirely new.

Having trouble recognizing, really feeling, this overarching, essential truth? Doesn't feel at all as if pure, powerful, peaceful essence is what you really are? Do you see yourself as a more or less random collection of thoughts, feelings, desires, wishes, satisfactions, disappointments, successes, failures, emptinesses, fullnesses, habits, relationships, daily doings, intellectual and emotional energies? But you have some sense of what's underneath all that, and that whatever it is, is worth getting in touch with, otherwise you wouldn't be here. The fact that you believe, you inherently know, that there's something more, something deeper, something that will give you an insight into what's really going on, is in and of itself proof to you that there is indeed a deeper level of awareness of your Self, of consciousness.

True creativity happens at a Soul level. All art, inspiration, imagination, innovation, invention comes from the Soul, however the individual artist, scientist or inventor conceives it. Yes, of course, creative ideas reside in the mind, and cerebral ones in the intellect; but underneath those is the unique You, driving your ambition to know, to understand, and to express.

This is the creativity, the power, the energy of the Soul. Of You. It's a mental puzzle, a conundrum that can itself help your breakthrough into inner space; You the Soul, being energy, are incapable of being destroyed and therefore, logically, of being created, but it's this process of self exploration, of self knowledge, that is the ultimate creative act. You create your Self. At a mental level you create your thoughts, your feelings, your attitudes, and deeper down at a spiritual level, your powers. You create them, and they create You. And as you engage with that idea – really feel it, experience it – automatically and without effort you create the world around you, your immediate environment. New habits; new habitat.

Every single human soul creates thought. If you're thinking, you're creating. But most religious or spiritual traditions, certainly the 'mystic' subsections of them that include meditation or contemplation, see the mind, where thoughts are created and experienced, as not the true You. The idea of meditation is to still the mind, to reduce the speed and quantity of thoughts down to nearly nothing if possible, so you can dig deeper and experience the silent power of the Self. This is the starting point for the process of balancing your inner ecology, but it's not a hard discipline of meditation. We base our effort on the easy 'Magic Minute', for the simple reason that we need to keep this process accessible and practical, and I know full well that if I ask you to devote an hour a day to meditation and to wreak radical changes in your life, we won't get anywhere. It has to be easy, at the start anyway. This way, change sort of creeps up on you; you will look back and see your behavior has changed, and know how that happened. Your actions have changed because you have changed your mind – not created but re-created, renewed it. Maybe this is the true meaning of recreation.

The Power of Creativity Meditation 1: Reproduction

> Let us investigate more closely this property common to animal and plant, this power of producing its likeness, this chain of successive existences of individuals, which constitutes the real existence of the species.
> *Comte Georges-Louis Leclerc de Buffon,* De la Reproduction en Générale et particulière, Histoire Naturelle, Générale et Particulière, Avec la Description du Cabinet du Roi (1749), Vol. 2, 18. *Trans. Phillip R. Sloan*

Reproduction is one of the greatest, if not the greatest, of our creative powers, and one that we share with every other living being. That in itself is worth a good few minutes' silent contemplation. We're talking about sex, just in case you've missed the connection. The urge to reproduce is a primal power in and of itself, a force of nature that flows through us all and drives our actions from a very deep level, however far away from the natural world we are in our daily urban lives. Being human – again arguably – separates us from the planet's other living beings because, as far as we are aware, we have the self-consciousness, the self-awareness that they don't. But every single living being on the planet, from amoeba on up, has the inbuilt ability to reproduce. Worth pondering on, in your silent Magic Minute.

But – strictly physical, you think? The same bodily power that every adult on the planet has, one way or the other, bar a few medical exceptions? What's it doing in this list of mental or spiritual powers?

Well, for a start, not all the meditations which underlie and support your understanding and your experience of your innate Powers have to focus on the strictly non-physical realm. We have already established that the physical affects the spiritual and the other way round, right? Not to be confused with each other, but those dimensions interact, intertwine and affect each other. And as far as creativity is concerned, no one would deny that this particular area of physical experience is: a) within us all; and b) overwhelmingly, profoundly, primally powerful.

This meditation focuses your attention on the idea of a seed, both mental/spiritual and physical. The parallel is a neat one. In your silent Magic Minute(s) you plant a Power Seed of thought that, like all seeds, holds an entire universe in itself, in pre-programmed and pre-physical form; part of your Power Seed is thinking about the biological seeds that you physically make, and from which our physical existence springs. Women, focus on your innate power to grow another human inside your body, the seed that is fertilized; men, focus on your power to produce the seeds that fertilize.

These familiar concepts lead you to experience the subtle energy flowing inside you – Prān, Ch'i, the life force. You the observer, a form of spiritual energy, are focusing on the observed physical phenomenon, the flow of life. Keep it at that universal level, and keep your mind away from thoughts about sex. I'm not suggesting that you eliminate or ignore your sexuality; it's vitally important, in fact, and very much a part of a balanced spiritual ecology that you understand it and have a close, respectful and loving relationship with it. But not here and now. This is your crucially valuable Magic Minute, and giving sex your attention now will waste your mental energy. The whole point is to dive under or rise over physicality, harnessing the power of your mind to discover the much, much greater power behind the mind, which you can only do when you still it.

This process opens a door directly into the universe, just as if you were in a science fiction fantasy, and opening the door to leave home one morning, you found yourself facing infinite space instead of your front yard. The thought process itself will calm your mind, slow it down; you enter inner space, and by placing your full, silent awareness on your Self as owner of this reproductive power, you tap directly into the universal Power of Creativity. Nurture it. Your mind is changing; you are changing your mind. When you are truly experiencing your Self like this, you are really heading for a balanced internal ecology, a healthy spiritual ecosystem. And by the way, in that balance you will also find a new depth, power, and transcendent beauty in your loving sexual experience. Can't be bad.

The Power of Creativity Meditation 2: Joy

> Where there is joy there is creation. Where there is no joy there is no creation; know the nature of joy.
> *Maitrayaniya Upanishad,* c800 BC

It's easy to forget, among all the hustle and bustle, the daily life, the going and coming, the work, the family, the worries, the getting and spending. It may even seem like an alien concept. We are creatures of delight, of joy, put here on this earth to have fun.

No? Too far-fetched? Completely missing the point of our serious existence? Too flippertigibbet, superficial, lightweight? Aren't we engaged in a process of self transformation here, the power of silence, the quiet contemplation and rebuilding of our inner selves, which leads to changed actions and ultimately a changed world? What could be more serious than that?

Well, have a think about this; no reason why you can't be serious and effective but also experience the deep joy, the delight of being, the 'high' that comes from you knowing and feeling your natural state as a conscient, non-physical entity. The word 'fun' may be a little misleading in this context, true; it's not a matter to be taken lightly. But it does get at the point that we have missed, which is that anxiety, discontent, stress, sadness, fear and anger are not our default settings. Strange though it may seem, happiness is. Otherwise why would we be seeking it in so many ways? To be truly aware of your true Self is to be truly joyful. I'm not suggesting inappropriate behavior, like having a fit of the giggles at a funeral, or asking you to find the delight in some nasty task like cleaning up after someone (your child, your mother-in-law, your best friend, your dog) has been sick on the rug. The joy is underneath all that.

Contemplation of the simple idea of joy brings you quickly to spiritual joy, contentment, peace. To 'bliss', to use a beautiful and powerful word, which describes the ultimate meditative experience, when you are a silent light floating in a silent sea of light. (Enlightenment, geddit?) Although that state doesn't come easily, even the journey towards it feeds your everyday joy, your natural happiness. Surprise, you are essentially a happy being!

Joy is your natural state because You the Soul are a node of pure, peaceful, silent, spiritual energy, conscious of Your Self as a Soul and of the physical and subtle energy constantly flowing through your body. If you have managed to calm the naughty child that is your mind for long enough to break through to this deep awareness, and to settle into the full realization that it is this peaceful Self that is You, and not the chatter on top, you emerge from it smiling. Grinning, even. That has to tell you something, surely; you just tapped into an infinite source of happiness with no expense and virtually no effort, in the comfort of your own home (or car, or bus, or subway, or workplace, or anyplace). It was inside you, all this time. How can that not affect your life and that of those around you?

The happiness you get from everyday life can be powerful; let's not disrespect it. Your love for your family, for your sport, art or music, natural beauty, your garden, even that new phone, kitchen or car, are joys that keep us going through our days and nights, through the grind. But the deep-down joy you are connecting to means peace. Joy means power, joy means bliss, joy means love. It is a definition of the conscient energy that is You. The physical is always moving, always in action – which is why we seek joy and connection to it through physical means – the art, music or nature I talked about. The spiritual is still and silent, but alive, conscient. This is where you're headed. To get in contact with that single, still source of incredibly powerful energy that is You.

Consciousness, including thoughts, feelings, desires, fears, atmospheres, emotions, memories, perceptions – all the activity by which we define ourselves at an everyday level – is energy.

And therefore indestructible. And if 'You' are energy that is also somehow individual, then you are an energy form, a node, with unique characteristics. 'You' are indestructible; you will just change as you move on. You are affected by physical energy, and you in turn affect it; your body affects your feelings, and your feelings affect your body. Physical energy flows and vibrates; the pure spiritual energy that is You is stillness, in perfect peace – but it is still giving off a vibration.

All that these meditations do is bring you to an awareness of your Self as that energy, and not as the thoughts, feelings, desires, fears, atmospheres, emotions, memories and perceptions aforesaid. And when you have that awareness – when you are Soul Conscious as opposed to body conscious – you see yourself as an infinitesimally small particle of energy, a spiritual neutrino if you like, burning like a light or a flame but never consuming itself, never going out; still, silent, peaceful and powerful, but like the flame or the light, alive and vibrating at the same time. And if you don't find yourself connecting to unlimited Joy as you kick into that awareness, then try again. You just haven't got to it yet. I can't take you there; you have to take yourself. You don't have to create it. It's already there. You just have to connect.

The Power of Creativity Meditation 3: Enthusiasm

(ένθουσιασμός)

> The secret of genius is to carry the spirit of the child into old age, which means never losing your enthusiasm.
> *Aldous Huxley*

> Enthusiasm is the yeast that makes your hopes shine to the stars. Enthusiasm is the sparkle in your eyes, the swing in your gait. The grip of your hand, the irresistible surge of will and energy to execute your ideas.
> *Henry Ford*

Enthusiasm is a primary ingredient of the Power of Creativity, firstly because it describes the intensity of the creative process, particularly at the start, and most importantly because it defines your relationship with that process. Just in case you are thinking that this is not for you, because you don't see yourself as a creative person and the creative process means nothing to you, remember that the Power of Creativity is one of your essential powers, inherent in and defining You the Soul. Remember that there is no human being on this earth who isn't creative, because we create thoughts, feelings, actions – and we reproduce. You are on a journey to rediscover and nurture those powers, dormant in the fundamental, essential You.

It's always useful to go back to definitions, because they show us the intimately creative relationship between language and thought. The *Shorter Oxford English Dictionary*'s entry for enthusiasm quotes the Greek ένθουσιασμός (enthusiasmos), by which Plato meant 'inspired or possessed by the god'. ''Eν', inspired, θεός', god. It goes on into later English usages: "Possession by a god, supernatural inspiration, prophetic or poetic ecstasy; fancied inspiration, a conceit of divine favour or communication." In the 18th century it was used to denote "ill regulated religious emotion or speculation" (both quotes from the *Shorter Oxford English Dictionary*). And the Enthusiasts, we learn, were fourth century 'heretics' who laid claim to special revelations. So no question that the word – and hence the idea – originally expressed transcendence; connection or communication with 'the Divine', which is simply a way of saying "a power which we can't know or define using our senses or intellect". Enthusiasm is one of the many ways in which you experience the power of your mind when it is really focused, and below and behind that, the creative power of You the Soul which underpins all that mental, sensual and emotional energy. Enthusiasm is one of the routes to the self awareness which is essential to a balanced Ecology of the Soul.

There is a personal, private fire that burns in the heart of those people lucky (or unlucky, depending on how you look at it) enough to have a cause, a mission or a project in which they passionately believe and to which they are profoundly committed. That flame is lit from the same source of energy which drives the enthusiast in the sense of artist, sportsperson or even hobbyist; they are continuously engaged, they have continuous desire for improvement, to be better, to achieve more, to have more (which, if it's just ownership of more things, may prove self defeating). They don't mind personal discomfort, they often make sacrifices for the sake of their enthusiasm, which it's easy to see as selfishness. Artists can be difficult people, driven to create while other aspects of their life lie neglected. If your enthusiasm is for adrenalin-fueled activities like mountain climbing, skydiving, motor sport or extreme skiing, you happily take on danger, discomfort and expense, separation from your loved ones and even the risk of physical harm, which also of course harms your loved ones. Less extreme enthusiasms such as chess, fishing or computer games don't perhaps demand that you risk your life, but they are nonetheless consuming and exclusive. Unless you share your enthusiasm with those unfortunate loved ones, they are likely to take second place. Your enthusiasm takes you out on your own.

Not, on the face of it, a great recommendation for enthusiasm. But that private fire burning in your heart – even if it's only for a particular TV program which demands that everything else stop while you watch it – gives you a way of defining yourself, of knowing yourself. And that is the link to the Power of Creativity, because knowing yourself leads directly to creating yourself. And creating (or re-creating) your Self. With or without self awareness, you create your thoughts, your thoughts create your feelings and your actions, your actions create you with a small 'y'. Which creates your thoughts, which create your actions… and so on, round and round.

So. If at the everyday, physical level of normal life, one of the ways you create a sense of your 'normal' self is through your enthusiasms, it follows that you can turn them towards an understanding of your spiritual Self. Keep looking below the surface, giving thought to why you are so keen on this particular thing or activity. Perversely, it seems that it is because it takes you 'out of yourself'. So totally absorbed in something do you become that you 'forget yourself'. What you are forgetting, fortunately, is the everyday self, the one that's dealing with all the complications, the worries, the things that should have been but aren't or shouldn't have been but are. While you're doing this, nothing else matters. You're in touch with your deeper Self. The electricity bill is not relevant to the here and now.

Like everything else, enthusiasm is energy. It is creative energy, because although it applies itself mostly to external worldly things, it comes from You the soul, which is conscient, aware, living spiritual energy, not the dumb, flowing, universal life force. The dumb one is creative in the sense that it makes flowers grow and birds fly, but it is creation without awareness. It is not self aware, it is not conscient. Your power and privilege as a unique and individual node of conscient energy is to know the creative power of your Self. Enthusiasm, like many other forms of awareness, is a route to this knowledge and this experience.

The Power of Creativity Meditation 4: Imagination

Imagination is usually regarded as a synonym for the unreal. Yet is true imagination healthful and real, no more likely to mislead than the coarse senses. Indeed, the power of imagination makes us infinite.

Naturalist and champion of Yosemite *John Muir*, The National Parks and Forest Reservations *Sierra Club Bulletin*, v. 1, no. 7, January 1896

Some of us might not think of ourselves as creative, and others of us might struggle to see enthusiasm, or even joy, as an inherent part of our personal makeup. But everyone, surely, knows they have imagination. If people accuse you of having no imagination, it doesn't mean you have none, it just means you don't have the same one as they do. Which is hardly surprising, given that each and every individual human soul on this earth is unique. If you did have the same imagination as them, there'd be trouble.

Our goal is to balance the Ecology of the Soul, of which the mind is a part. And imagination resides in the mind. The received wisdom from generations of philosophers and psychologists tends to be that imagination is a bridge between 'unreality', the fantasy of the unconscious, and conscious reality, which is somehow better because it's more real, ie in the physical realm. It is indeed your bridge, but between two sorts of reality – the physical and the non-physical – not reality and 'unreality'. Remember that spiritual and mystical traditions see the non-physical as real, and the physical as illusion.

Most of the time your mind occupies the physical space. You get up in the morning, you lead your daily life: home, family, friends, work, play, getting and spending, eating, drinking, relaxing. You need to pay attention to those physical things; and to more 'cerebral', less physical activities like reading books or newspapers, listening to music, watching TV, having conversations. But all the time you and your daily life are getting on with each other, your imagination is whirring away on a separate track.

There is the idea of separation between the 'reproductive' and the 'productive' imaginations, or functions of the imagination, which goes back to the early days of psychology and appears, for example, in James Rowland Angell's *Psychology: an Introductory Study of the Structure and Function of Human Consciousness* (1906). Unless I've woefully misunderstood, it is to distinguish between what we would otherwise know as 'visual memory' (we conjure up pictures and experiences of events, things that happened or are about to happen, a sort of reliving) and the more directly creative function which generates all our 'original' ideas, images, words, music, literature, poetry, art, design, architecture. This is the truly imaginative stuff, where people bring things into the world that were apparently never before heard or seen, and that somehow shed light on what we call 'the human condition' – making a stab at the 'meaning of life'.

Which is the part we're interested in, because: a) it's the truly creative part; b) that truly creative part is the one with which the majority of people don't identify – they don't see themselves as 'creative'; and c) it turns out that the truly creative part is actually not creative at all, in the sense of making something out of nothing, but 're-creative'. I don't mean that everyone who reads this book or begins to achieve balance in their internal ecology will automatically turn into an artist or musician. I do mean that turning your attention inwards towards your spiritual, inner, true Self gives you an insight double whammy; at the same time as your new awareness allows you to connect to the 'dumb life' flow of energy, you are fully experiencing the unique, individual node of 'smart consciousness' that is You.

Making that connection, in the early stages at least, uses the imagination. Meditation starts with visualization, which is another word for (one type of) imagination. You see your Self with your mind's eye; your imagination is your tool. The real nub of the matter is that you are not imagining something into existence, creating something that was never before heard or seen; you are visualizing something that is already there. The more you experience it, the less you will have to 'productively' imagine it, because truly experiencing it happens at a level of consciousness below (or above) your mind. In fact, you can't get there without shutting your mind down, or at least temporarily suspending its activity.

Want to take the logical, intellectual route? Test the premise that all the inner power and peace you need to become your true, balanced, resilient, loveful and joyful Self are already present but dormant, waiting to be unlocked? Consider this. Every human being has an idea of Heaven. The awareness of a place – or a state of being – of peace, happiness, harmony and beauty. We couldn't come up with such a concept if we didn't have experience of it at some profound, deeply buried level, way down in the foundations of our multi-generational awareness.

Which is to say, you can't imagine what you don't know, can't bring into being in your mind something that in some way has not already been part of your own individual or the collective human experience. The relationship between thought and language revolves around a similar idea; you can't think something for which a word doesn't exist. In the realm of imagination, every original idea you or anyone else ever had comes from a combination of what you have done, read, seen or heard, and the accumulated experience of all the generations in human history. In simplistic terms, there's no such thing as a completely original idea. It goes to persuade you, again quite simply, that since you are here working on ways to create (re-create) a more peaceful, powerful You, that peaceful, powerful You has already existed. If it hadn't, you couldn't be engaged in the effort to create (or re-create) it. Give thanks that you have the imagination to show you what's possible.

The Power of Creativity Meditation 5: Transformation

> The way of the Creative works through change and transformation, so that each thing receives its true nature and destiny and comes into permanent accord with the Great Harmony: this is what furthers and what perseveres.
> *Alexander Pope*

Transformation is an intrinsic part of creativity, the creative process. Take some lumps of wood and turn them into a table. If your name is Michelangelo, take a lump of marble and turn it into David. A vast tract of humanity's imaginative and cultural life – literature, art, fairy tale, myth, the supernatural – is about transformation. From Alice in Wonderland and the Ugly Duckling to Franz Kafka's *Metamorphosis* via Cinderella, Jekyll and Hyde or Superman, the psychic power of the idea is huge. In Christianity we have enlightenment, canonization, transubstantiation, angels becoming devils and vice versa. Can't get much shape-shiftier than blood into wine and flesh into bread. In magic, we have werewolves, vampires, wizards and death eaters. One thing turns into another. Which is real? In your sub- or super-consciousness, the reality is You, your peaceful, powerful, blissful true Self. To know and live that reality is the transformation you seek. Here, transformation is creation.

Creation. Regeneration. Renewal. Transformation. They are inevitable. You have to deal, not deny. You can't control or divert them for your physical self, however many expensive cosmetics you buy or hours you spend in the gym. Your body is subject to the degenerative and the regenerative laws of nature. But in the case of your mind and consciousness, you can control the process. You can choose to set your consciousness on a permanent path of growth, expansion, increase in power and capacity. Your creative, transformational power is that of the open mind, the willingness to listen, to experiment. It demands commitment, but hey, change is going to happen anyway. Might as well harness it to the good.

While you are working on the balance of the Ecology of the Soul that is You, unlocking your innate powers, there is the paradox that you experience yourself as creating your new Self, but in fact that new Self is your true Self which has always been there. You are rediscovering it rather than creating it. It is a creative process, but the raw material is already there. There is no realization more powerful than that. Transformation, despite (because of?) the enormous power of the idea, is simple. It is the result of that self discovery what happens next; changing yourself, on the ground, in daily life, simply means bringing the true You to the surface and driving your actions from that experience. Is it the transformation of your true nature? No. It's transformation of your thinking, your way of seeing, your attitude – your behavior – through understanding and experiencing your true nature. Yes, your behavior has changed; you have transformed yourself by opening up to the true You, your Self. The grub is becoming a butterfly.

In fact, when we really turn our close attention to what transformation means in the context of changing our awareness, our state of mind, our consciousness, our behavior – changing our Selves – we fetch up against the idea of perfection. Because if we set ourselves on a path of constant improvement, we automatically engage with the ultimate goal of such a path; though we might not choose to commit to it in our everyday lives, and see ourselves merely as working towards a better way of living, we are still on an upward curve that stops when that process, notionally or practically, stops. Which is at the achievement of bliss, the ultimate fulfilment, complete and total, unwavering, unshakeable happiness, transcendence. A perfect state of being.

No such thing in an imperfect world, subject to the laws of

change and decay, etc, etc, right? Of course. But the idea is still there, right? So where did it come from? Adam and Eve's innocence in the biblical Garden can be seen as a way of describing a state of consciousness where 'sin', in other words the mistaken consciousness of our Selves as our bodies and the resulting actions that come from that mistaken consciousness, does not exist. No mistaken or 'bad' action, no bad reaction. No suffering, no loss, no pain. Just fulfilment, satisfaction, contentment. Peace. Like, Heaven.

The practical change in your behavior is not going to be overnight, but the trigger to start the creation of that new mental landscape can be instantaneous. Inspiration, revelation, determination – you wake up one morning with another head on. You may decide to conquer your anger, to get a grip on your anxieties, or just to exercise more, to diet, to give up alcohol or coffee – as long as you persuade yourself to see it not as giving up but as adding to your improved state of being. If your change program is guilt- or shame-driven ("What a dick I am for drinking that much when I promised myself I wouldn't drink at all"; "What a fool I am for letting him make me feel that way again after I promised myself I would rise above it and ignore him"), there's already resistance, and it won't work, because it comes from self-hatred. You can only make it happen by treating yourself with love. Even then, you will almost certainly make progress, then fall back again. Always look on yourself with the love and compassion that history's best humans have genuinely felt for all souls. You are beautiful, after all. The essential, true You is a living light, and there is nothing more beautiful than that. When you are still and silent, conscious only of your Self as a light steadily shining, it's easy to make that experience real. This is the nub, where creativity and transformation meet and become the same thing. It's as near as we can get in the here and now to a perfect state of being.

The Power of Creativity Meditation 6: Self Creation

> Whoever undertakes to create soon finds himself engaged in creating himself.
> *Harold Rosenberg*

> As human beings, our greatness lies not so much in being able to remake the world – that is the myth of the atomic age – as in being able to remake ourselves.
> *Mahatma Gandhi*

Creation, self creation, recreation, re-creation. When it comes to the Self or Soul we are at the heart of the matter, where we explore the nature of mind, thought, feeling and their relationship to action. (We're here to change our actions, remember?) We're dealing with levels of consciousness above or below the mind, and only by stilling the mind and taking it out of gear will we get to those levels where the understanding comes directly from experience.

But the process of balancing the Ecology of the Soul starts at the mind and intellect level, where we do our thinking. We focus first of all on our 'mental ecology', by which I mean the inner world we inhabit, the nature of our thought patterns, emotions, imagination, hopes, fears, ambitions, delights, preoccupations. That mental ecology affects and is affected by the 'real', ie the physical, world. Then we dig deeper and come to an awareness of our *spiritual* as distinct from our *mental* ecology – the Ecology of the Soul, of which your mind is but a part.

It takes a lot of meditation practice to get to the place where you have literally no thought, but by the time you get there – and on the journey even – you are abundantly aware that You. Are. Not. Your. Mind. You have been watching Your mind, getting the measure of it, starting on the process of controlling it; You are something different from it. You are separating out the levels of your consciousness, becoming aware of the difference between the observer and the observed, and which one is really You. You are a unit of non-physical, conscient energy that is aware of itself, that is itself awareness, that thinks and feels, is light. A light burning, shining, glowing, without ever consuming itself.

In this powerful process of creating, or re-creating, your Self, you unleash the true Power of Creativity in your Self. First, by refining your understanding of which bit of your consciousness does what; then turning that understanding into real life experience; then feeding that experience back to the 'thoughts and feelings' level where it automatically triggers the change, or creation, process. 'Automatically' doesn't mean it can be done without effort, but it does mean that as your consciousness changes, so your thoughts, feelings and attitudes change. You need mental and spiritual power to do this, which is precisely what study of the Ecology of the Soul will give you. This is all about revitalizing your original, natural, innate powers. By tapping into, in this case, your Power of Creativity, you encourage it, increase it, enhance it, nurture it, expand it – renew it. Like exercising muscles you never knew you had.

The process of creating (re-creating) our Selves and hence our actions demands a clear sense of the difference between the pure, peaceful, powerful spiritual Self, the true You, and its ordinary, everyday subdivisions which connect directly to action; where the power comes from, and where it goes.

The thousands of inspirational, motivational, meditation or self-improvement texts that have been written and read over generations, however diverse their philosophies, all have one thing in common: a focus on the power of thought. Deep or shallow, they teach that the mind is enormously powerful, that its thinking is mostly uncontrolled and that to control it will break us through to the experience of the true Self – or to the health, wealth and happiness we feel is our birthright – or to both. The power of the mind (some say) will make everything you desire come true. But there is also the great trick we have allowed our minds to play on us, making us mistake our bodies for our Selves. The power of the mind is a means of escape from this illusion, freeing itself from its own waywardness.

How, practically, can we break the old thought molds and create new ones, which lead to new actions, new behaviors? For me, the teachings of Raja Yoga make the most sense of this profoundly powerful subject, because they break down the 'faculties' of the Soul, if you like, into three: Mind, Intellect and Sanskars (inadequately translated into English as 'Impressions', or even 'Personality', which I think is a little misleading). They are not separate departments as such, more like aspects of the conscient unit of non-physical energy that is You the Soul, working on different levels. "Just as electrical energy produces warmth, sound or light depending on the device through which it passes, similarly, the energy of consciousness functions through three different but closely connected faculties, referred to respectively by the terms mind, intellect, and personality," says the 'Consciousness and Self-Realization' section of the Raja Yoga Meditation course on www.bkwsu.org, the Brahma Kumaris' official site.

Through the mind, says the teaching, one imagines, thinks and forms ideas. The thought process is the basis of all emotions, desires and sensations. The intellect is the critical faculty, the one that carries the power of understanding, reasoning, analysis, judgement, assessment. It is what we use to memorize, discriminate and make decisions – not to be confused with the brain, which is the physical 'control panel' by which the Soul's non-physical activity is brought into the physical. Soul sends messages to brain; brain sends messages to body.

The third and most 'difficult' faculty gives an understanding of how we come to be who we are in the everyday, personal life sense, with our accumulated baggage of history, physical identity, attitudes, relationships, circumstances and behavior. 'Sanskars' or 'sanksaras' is the Sanskrit word used to describe this aspect of consciousness: the recorded results of all our actions through all of our lives. Essentially, the concept takes the universal Law of Karma and puts it into a useable framework for self-examination and behavior change.

Karma means, simply, action. Everything you do or have ever done, in this and all your lives, leaves an impression on the Soul, cumulatively creating the unique individual that is You. Action creates reaction, which creates more action – we all know this if we've ever had a habit that we've tried to control or stop. The more you do it, the more you do it. Do it less, and the impulse to do it fades away. The law of karma, the universal law of action and reaction, is Newton's third law of the physical universe: 'For every action there is an equal and opposite reaction.' It's also the spiritual or ethical law: 'As you sow, so shall you reap', 'You get what you give', etc, etc.

But the intricacies of cause and effect over thousands of generations are so unfathomable, it's a waste of mental and spiritual energy to try. Here and now, we can apply this beautiful knowledge to the job in hand – changing ourselves back to the pure, powerful, peaceful Souls that we once were. If we create new actions, we create our Selves anew. And a newly created Self will create new actions. Which in turn feed back to the Self-creation process. Or re-creation, because that is our original state. Or recreation, because let's not forget amongst all this mental and intellectual activity that our original state is one of bliss, delight, joy, love, happiness, power and peace. And that is recreation that we all need, God knows.

The Power of Creativity Meditation 7: World Creation

> We are one human family and one Earth community with a common destiny. We must join together to bring forth a sustainable global society founded on respect for nature, universal human rights, economic justice, and a culture of peace. Towards this end, it is imperative that we, the peoples of Earth, declare our responsibility to one another, to the greater community of life, and to future generations.
> *Earth Charter Preamble,* 2000

> If the world is to change for the better it must start with a change in human consciousness, in the very humanness of modern man.
> *Václav Havel, Disturbing the Peace: A Conversation with Karel Hvizdala.* English translation by Paul Wilson (1990)

The aim of this meditation is to firmly implant in your mind the certain knowledge that a change in your own consciousness changes the world. To do it alone, as one among seven billion, is kind of a tall order, obviously. So the proposition is that the more people begin to change their consciousness – by any route – the more the world changes.

This idea, this experience, depends on a clear understanding and acceptance of the idea that mind affects matter, but also that matter affects mind. Everywhere we look we see that what we are doing to the earth and how we ourselves are living is unsustainable, because it is all driven from a basic mistake we have made about the true nature of our Selves. We have been working on the idea that we are our physical bodies, and that the happiness we all seek can be gained by having physical things, things and more things. Makes sense that if that mistaken mindset has created this mess, then we need an 'unmistaken' other one to fix it. In fact, we can't begin to fix it unless and until we change the way we think – and feel, and perceive – and act. Which is where the change in consciousness having an effect on the state of the world comes in. Here we're talking about the effect of the subtle, the non-physical, on the physical; the impact of thoughts and emotions on the material world.

Matter is energy, right? I think we all, with Mr. Einstein's help, have established that much. Right down at the subatomic level, where the quarks and neutrinos play, every single building block of material substance in or on this earth, everything that makes the earth or indeed the known universe, is nothing more than a handful of infinitesimally small particles whizzing about in what to them is infinite space. Matter is energy is motion, vibrating, flowing, at frequencies which we as conscious, conscient beings (a different kind of energy) pick up. We also generate vibrations or frequencies with our own mental and spiritual activity – we put out our own 'vibe'. Walk into a club or bar where you don't belong, for whatever reason, or find yourself in the wrong section of a sports stadium, and you will feel an atmosphere, created from the thought frequencies of those around you. If you're not wanted or welcome, you'll feel it. Churches, temples, prisons, hospitals: you name it. It's what people think, feel and do that create the atmosphere; their mental and spiritual activity.

You just need to consider what people call the 'power of the mind' to know how our own conscient energy affects our physical environment. There have actually been scientific experiments to prove this,[1] although doubtless there are still doubters. At a personal level, we know very well how our mental and emotional states affect our heath and well-being, our sex lives, our ability to perform in any activity. In yoga we are very

---

1 Garrett Moddel & Kevin Walsh, PsiPhen Laboratory, University of Colorado, 2007; http://psiphen.colorado.edu/Pubs/ModdelSSE07.pdf

familiar with how physical activity stills the mind and how that still mind in its turn opens and releases the body. If we love plants, we know that showing them that love in a subtle, nurturing way makes them grow better. Logically, we conclude that of course, with enough people with powerful minds focusing on the same end, our transformational effect on the physical world is guaranteed.

Sometimes after a session of yoga or meditation I sit silent, enjoying my gradual return to daily consciousness from a place of light and peace, and our cat, an ill-tempered and unpredictable creature given to lashing out without warning, will come and rub up against me, making contact with the peaceful energy she can feel. She becomes quiet and docile, lying back like a soft toy and purring as if she has plugged herself directly into this source of peace. Which, in a way, she has. My 'vibe' is spreading out, and so will yours, subtly affecting the energy of the immediate environment. If we want to make the polar ice caps come back, we have to build our powers into something spectacular, learn to focus them a great deal more precisely, and work in unison with the other 6,999,999,999 people on the planet.

Not every single human being is going to sit down and meditate all at the same time, of course, but the idea does lead us to the next step – a communal consciousness. As inhabitants of the natural physical world, driven by the non-physical energy of consciousness, the link between our 'micro' inner Selves and the 'macro' environment is inherent and obvious. That macro environment is mental and spiritual, not just physical; we feel that nature too, though it is physical energy alone, can have an emotional or spiritual element. The angry wind is cruel, the soft breeze is kind. But other people, who are – like you – chunks of physical energy controlled by spiritual energy, are also your environment, and after your Self your first port of call in the consciousness journey is them. Can't avoid it really, because as we have seen above, the people close to you – and soon, not so close – will be bound to pick up your 'vibe'.

The idea of a 'New World' means a change of general consciousness – in time. There is the world we have now, and the one that is coming. "When the ecology of the Soul is in balance" – to quote myself – "we live and thrive in this world – and create the new one – with grace, harmony and beauty. As we rediscover, reconnect and recharge our innate peace and power, the world changes along with us." Our enhanced, true perception of our Selves creates a powerful spiritual 'vibe', changing our environment with mind as well as action. As more and more of us achieve that individually, we achieve it together. We don't have to all sit down together because the connection is subtle and takes no notice of physical distance, but it helps because we feed off the cumulative power of the group as we feed into it. We become uplifted, completely living the experience that this power, of silence, peace and love, is not only the greatest power in humanity, but actually the only one. As the old world crumbles, this consciousness makes sense of what is happening around us right now and gives us a vision of the new world we are making. Which looks a lot like Heaven.

The Power of Creativity Practice 1: Plant a Power Seed Every Day

For this exercise, see your mind as a garden, or at least a patch of fertile soil. Thoughts and feelings grow in it, like plants. It's a riot of tangled and intertwined mental vegetation, much of it good and useful – and most of it neither good nor useful.

Use Power Seeds to grow a new garden of consciousness. They are mental devices, thought triggers to create, enhance or encourage Soul Consciousness, and hence change your actions. They are a bit like the Zen 'kōan' (eg 'the sound of one hand clapping') that kick your mind out of gear and raise the level of your awareness. You can't be – or act – greedy, angry, jealous, anxious, depressed or hostile when you're Soul Conscious – alive to the knowledge of your Self as an infinitesimal pinpoint of conscient light and life, burning steadily without consuming itself, giving off the vibration, the spiritual energy, of peace, power and love.

That's the idea, anyway. You are going to have to treat yourself with love in this process, because it doesn't happen overnight. This is partly because I am suggesting you start with a mere 'Magic Minute' each day – just a minute, 60 tiny seconds – for the simple reason that at that level it is easy and requires no major change in lifestyle to adopt. Get up a minute earlier each day? How hard can that be?

It's a trick, of course. If you have managed to focus, really focus all the innate power of your calmed, stilled mind, on your chosen Power Seed for 60 full seconds, that thought pattern will repeat and recur throughout the day, accumulating much more than a single minute of your mental activity. It's meditation in action, because the meditation is about action.

See Part I, the Introduction section on The Seven Powers, Power Seeds and the Magic Minute for a detailed explanation of the technique, and Part III for more examples from which you can choose according to specific areas of your consciousness and behavior. Ultimately, as your Self knowledge increases, you will be creating and planting your own, specific to your own circumstances.

To experience the Power of Creativity within your Self, as your consciousness of your breathing kicks in and you feel your mind slowing down, plant one of the 'introductory' mental Power Seeds that appear on the following pages.

Examine your own thoughts.
Look at the pictures.
Listen to the chatter.
Who is looking?
Who is listening?

Everyone is creative.
Everyone has creativity.
What is your strong suit?
Which private part of your world holds your true creativity?

Mind creates action:
action creates mind.
Create a beautiful mind.

The True You, the Soul, is no more nor less than energy.
You cannot be destroyed and You cannot be created.
But knowing your Self, transforming your Self, is the ultimate creative act. You create Your Self.

Creation is re-creation.
Creation of the Self is re-creation.
It is also recreational.

Reproduction starts with the seed.
Know your physical reproductive power, lying in the female seed that is fertilized or the male seed that fertilizes.
Now apply the knowledge of that power to non-physical thought seeds.
All the programming is already there. It just has to be brought into action.

Focus on the center of your forehead. You, the infinitesimal point of light, are sitting there, controlling this enormous

physical body.
Separate your Self from your physical identity.
Become Soul Conscious.
Become aware of your Self as a being of light, power and peace.
You are light.
Shine.

These 'general' Power Seeds lift your consciousness into meditations on the Power of Creativity. As your practice develops, get specific. Think about the day ahead (or behind, or either side) of you. Is there a situation or scenario in your life that you want to influence or change, that must improve? (Of course there is.) Is there a particular problem nagging at you? Choose or create your own Power Seed aimed directly at that problem or situation. If it will come up today, what are you going to do? How are you going to deal with it differently, knowing your Self now as you do?

As your new mental tracks bed in, you will come up against tougher mental challenges. Generally the solution is always positive thought. As your mind stills and quietness takes over, observe the problem as if it was floating in front of you but didn't belong to you. Detach from your mind. See yourself seeing your Self.

Remember that this is your mind, it is not You. And that it is absolutely unacceptable that your mind controls your mood. You are in control, not your mind. Take the wheel and drive, for God's sake. Your problem, anxiety or bad state of mind may not disappear in a puff of smoke, but you have at least got a grip and rebuilt your positive mood. And every problem diminishes when you face it in a positive mood, right?

The Power of Creativity Practice 2: Yoga Seeds – Salute to the Sun (Surya Namaskar)

Position 2: Forward Bend (Uttanasana)

The Salute to the Sun, like most things in Yoga, has many variations. The one we use here consists of seven 'asanas', to use the Sanskrit name for positions, done in a 12-step sequence. This posture is one of the Iyengar yoga system's basic components, used as a relaxation between more strenuous positions, although until the backs of your legs lengthen nicely it's hard to see how it can be relaxing!

'Ut' indicates deliberation or intensity and 'tān' means to stretch, extend, lengthen. The head-down position slows the heart and soothes the mind, giving an extreme stretch to the spinal column, which rejuvenates the nervous system and gets the Prān (or Ch'i, or life force) really flowing.

Uttanasana – Forward Bend: The Asana

It's also, if you're not already very limber, excruciating on the backs of the legs, which have to be kept ramrod straight with the knees locked, the kneecaps pulled up at all four corners. So there are intermediate positions on the way where you can use blocks to rest your hands, or even lean against a wall and stretch your arms out to a chair or suitable surface at the right height.

As in all asanas, the trick is keeping one (or some) parts of you energized and tight, which allows other parts of you to relax and let go as much as possible – which is how you get the stretch. Only by creating a strong and solid framework or foundation from which to 'hang' the parts that you want to go loose will you be able to let them go and get the full benefit of the stretch.

This is the second posture in the sequence, so you are coming to it from Tadasana, the standing mountain. Your arms are stretched to the full vertically above your head, the fingers linked and ideally the palms flat and facing outwards and upwards. Your coccyx is tucked in, the bottom of your pelvis tipped forward a little to flatten out the 'lordosis', the inward curve of the spine above your buttocks. On the outbreath, bring your arms, still straight, down to parallel with the floor at your eye level, then use them to continue downwards and stretch outwards as you bend at the hips. Take another breath if you need to, and go down on the outbreath. It's crucial to keep the top half of your body open as you bend. Don't curl up your spine and scrunch up the front of your body, but keep your head up and your back straight, bend from the hips and, still keeping your head up and your back in an upward curve, let your hands head for the floor. At their nearest point – ideally on the floor, but this won't happen if you're new to this position, unless you're unusually limber – legs still locked solid and straight, kneecaps pulled up, you let your head and neck go and allow gravity to do the work of extending them towards the floor. Pay particular attention to the back of your neck, which is usually under extreme tension because it has to hold your heavy head up all day long. Just let it go, feel it lengthen. Let go in the shoulders and between the shoulder blades.

If it's hurting the backs of your legs, which is pretty much a given when you start, try to get that trick of relaxing into the stretch. A lot of the result comes from being able to 'make space' in the hips, which allows the top half of your body to lengthen and come closer to your thighs. Feel your vertebrae separating and your whole spine stretching. Don't push. Never push, it won't work. Let go in your hips, feel the stretch on the muscles in the backs of your legs, and selectively pull them up towards your hips, which act as a pivot from which your lengthening top half will continue to lower towards the floor.

If the backs of your legs are shrieking so much that you are tensing up, especially in the back and shoulders where it is most likely to happen, give yourself a break and do it in stages. Use blocks or bricks or anything that raises the level to which your hands will drop, or do the chair and leaning against the wall thing. The benefit of this pose rapidly becomes apparent. It automatically quietens your mind. On each outbreath you can feel the top half of your body getting a little longer. Blood goes to your head, which is good, but if you feel dizzy, come up – always leading with your head, your back as open and extended as you can make it.

Next pose is the forward lunge to your right leg. Detail at the end of the next chapter.

Chapter 3

The Power of Endurance

Manipura, the Solar Plexus Chakra

In this chapter:
Introduction
Acceptance
Persistence (Doggedness)
Faith
Hope
Optimism
Serenity
Stillness
Power Seeds for Thought
The Salute to the Sun: Forward Lunge

Endurance is one of the most difficult disciplines, but it is to the one who endures that the final victory comes.
Buddha

Some days there won't be a song in your heart. Sing anyway.
Emory Austin

Endurance: It is the spirit which can bear things, not simply with resignation, but with blazing hope. It is the quality which keeps a man on his feet with his face to the wind. It is the virtue which can transmute the hardest trial into glory because beyond the pain it sees the goal.
Anonymous

Introduction

What is it that keeps us keeping on? That gives us the power to continue, to persist, to carry on when it would be far easier just to give up and sink beneath the waves? Not as bad as all that of course, we could probably just sit down on the couch with a beverage and watch TV. But whoever else we fooled, we'd know for ourselves that we gave up.

Endurance is what you need to survive without apparent encouragement or support. Endurance is entirely about depending on yourself, pulling the best out of yourself – which means managing yourself, looking after and nourishing your energies, both spiritual and physical. Tenacity, perseverance, self preservation, self management.

'Durus' is the Latin for 'hard', and 'indurare' translates as 'to harden'. How durable are you? Endure has the sense of 'last a long time', but also sustain, undergo, bear, support. To endure is to put up with, to cope with, to suffer without resistance, to tolerate. Endurance is strength, but lasting strength. It carries with it the wisdom that knows when to bend with the wind, and when to stand up straight.

This mental strength draws on the courage that comes with detachment, in the first instance from the body. If you distance yourself from your body, remembering that you are not it and detaching yourself from its experience, you can observe what it's going through without being drawn down into it. It gives you the power to carry on – with love, remember, you are not punishing yourself. Detachment in the wider sense, more a product of the Soul Consciousness that sees the physical world and the drama that plays out in it as a series of scenes in which you also have a part to play, gives you the power to deal with disappointments and setbacks. Aren't you achieving your goals quickly enough? Ask yourself – quickly enough for what? Are we on a deadline here or something?

It's always possible to find an argument, a sequence of logical, persuasive steps, to make yourself keep on. But though it might be clear and logical in your head, an argument isn't usually enough to drive feeling and actual committed action. You have to really want it.

Endurance is Self determination.
Endurance is Self knowledge.
Endurance is Self love.

Self determination: be clear about who you are and who you want to be, and move inexorably towards that. It's a phrase used in politics and diplomacy; a new nation wants self determination, which is to say it wants to define itself and to take responsibility for its own destiny. Determination, as we discuss in the Power of Focus, has two significances: that of discrimination, analysis, decision and conclusion, and that of strength of purpose. Once you've got one, the other falls naturally into place. Self determination is being certain about your own destiny, and making it happen. Strength of purpose comes from clarity of purpose, which comes from clarity of Self awareness.

Which is another way of saying Self knowledge. Which is what this whole book is about; from Self knowledge, everything else flows, including the energy and stamina you need to progress on your chosen path. This is not to say that the path is relentlessly hard and you will need to call on all your reserves of stamina all the time; no, it's not that difficult. But things will come less easily on some days than others, and that's when you need the urge to push on, to reach the top. It's the same process with Self knowledge itself; you don't get the whole experience of Soul Consciousness delivered in one spectacular moment. It's gradual; your realization develops, deepens, and takes another step forward as you assimilate and put it into practice.

As in so many other instances in the book, Self love is perhaps the final and ultimate key. We need this strength, this power, the particular kind that endures; we also need to balance the pushing, the determination, with a loveful and compassionate treatment of ourselves. Just as you don't get anywhere on this path without Self knowledge – in fact, it *is* the path of Self Knowledge – so you won't make any progress unless you treat yourself (with a small 's', meaning the ordinary everyday self, the one that is aware of making the effort) with the love that is the energy that is You. It's your true and natural nature; the stuff of which you are made is love. (See Chapter 4: The Power of Love for more explanation.) So as you tread this path, making progress then falling back, getting a bit lazy maybe, or being taken out of your routine for some entirely genuine reason such as a holiday, you have to learn to handle yourself with love. If your willpower falters and you lose ground, if you're not sticking with it as you feel you should, don't beat yourself up; that is counterproductive. Pick yourself up, dust yourself off, return to the fray with love. Press on. Hey, that's the power of endurance.

Not surprisingly, Manipura, the solar plexus/navel chakra (depending on which authority you're reading) where this power is seated, is directly associated with will, dynamism, energy and achievement. This is the one where your stamina comes from. The name actually means 'Place of Resplendence', or in another translation 'Jewel City', which is helpful for focusing your mind on the beauty and power of your core strength. It is also more closely associated than any of the other chakras with Ch'i, the life force, the flow of subtle energy that we also know as Prān, which Manipura radiates throughout the body. Here again we find ourselves in that fascinating borderline territory between spiritual, subtle and physical energy, and the impact they have on each other. Prān is a physical phenomenon, although expressed as 'subtle'. It is not consciousness itself – but our consciousness of it enhances, enlightens and uplifts our consciousness. Clumsily expressed perhaps, but beautifully experienced.

It's willpower, isn't it, that's what we're talking about.

Determination, which also comes up in Chapter 6: The Power of Focus. That inner drive, the impetus that can't come from anywhere other than your own personal resources. But your personal resources are not in static supply, to be drawn on, depleted and gradually exhausted. Far from it. The more you draw on them, the more determined you become, the more power they deliver. If I may use the running analogy: once you have cracked the five-mile barrier, you know you can do more. The more you do, the more you know you can do. It's self-feeding, as well as self-preserving: Manipura governs the digestion, the distribution of physical energy from food round the body, but spiritual energy generates itself. The more you use it, the more you've got to use. And the more you know about who you are (a single, indivisible, indestructible unit of non-physical energy) and where you're going, the more in tune you are with the physical energy that flows through your body. Hey presto, your power is increasing.

The Power of Endurance Meditation 1: Acceptance

> God grant me the serenity to accept the things I cannot change, the courage to change the things I can, and the wisdom to know the difference.
> *Reinhold Niebuhr*

If, as is the case for us all, our project and our process is self improvement or self enhancement, then we have to be ready to accept change; to accept failure; to accept success (in some ways much harder); to accept love; to accept gifts, help, succor and support; to accept hardship and disappointment; to accept unfamiliar and uncomfortable ideas, in what we might call a leap of faith (see the meditation on Faith in this chapter) to accept ourselves with a small 's', with all our faults and problems; and, finally, and perhaps most difficult, to accept others.

The trickiest thing about acceptance – which is, when you come to think of it, a key mental attribute for those engaged in a self-improvement or self-enhancement process – is balancing the passivity with the activity. How do you remain calm and unperturbed, accepting whatever misfortunes befall you on your way, without giving up the determination to progress, make the changes you know you need to make? If all you do is accept, then you're a doormat for other people to walk on, right? If all you do is accept, where is the impetus, the action, the commitment to change things? Because of course we're talking about real life here, lived in the real world, where external circumstances demand to be dealt with – accepted or rejected – just as much as the 'internal circumstance' of our own personal growth.

It's a balance, is all. A matter of attitude. You maintain calmness, remain centered and balanced in that center, but out of that serene center comes enough energy to spring into action whenever it's needed. Remember that our project here is achieving a balanced Ecology of the Soul, which essentially means all our powers are used in the right way at the right time. The payoff in the Reinhold Niebuhr prayer above is the wisdom to know when to accept and when to make changes. For 'wisdom', read 'discrimination'. It's chicken and egg again; the more balance you have, the easier it is to achieve balance. The more clarity you have, the easier it is to decide what you should stoically accept and what you should fiercely refuse to accept, ready and willing to move heaven and earth to change.

That wisdom, or discrimination, comes from detachment – which is another way of saying acceptance, which makes the whole thing circular. Attachment is the 'ownership' principle at work; the thought that, for example, "This is my idea and I should benefit from it." Accept that you cannot own an idea (much to the confusion and despair of intellectual property lawyers). Let go. Detach.

But it's a conundrum, because what if you don't *want* to let go? Do you have to, against your 'better judgement'? This is everyday life, remember, not the path of renunciation, the begging bowl and the mountaintop. Particularly if you work in a creative context, where ideas are everything, or even in normal work and business, you want to – have to – protect your idea to make sure you and/or your company profit from it. It's a similar process to finding the balance between passive acceptance and active engagement in change. The discrimination you use, which is part of the determination process anyway – see Meditation 5 in The Power of Focus – has at its center the very stillness and clarity you get from Soul Consciousness, self awareness. You, in fact, are centered, and from this state of consciousness in a subtle way you are able to find the stillness in the center of the action. You are confronted with a circumstance or behavior, in yourself or others, that you know you can't abide. It must be dealt with. It won't change with force. Your solid foundation of calm is the best – the only – platform from which to really effect change. Accepting, absorbing, and committing to determined activity at the same time. Knowing when to hold on and when to let go. Not an easy trick to pull off; Soul Consciousness is the only way. And – to repeat – don't beat yourself up if things go off course. Push yourself, of course. But love yourself. Your Self.

There is a story about a Zen Master who was falsely accused by a young girl in his village of being the father of her illegitimate child. The girl's father came to the Master and handed him the child, saying: "This is your baby. Look after it." All the Master said was: "Is that so?" He took the child and raised it as his own for a year, shunned and vilified by the villagers, who saw him as a cheat and a fraud. A year later, the father reappeared with a hangdog youth in tow, who admitted that the baby was indeed his, and he and the girl would take responsibility. The Master's only comment, as he handed the child over: "Is that so?"

I struggle with this story, I suppose because it proposes acceptance to what most people would see as an impossible, self-defeating degree. It's also true that most Zen stories are about monks whose high path of renunciation has taken them on the begging bowl and mountaintop route, so their example is to inspire and educate, but not necessarily to be followed by ordinary everyday people – although here, it's true, we do have someone living in a village and engaging, to all intents and purposes, with its people and their affairs. It's an extreme example, put there to demonstrate an extremity of unperturbed acceptance, showing the extent to which someone who is truly enlightened can go. It doesn't tell us anything about the Master's childcare skills – one can hardly imagine him being an enormously affectionate surrogate Dad – or indeed how the baby coped. One bowl of rice a day isn't what you'd call the ideal infant diet.

Remember. When to hold on, and when to let go. The committed, energetic action is inside the stillness and peace of acceptance. Silence is a safe, solid ground from which to come out fighting. And, last of all, acceptance is not giving up. Don't confuse them. Never give up. Never. Which leads us to…

The Power of Endurance Meditation 2: Persistence (Doggedness)

The art of love is largely the art of persistence.
Albert Ellis

As long as we are persistent in our pursuit of our deepest destiny, we will continue to grow. We cannot choose the day or time when we will fully bloom. It happens in its own time.
Denis Waitley

We are made to persist. That's how we find out who we are.
Tobias Wolff

O snail
Climb Mount Fuji
But slowly, slowly!
Kobayashi Issa

Persistence: let's look at a few definitions. Amazing how the thought defines the word as the word defines the thought. The *Shorter Oxford English Dictionary* defines persistent as "obstinate, stubborn, pertinacious". 'Pertinacious' is defined as "persistent or stubborn in holding to one's own opinion or design; resolute; obstinate". 'Persistent' and 'dogged' define each other: "persistent in effort; stubbornly tenacious: a dogged worker". Is this an attribute we associate with spirituality at all? Not perhaps at first glance, but for our enlightened purposes here and now, persistence equals holding power as well as pushing power; the stamina to consolidate and stay in one place, even if forward progress is halted.

The meditation seems to be using combative, proto-military, strategic or tactical language. 'Consolidate'. 'Hold an opinion (ie a position)'. 'Forward progress'. And we have 'attack' and 'defense' appearing below. Are we fighting anyone? Other than ourselves? Is persistence always about overcoming; is it always *against* something?

Not when it means abiding, long lived to the point of eternity, a persistent existence. But the language of battle is occasionally appropriate, because there's no doubt that this path is sometimes a struggle, and at those times you do indeed need a fighting mentality. Just how far this is from the pure, powerful, peaceful Soul that you really are is a moot point, the sort we often come up against in the search for positive, proactive action. Let's say, it's not as far as you think. Right under your spiritual nose, in fact. It's the nub of the meditation; how you find forcefulness and momentum at the heart of silence, while you're floating in an ocean of peace.

That forcefulness and momentum obviously comes from the very center of yourself, the true You, the peaceful, powerful Soul. Can't be anywhere else. Power grows from peace; peace *is* power. Peace does not grow from power; it comes first, because that is what You are made of. Then when it comes to power, persistence mostly carries with it the sense of grim, dogged determination, the holding power. But that strength is the foundation for both the pushing power, the outward attack, and the inward holding power of defense or consolidation.

This meditation is the 'never give up' one. It comes with a subtitle in parentheses which it doesn't really need – everyone knows what Persistence means. But I kept 'doggedness' in because it has that sense of plodding, trudging, slow, often painful, progress. You need a lot more head-down, teeth-gritting determination (that word again – and we'll see it a good few more times in this chapter) than a typical dog. Persistence keeps you keeping on, against all contraindications, against the indifference, unsupportiveness, blank incomprehension or downright hostility of others, even against your own powers of self persuasion. Why not stay in bed this morning? You did your meditation yesterday, you'll do it tomorrow. Give yourself a break. You're tired.

Which, if we're honest, is occasionally not a bad idea. If you genuinely are tired and you're considering the reserves of energy you'll need that day, and the likelihood is that if you try and meditate you'll doze off anyway, you should give yourself that break. A bad, timewasting meditation where your mind wanders and you get into the 'nodding dog' routine of alternately fading towards sleep and bringing yourself back with a jerk is – arguably – worse than no meditation at all.

This is why persistence, like acceptance, is not remotely as simple as it sounds, and – again like acceptance, and indeed a good many of these meditations on behavioral attributes – is defined by its paradoxes. Part of persistence is knowing when to give way, to back off, mostly so you can recoup your energies ready to give it another go and get back to the active, energetic, even aggressive part. But that break that you give yourself has to come from the right place – of self management with love. If it's laziness that's won yet another little battle, be careful you aren't losing the war.

There's another way of seeing persistence of course, and one that might well help with this paradoxical process that requires the co-existence of inner silence with outer activity. The key is in the words 'energies' and 'energetic' in the previous paragraph, although there they are used to mean mental and physical energy rather than spiritual. This is where 'persistent' equals 'eternal', because, come to think of it, you are in and of your Self persistent spiritual energy, in the sense that You were neither created nor shall You be destroyed. And if you have a slight problem with viewing yourself – your Self – as eternal, consider that even at the physical level, energy, aka matter, can neither be created nor can it be destroyed. It only transforms. You the Soul, as an indivisible, individual, unique unit of non-physical energy, cannot be broken down into component parts, nor are you an amorphous, swirling collection of miasmic particles that somehow belong to a universal consciousness at the same time as exhibiting an individual one. You are your Self, always have been and always will remain so. Yes, you go through changes, but not in form – if you can call an infinitesimally small pinpoint, a being that has location but no size, a form.

That should give you enough to chew on. If your dogged persistence is weakening, remember that you are eternal. You persist, through the eons of time. Feeling stronger already?

The Power of Endurance Meditation 3: Faith

> Faith is believing that which you know to be untrue.
> *Anonymous schoolboy*

> Faith is to believe what you do not see; the reward of this faith is to see what you believe.
> *Saint Augustine*

> Faith is the bird that feels the light when the dawn is still dark.
> *Rabindranath Tagore*

> If patience is worth anything, it must endure to the end of time. And a living faith will last in the midst of the blackest storm.
> *Mahatma Gandhi*

> To one who has faith, no explanation is necessary.
> To one without faith, no explanation is possible.
> *Thomas Aquinas*

Faith. The first thought being, "Why do we need it?" If faith is that which keeps you going through the darkness of ignorance and adversity, we've already got light, haven't we? The answers are all here, or at least a combination of here and a few other places. We've got the information, and we've got the experience. Ignorance is banished, and it's only when we're in ignorance that we need faith, right?

Well, of course, no. Not right. Easy enough to see where that leading question was leading. We may not need it (we might ignorantly think), but we have it anyway. Faith is inbuilt. It comes with the package. It is one of our deepest sanskars – that department of the Soul that represents individual character, the recorded results of countless actions over the full number of our births, that lead to creating more and similar actions. And this is not one of those sanskars (ie nasty habits) that we need to erase, believe me.

Most of the wise quotes that you can find about this challenging concept come from Christianity, where you are asked to believe that which you cannot see, and your experience too comes from giving yourself to the immortal, ineffable God – whom you cannot see. You have to trust (have faith) in prayer, offer yourself up for experience, and be thankful if, as and when it comes. Other spiritual paths like this one focus more on the direct experience of meditation, and as that takes hold it's tempting to conclude that we don't have to have belief in that which we cannot see. The first experience firsthand is the experience of the Self, no 'leap of faith' required.

But that experience, perversely, *gives* us faith in our Self. And when we know – and feel, tangibly – who we are and what kind of being we are, that also gives us faith in ourselves (small 's'), not only in our ability to stay the course, but also the sense of worth, the feeling that yes, we are being lifted up, and yes, we are privileged, lucky. We keep faith in our own divinity, if you like – although this is not the same divinity as God's. Not everyone has the opportunity to seize this peace and this power in this life; our luck – which is another way of saying karma – is to be given a clear route to it, the clarity to recognize it, and the will to reach it.

Notice I say 'given' when we are debating the rôle of faith as 'necessary' or 'unnecessary' to someone who, on the face of it, is dependent entirely on his or her own efforts. No outside help. Which leads me to a little story. My first experiences of meditation in the Raja Yoga World Spiritual Museum in Mount Abu were frustrating, of course. I just couldn't seem to make the connection. In the Christian context, when I was preparing, for instance, for confirmation, the whole process had been based on philosophy, ethics, ideas. So too was my introduction to Raja Yoga, whose core is experience, but whose ideas I found outlandish and difficult. More difficult still was the change in attitude I had to make: the critical exchange, the familiar 'thesis – antithesis – synthesis' process was no use here, in fact considered actively disrespectful. So I was struggling. I just had to accept the different intellectual approach, and see what happened. It only demanded a very small leap of faith – in fact, was it even faith? "Oh well, might as well try it," could hardly be called the kind of faith that moves mountains. I had to set my Western intellectual training aside for a moment and open my mind. Yet with that small leap, I remember very clearly how it felt. I was pulled, uplifted, into the depths and heights of experience without apparent effort on my part. One day, after lengthy and at times frustrating discussion as usual, I went to sit in meditation, and will swear to my dying day that I was literally taken. Meditation was exactly the same as yesterday: sit in the cushioned room, stare at the red plastic oval on the wall, repeat to self, "I am a Soul, a tiny pinpoint of light in the center of this forehead of this great big body." And bang. As if I'd been hooked up to a wire or something, and just pulled upwards. It was a most extraordinary experience, a 'whoosh' like being in a high-speed elevator. Say or think what you like about who or what that might have been, but to me it was clear as day. I definitely had outside help.

Which is the kind of experience that you only need once. Or once every 30 years or so. It was enough to drive doubt from my mind, but I wasn't really doubting anyway. I was questioning. Did I *want* to believe? Was it that that drove the experience? Was I pulling it towards me anyway? I don't think so. I was interested, but I had an itinerary which I wanted to stick to, and at the time I was on my way to Pune to study hatha yoga with BKS Iyengar. I wasn't looking for diversions. But this diversion turned out to be the main route. Suffice it to say – as I do elsewhere – I never got to Pune.

The Power of Endurance Meditation 4: Hope

Hope springs eternal in the human breast;
Man never is, but always to be blessed:
The soul, uneasy and confined from home,
Rests and expatiates in a life to come.
Alexander Pope, "An Essay on Man"

Our old friend the *Shorter Oxford English Dictionary* defines hope as "Expectation of something desired; desire combined with expectation." Or as a verb: "To entertain expectation of something desired; to expect with desire, or to desire with expectation." Other definitions include "Expect with confidence" and "Cherish a desire with anticipation". So clearly, hope brings us face to face with the knotty problems surrounding desire. If it's desire for enlightenment, it's OK, right? – although I'm not sure a Zen master would agree. But then we get desire for material goods, or happiness as delivered through romantic or sexual love, or money; and that is most definitely not all right. Not in the context of our path to enlightenment, anyway.

The philosophers and psychologists pin their hopes, so to speak, on the future. The 'positive psychologist' CR Snyder links hope with a goal and a determined plan for reaching it.[1] He saw the connection between hope and mental willpower, which includes a realistic perception of goals; in this understanding, the difference between hope and optimism is that hope includes practical pathways to an improved future.[2] He even had a scale to measure it, which essentially measures, by a collection of questions, an individual's determination to achieve their goal. Dr. Barbara L. Fredrickson maintained that hope kicks in and becomes useful in times of crisis, making us more creative to deal with it.[3] With great need, she says, comes a wide range of ideas and positive emotions such as happiness, courage and empowerment, drawn from four different areas of the Self: cognitive, psychological, social or physical.[4] Philosopher Richard Rorty, coming at it from a different direction, claims that hope is a "metanarrative", a story that serves as a promise or reason to expect a better future.[5]

But like faith, Hope is inbuilt in the Soul's breast. Be careful to distinguish it from optimism, which comes next and which is either an embedded character trait or a learned response. That hope, like faith, sits in a place defined by ignorance is not to disrespect it; it looks towards a notional future for those on a path more of worship and devotion than of meditation and inwardness. But here at the Ecology of the Soul, in the light of the knowledge and understanding we're gaining, we appear not to need it. Is that smug? No; everything is down to our own efforts, and we ourselves can see how we are standing or falling.

Does this mean then that we have nothing to hope for? Hope is about uplift, the forward looking, upward looking path, the path to a higher plane. Again like faith, it lives in our hearts as a key ingredient of the Power of Endurance. It's actually a key ingredient of ordinary everyday consciousness, at the ordinary

---

1 Snyder, CR and Lopez, SJ (2007) *Positive Psychology: The Scientific and Practical Explorations of Human Strengths*. Thousand Oaks, CA, US: Sage Publications

2 Snyder, Charles R. *The Psychology of Hope: You Can Get There from Here.* New York: The Free Press, 1994, pp 7–8

3 Fredrickson, Barbara L. (2009-03-23) "Why Choose Hope?" *Psychology Today*. Retrieved 2012-10-02.

4 Fredrickson, Barbara L., et al. (2008) "Open Hearts Build Lives: Positive Emotions, Induced Through Loving-Kindness Meditation, Build Consequential Personal Resources." *Journal of Personality and Social Psychology*, 95, pp 1045–1062. Retrieved 2012-10-02.

5 DL Hall, *Richard Rorty* (1994) pp 150 and 232

everyday mind level, let alone Soul Consciousness. It's the priming fuel, the shot of high-octane gasoline injected directly into the Soul's combustion chamber that gets us out of bed in the morning and ready for another day. Widen the definition of hope in your mind for a short spell. Look at it as 'hopefulness', which makes it chime with positive thinking, in all its myriad forms and definitions. I repeat, not to be confused with optimism, but understood as one of the basic, first-principle characteristics of the Soul. There is more than one 'prime mover', the things that get us up in the morning, deep down there in the Soul's basement. The things that bring us back up to the struggle (Yep, sometimes it's a struggle. Not all easy, not at all.), that give us the impetus to keep on keeping on. Hope, or hopefulness, is one of them, and a very main one indeed, because it's upward looking, and if you are looking upwards, you can't fail. Sooner or later, you will fly for sure.

You can tell whether it's in place and working, because if it isn't you're downward looking, into the black hole of despair. Sounds rather radical and desperate, and it's also hardly ideal to define a characteristic by its opposite. But here, the alternative route helps to pin down this elusive quality and bring it into sharp focus. If you're not being driven by hope, you're being driven by despair. You can swap from one to the other, at different intensities, but essentially it's one or the other.

Catholic theology categorizes despair as a vice, a sin, because it is where the Soul turns away from God and makes itself 'unsaveable'. Looking at that same theology's idea of hope – expectation of and desire of receiving; refraining from despair; the capability of not giving up – returns us to the knotty one about desire, which we, Zen masters notwithstanding, simply must accept as an indispensable kick-starter of our efforts towards enlightenment. As for 'refraining from despair' (as if we were in control of such things), hope – and faith – protect us from the black hole, but they need to be nurtured with love and compassion for yourself and your Self. Hope's deep down message is not so much 'Never give up' as 'Never give up hope'.

Again at the risk of sounding smug, the Soul conscious soul can avoid some of the most difficult issues, the ones that demand the leap of faith in the dark, or the maintenance of hope in the absence of encouragement, simply because said Soul has been given the tools to know itself as a being of light. It's a mistake to think that because we've been blessed with that extra knowledge and experience of the Self, we don't need hope, or faith; they are inbuilt in the Soul just as love is. It's what you're made of.

The Power of Endurance Meditation 5: Optimism

A pessimist sees the difficulty in every opportunity; an optimist sees the opportunity in every difficulty.
Winston S. Churchill

Man often becomes what he believes himself to be. If I keep on saying to myself that I cannot do a certain thing, it is possible that I may end by really becoming incapable of doing it. On the contrary, if I have the belief that I can do it, I shall surely acquire the capacity to do it even if I may not have it at the beginning.
Mahatma Gandhi

Only those who attempt the absurd can achieve the impossible.
Albert Einstein

"It's snowing still," said Eeyore gloomily.
"So it is."
"And freezing."
"Is it?"
"Yes," said Eeyore. "However," he said, brightening up a little, "we haven't had an earthquake lately."
AA Milne

Always look on the bright side of life, says (or sings) the optimist, who has, either learnt or inbuilt, one of the key attributes of the Power of Endurance. Optimism is no more nor less than positive thinking, but it operates in time; it's not about the present or the 'presence', but always the future. Does this compromise our ability to remain present? If we want to be optimistic, can we also avoid the strength-sapping habit of always having our mind in some other place from the one we are actually in, here and now?

Yes, because the 'here and now' mantra is to help people become present whose entire habit of mind is formed around what has been, what should have been and what shouldn't, what will be, what might be, what should be and what shouldn't. They are somehow never right here in the moment. If we've managed to gain even a smidgeon of Soul Consciousness in the Ecology of the Soul's meditations, it has given us a nascent ability to place ourselves in the present and refer to, or tap into, that experience at will. Which in turn gives us the ability to deal with intentions, plans, desires and eventualities up ahead without losing our balance in time. Our optimism itself stems from this solid, centered, grounded consciousness. Without it we wouldn't have the positive view. It is the now, it can't be anything else. If it is anything else, it isn't the now, and therefore isn't on that solid foundation. So, perversely, the optimism that looks ahead is dependent on the transcendent experience of the moment that doesn't admit the existence of past or future.

'Optimum' means the best. We optimize – engineer, edit or adjust – our outcomes to be the best. We 'make the best of', which in a sense is the truth of optimism: always look for the best outcome, always find it, but if the outcome is not what you desired or judged to be the best possible, you make the best of it. Dig down to the bottom of this idea, and indeed all ideas since no idea can exist without words (can it?), with our Old Reliable *Shorter Oxford English Dictionary*. Having established that the Latin *optimum* and *optimus* translate as 'best', the *SOED* then quotes Gottfried Wilhelm Leibniz's doctrine of optimism from his *Theodicy* of 1710. Leibniz held that this world we inhabit is the *meilleur des mondes possibles*, the best of all possible worlds, "being chosen by the Creator as that in which most good could be obtained at the cost of least evil." (The quote is from the *SOED*, not Leibniz himself.) This presupposes a God who has physically created the world, who has active input and engagement in the karmic cycle, whereas the Ecology of the Soul understands Him[1] to be uniquely karmateet, that is, non-physical, free of the bonds of action and reaction, above and untouched by karmic law, because He is incorporeal, a soul with no body. Perfect knowledge, yes. Actual action, no.

The Leibniz debate – as you can imagine, his doctrine came in for considerable stick from other philosophers, and even Voltaire's *Candide* is seen by some as a jokey rebuttal of the proposition – tends to lead us astray, however surprisingly affirmative and encouraging it may be, because it is essentially an attempt to accommodate the existence of evil in the human psycho-spiritual system. We end up feeling (sort of) OK about all the evil in the world, goes the thinking, because on balance there is more good. But this is not really the point of optimism for us, working to balance the Ecology of the Soul; we're looking here for attributes of the Power of Endurance, ingredients in the recipe of this potion that keeps us going, head down, teeth gritted. Which is why we go back to the point about optimism being defined in time; we're looking ahead.

The *Shorter Oxford* finally gets to our point, in definition 3: "Disposition to hope for the best or to look on the bright side of things under all circumstances". This kicks us back to hope, the subject of the previous meditation, which we differentiated from optimism by saying that optimism is either an embedded

1 God is a Soul with no body, not a human being, so it's no more accurate to use one pronoun rather than any other – Him, Her, It, Father, Mother, Neuter. For the sake of clarity and ease of language, I have (after numerous attempts at the Him/Her/It thing, or alternating personal pronouns, which is worse) decided to stick with 'Him'. For those who accept the idea that God is an individual entity, 'Father' seems to make most sense and is the most recognizable relationship.

character trait or a learned response, whereas hope is a primary, inseparable component of consciousness – at the level of the mind. Those philosophers I quote in Meditation 4, Hope, add that hope comes with a specific outcome attached, but this is: a) arguable; and b) again not really to the point, because for us Ecologists, hope is a basic building block of consciousness. At an ordinary everyday level, yes, hope usually expresses something like: "I hope the bus is on time," but that thought pattern can also be seen as worry. What will happen if the bus isn't on time? Either way, it's a waste of mental energy, because there's nothing we can do about it. Maintain a positive (optimistic) state of mind and focus it on those things it can control, like its own thought patterns.

We have either the optimistic 'disposition' – the embedded character trait – or the 'learned response', which brings us directly to the positive thinking department. It's true, even if you don't have that disposition, you can teach and train yourself to accentuate the positive in all circumstances. Eliminating the negative is harder because, as we see above, what might appear to be positive can come with its own negativity inbuilt. It's also hard to maintain that positivity when things don't go your way; oops, the bus was late anyway. Must not be 'thinking positive' hard enough. Which again is a mistake. Never a good idea to beat yourself up over your own habits of mind. The late bus is merely a test to strengthen your positivity.

The interesting thing about the Law of Attraction version of positive thinking, optimism, call it what you like, is that its proponents insist that to make your desires come true you mustn't allow yourself to think: "I really want that bus to be on time." If you're admitting that you want something, you're admitting that you lack it ('want' is old English, sometimes still used, for 'lack'), and your mental focus is on the lack rather than the presence of said thing. And you get what you focus on. So somehow you have to trick yourself into creating the state of mind that takes it for granted that the bus will be on time. And lo and behold, there it is. Or not, in which case the LoA people would just say you haven't got into the zone yet, where the Universe serves you. We should be so lucky as to ignore the laws of karma, I say. They certainly won't ignore us.

The Power of Endurance Meditation 6: Serenity

Boredom is the feeling that everything is a waste of time; serenity, that nothing is.
Thomas Szasz

Despair is the damp of hell, as joy is the serenity of heaven.
John Donne

Peace is present right here and now, in ourselves and in everything we do and see. Every breath we take, every step we take, can be filled with peace, joy, and serenity. The question is whether or not we are in touch with it. We need only to be awake, alive in the present moment.
Thích Nhất Hạnh

Serene or serenity, from the Latin *serenus*, meaning peaceful, calm, clear, seems originally to have been a term to describe weather. Then it becomes 'cheerful tranquility (of mind, temper, countenance etc)' – notice the 'cheerful' – and has also been used to mean 'most high or august' when used as a royal epithet, eg 'His Serene Highness'.

Serenity is acceptance, serenity is faith, serenity is hope, serenity is optimism. Serenity is detachment.

Serene is calm, serene is still (though it is not stillness), serene is quiet (though it comes from silence, it is not silence). Serene is beautiful, graceful, elegant, transcendent. Serene is floating, untouched and undisturbed, even in the face of circumstances that conspire to touch or disturb; there is a sense of invincibility about it, an underlying resilient strength that supports and protects the calm. It can look like refusal to engage, to care, because the calm doesn't turn into panic, despair or alarm when confronted with said adverse circumstances, but the truth is that action – if it's required – is more effective and efficient when it comes from the quiet, focused, self-aware space. Just because we don't jump up and down and make a fuss, it doesn't mean we're devoid of compassion. Our path commits us to gaining enlightenment for the sake of all living beings, right?

This is the paradox at the heart of many of the attributes and powers that we are working on to build a balanced Ecology of the Soul. Deep within the pure peace and bottomless silence that are the Soul's true nature are the powerful seeds of strength, action and effectiveness. When a Soul Conscious Soul comes into action, it does so with full awareness of the karmic picture, of intentions and consequences. It does so without mental chatter and dispersed energy; everything is focused, everything fits. The Soul Conscious Soul is detached, remaining centered in the midst of a storm of activity, able to discern where its energy is best expended and pinpoint that place for effort – which somehow seems effortless anyway, because it is so efficient.

'Efficient' is the language of physics, mechanics or productivity, hardly what one expects to hear in the context of a quest for mental and spiritual balance and a chosen path to upliftment. But the word does hit the spot, plus it gives an insight into this tricky 'detachment' idea, because in all contexts 'efficient' means no wasted energy. That calm serenity, that apparent insouciance and refusal or inability to engage, overlays a readiness, if not an actual eagerness, for action which will further our own enlightenment and contribute to others'. (Just in case this talk of enlightenment puts you off, by the way, remember that the enlightenment you gain through balancing the Ecology of the Soul is accessible and manageable. It doesn't demand that you renounce your worldly life, friends and family, home and possessions. This is enlightenment for real people in the real world.)

Since we're in paradox territory, consider the relationship between inner, silent stillness and outer, noisy action. Everything

– every single thing, tiny or large – that you do day to day, and indeed even unusual and uncommon things that you do only rarely, will be improved, enhanced and refined by the detachment you achieve from seeing yourself as a Soul driving a body doing the actions. Although we must tread carefully claiming perfection for the imperfect human Soul, there is a time and a dimension in which your existence is perfect, simply and precisely because you are not engaged in any action and therefore not creating, adding to or subtracting from your karmic 'account'. From here, the state of perfect peace, you apply your self knowledge to action, and since in some sense at least you are coming from perfection, naturally your tasks and actions, and the way in which you perform them, automatically carry that quality. Thus, logically, the more you experience serenity in your Self, the more it becomes a stable, solid platform for action. No more running round like a headless chicken, no more dubious decisions, no more errors of judgement, no more fudged or 'make-do' results. Yes, a tall order, certainly. But keep floating on that sea of serenity, and the super-efficient, super-effective action will follow. It's inevitable, because it makes perfect sense.

Just in case you're thinking there might be a connection with serendipity, which would seem to have the same etymological root and which is usually taken to mean a happy combination of circumstances or a pleasant but accidental surprise, there isn't. Although most of us think Mary Poppins invented it, it was actually coined in 1754 by the English art historian and man of letters Horace Walpole, who referred to the Persian fairy story *The Three Princes of Serendip* (the ancient name for Sri Lanka) to explain one of his discoveries. The Princes were "always making discoveries, by accidents and sagacity, of things which they were not in quest of". Nice, but not the same thing at all.

The Power of Endurance Meditation 7: Stillness

Inner stillness is the key to outer strength.
Jared Brock

To know yourself as the Being underneath the thinker, the stillness underneath the mental noise, the love and joy underneath the pain, is freedom, salvation, enlightenment.
Eckhart Tolle

The power of stillness is such that it is almost worth listing as a Power in its own right rather than a subsection of, or meditation upon, another one. Make no mistake, this quality is right at the heart of Soul Consciousness; it is part of the definition of the experience, if not of the actual experience itself. Speaking through the earthquake, wind and fire, goes the hymn, the still small voice of calm can be heard in the silence. Your peaceful, powerful Self sits in the eye of the storm of emotions, needs, wants and desires, remaining aware of itSelf, but driving – if you've got it right – Soul Conscious action.

Stillness and Silence (the first meditation in the Power of Nature) are intimately related. You can't have one without the other, but they are not the same thing. One, on the face of it, is the absence of movement; the other – on the face of it – is the absence of sound. But for us Ecologists of the Soul, neither of these qualities are anything like adequately defined or understood in the negative, by absences. Both are powers, or at least, both are underpinned by power, which is why Stillness comes in the key end position that encompasses the other meditations in this chapter. No acceptance, no persistence, no faith, no hope, no optimism, and, above all, no serenity – without stillness.

No endurance without stillness either, which is the overarching theme of this entire chapter, and which to some extent we are anatomizing and dissecting as we go through the seven separate meditations. Two of them you can see as components of the power (acceptance, persistence), another four are *sine qua nons*, the essential elements without which the power will never get off the ground (faith, hope, optimism, serenity); all together come to a point within stillness, which is the bedrock, the foundation of the power, both complex and simple at the same time, because it is a quality of consciousness itself. It's a quality you can comparatively easily reach through meditation, vaulting over or diving under the processes of mind and intellect and arriving, if you like, in the Chamber of Stillness, but it also demands the understanding reached through those active mental and intellectual processes that you have just bypassed. This is because, as we say above, stillness is not just absence. It is very much presence, and indeed the place where you the Soul can – and must, if you want to make anything of the Power of Endurance – settle your Self, understand your Self, experience your Self and be your Self, completely in the now. This presence is not just presence of mind, which usually means an ability to think quickly and accurately; stillness is reached through both the activity of mind and intellect and the calm inactivity of consciousness contemplating itself. We are also looking for the stillness that can be found inside actual physical action, not just mental and intellectual. Meditation in action and as action, as we see elsewhere (Chapter 6: The Power of Focus, Meditation 7, Mindfulness).

Doesn't take long to come to the water analogy. Meditation texts are often accompanied by images of still water, with perhaps one drop arriving on the surface and creating a slow, languid series of ever-widening circular ripples. 'Still waters run deep', goes the saying, which I have always thought was literal nonsense, because if water is still, it can't be running, can it? It isn't figurative nonsense though, because it's giving us a glimpse of the 'alternate' dimension; still on the horizontal surface, but vertically limitless beneath. Dive, and keep on going. There is this almost tactile quality about stillness, perhaps because our understanding or appreciation of it as applied to our state of consciousness is closely connected with the water image. It closes over your head, liquid, dark, silent and enveloping, absorbing and dissolving your separateness. Which, as we know, is not the return to a universal miasma of omnipresent consciousness, encompassing all living beings or even things. This sense of separateness is your body consciousness, your mistaken sense of your Self as a physical being.

Which leads us neatly to the place where you belong, the non-material dimension from which you the Soul come and to which you the Soul will return in the cycle of time, to start your series of lives all over again. This dimension – Raja Yoga calls it "Paramdham", or the 'Soul World' – has nothing of the liquid or dark qualities of stillness about it. Stillness it does have, however, in abundance. In fact, there is nothing else. It doesn't *have* stillness so much as it *is* stillness. It is not really a place as such because it is non-physical, a dimension of light, peace and silence where non-physical beings that have location but no size dwell. Pinpoints of consciousness, waiting to enter a body and come into action in the physical world.

If you are having intellectual trouble with this idea, if it's sounding more than a little like mumbo-jumbo, consider this: you are a non-physical being of light. Let's hope you've bought and experienced that idea by now, because if you haven't, you need to stop reading, sit down in a quiet place where you won't be disturbed and meditate on it. "I am a Soul, a pinpoint of light, an infinitesimally small, non-physical unit of human consciousness, living in the forehead of this physical body." Stay with that until you break through the chatter and find your Self floating in the ocean of peace, of silence. Of stillness.

As an eternal, indivisible, indestructible Soul, you cannot be created, nor can you be destroyed. It's the same with matter. Although physical matter does constantly change and reform, it cannot cease to exist nor can it come into existence. But the Soul is already an individual, unique unit of consciousness; always has been, always will be. Eternal, like I said. In which case, how come the population of the world continues to increase? (It's hypnotizing watching it grow, at websites such as worldometers.info.) Isn't this new souls just coming into being? Nope, because they can't come into being or stop being. They – You – are eternal, right?

So although your experience of the Soul World depends entirely on you being able to bypass the activity of the mind and the intellect, it does make intellectual sense as well. There has to be some where or some how or some way in which the eternal souls that make up the sum total of the human race are 'stored' before they arrive in the physical body of their first birth. There is. It's called the Soul World, and the only word we can rightly use for it is 'dimension'. It's not science fiction; it's real. Your natural habitat. The reason why you seek peace and bliss, why you turn away from physical things and towards the spiritual when you realize that ultimate fulfilment, inner peace and power do not come from engagement with the physical world. A world of stillness. Your Home. Or, as we might say if we liked puns, your Ōm.

The Power of Endurance Practice 1: Plant a Power Seed Every Day

Power Seeds are mental devices, thought triggers to generate Soul Consciousness, and hence change your actions. They are a bit like the Zen 'kōan' (for instance the idea of the sound of one hand clapping) that kick your mind out of gear and raise the level of your awareness.

Using Power Seeds, you grow a new garden of consciousness. See your mind as a garden, or at least a patch of fertile soil. Thoughts and feelings grow in it, like plants. Your mind is a riot of tangled and intertwined mental vegetation, much of it good and useful and most of it neither good nor useful. So it's a pleasant surprise that you don't have to struggle with the weeds. All you have to do is plant your mental plot with new seeds – 'Power Seeds' – which grow into thought, attitude, feeling, and action. Which feeds back and creates new thought and feeling. You have created a new mental and spiritual garden – and a new framework for your behavior.

If you really focus all the innate power of your calmed, stilled mind on the Power Seed you choose for 60 full seconds, that thought pattern will repeat and recur throughout the day, accumulating much more than a single minute of your mental activity. It's meditation in action, because the meditation is about action.

Plant one of the mental Power Seeds that appear on the following pages. The Seven Powers, Power Seeds and the Magic Minute section of Part I, the Introduction, gives the full explanation of how to prepare the mental and spiritual ground for your new garden; Part III gives you a whole range of Power Seeds to suit your circumstances. Ultimately, as your Self knowledge increases, you will be creating and planting your own.

Endurance is nourishing your energies, both spiritual and physical.

Endurance is Self determination.
Endurance is Self knowledge.
Endurance is Self love.

If your willpower falters, don't beat yourself up.
Handle yourself with love.
Return to the fray with love.

Spiritual energy generates itself. The more you use it, the more you've got to use.

Self determination is being certain about your own destiny and making it happen. Determinedly.

Strength of purpose comes from clarity of purpose, which comes from clarity of Self awareness.

The stuff of which you are made is love.
It's your true and natural nature.

Maintain calmness, remain centered and balanced in that center. Out of that serene center comes the energy to spring into action.

The committed, energetic action is inside the stillness and peace of acceptance.

Acceptance is not giving up.
Don't confuse them.

Never give up.

Never.

Power grows from peace.
Peace *is* power.
Peace does not grow from power, it comes first, because that is what You are made of.

You are – your Self – persistent spiritual energy.
You were neither created nor shall you be destroyed.

Your luck – karma – is to be given a clear route to peace and power, the clarity to recognize it, and the will to reach it.

The experience of the Self
gives faith in the Self.

Look at hope as 'hopefulness'.
It is the priming fuel, the shot of high-octane spiritual gasoline that gets us out of bed in the morning and ready for another day.

Hope and faith are inbuilt in the Soul just as love is.
They are what you're made of.

The optimism that looks ahead is dependent on the transcendent experience of the moment that doesn't admit the existence of past or future.

Serenity is acceptance.
Serenity is faith.
Serenity is hope.
Serenity is optimism.

Serenity is detachment.

Deep within the pure peace and bottomless silence that are the Soul's true nature are the powerful seeds of strength, action and effectiveness.

There is a time and a dimension in which your existence is perfect, simply because you are not engaged in any action.

Stillness is the foundation of the Power of Endurance because it is a quality of consciousness.

Have the stillness of the observer.

Have the stillness of the hunter.

Have the stillness of the deer hiding in the forest.

Stillness is reached through both the activity of mind and intellect and the calm inactivity of consciousness contemplating itself.

The Soul World is non-physical, a dimension of light, peace and silence where non-physical beings that have location but no size dwell.

As an eternal, indivisible, indestructible Soul, you cannot be created, nor can you be destroyed. Think about it.
You're eternal.

The Power of Endurance Practice 2: Yoga Seeds – Salute to the Sun (Surya Namaskar)

Position 3: Forward Lunge

The Salute to the Sun, like most things in Yoga, has many variations. The one we use here consists of seven 'asanas', to use the Sanskrit name for positions, done in a 12-step sequence: Prayer, Mountain, Forward Bend, the Forward Lunge we deal with here (one leg forward), Plank, Dog, Cobra, Child, Forward Lunge (the other leg forward), Forward Bend, Mountain, Prayer.

This asana doesn't seem to have a Sanskrit name, so its antecedents as one of Patanjali's originals are under question. Which doesn't really matter a jot, since it appears in many modern hatha yoga texts, and adds a specific transitional moment in the Salute to the Sun. It stretches and energizes you and prepares you for the next position.

You're coming from Forward Bend, Uttanasana. Head still down, hands to the floor, take your weight on your hands, arms straight, look up and leave your left foot forward while taking your right one back (it doesn't matter which side you start on as long as you do the other one on the way back). You end up with your left knee at your armpit, your left shin vertical to the floor and thigh parallel to it, your arms reaching down to the floor next to your foot on the left and in line with it on the opposite side. Depending on the length of your arms, you can put your hands flat on the floor or rest them on 'tented' fingers.

Your left foot is planted flat and firm on the floor. Your right leg is extended straight and true, as far back as it goes, the toes bent and the foot straight up and down. As in all standing positions and most sitting ones, you are opening your energy meridians by keeping your torso and limbs in as many straight lines as possible. Keep your back flat, firm and straight; stretch and extend your backward leg, keeping that as straight and energized as you can, especially at the knee; feel it in a long line all the way from the back of your heel to the back of your neck, then up and beyond through your head. Balance that with the energy you are directing to the floor through your left foot, so there is a kind of upward resistance from the floor running up your shin and then through your thigh. You can feel it most at the turn where the back of your thigh becomes your buttock.

There are variations on what you do with your head. Some teachers will have you look up and forward, stretching your neck as far forward as it will go; I prefer the 'head down' option, where you face the floor and can extend your neck without it having to go round such a sharp corner. Let the shoulders fall back, open out there. Don't hunch. It's crucial to find space in the shoulders, because somehow they act as a pivot point for the forces coming up from your right heel and your left flat foot. Relax them, open them, let your neck fall (or rise) out of them, twist them back and forth a little to settle them and make sure they are allowing enough combination of relaxation and tension to let the energy flow.

As you hold the position, feel the lift in the energy coming back up through your limbs as a result, if you like, of your active stance on the floor. Adjust your shoulders and neck constantly to make sure there are no blocks. Extend the bottom of your backbone down, and your neck up and forward. Remember the trick: you can't stretch until you let go. This is a very good pose to practice the mental discipline of separating out the parts of your body that are active and under muscular extension, and identifying the parts that you want to stretch and can let go. It's as I've described in other asanas: you make a solid framework with some of your limbs and muscles, which allows others to go soft and relax. Active relaxation, it might be called.

Next stop is Chaturanga Dandasana, Plank. Just leap your forward foot back to join the other one and you're there. Easy.

Chapter 4

The Power of Love

Anahata, the Heart Chakra

In this chapter:

God is Love, but Love is not God
Dadi Kumarka, Brahma Kumaris, 1978

Introduction

Love is the most important thing of all. You could say it is the only thing. The introductory part of this chapter is entirely concerned with spiritual love and consciousness; we don't deal with romantic or sexual love here. Both come into it, in the 'Passion' meditation of this chapter and elsewhere. But right here, right now we are concerning ourselves only with the power, depth and truth of Love as pure energy, both spiritual and physical.

As we consistently return throughout this book to the project of balancing the component powers that make up the soul's ecosystem, we continue to get new insight – and experience – into how achieving that balance sets us free and leads us to a place of perfect peace, power and stillness.

Love is the name of that balance. Love is the name of that place. Love is the name of that peace, of that power, of that stillness. Love is the goal, and love is the means to get there.

Our natural, original, perfect state of being is Love. We are love, we are made of love, we seek love, we seek to give love, we seek to give ourselves with love – or indeed, we seek to give ourselves *to* love. We don't seek hatred, fear, despair and misery, do we? They assail us and we find ourselves living inside them; but the true nature of even the 'meanest' and most negative of souls, who willfully turns away from the light, is Love and Peace.

Love is Light, and Light is Love – spiritual light, that is. That spiritual light is You the Soul, who – precisely because you are made of light – seeks enlightenment. Physical sunlight and fire are also love, but only in the sense that Love is also a name for physical energy. You the Soul are a unit of consciousness, of spiritual energy, aware of itself as light and as love. So the energy that is You is love, and the subtle energy that flows through your body – Ch'i, Prān, the life force – is love.

Energy is love. Love is energy. Energy is power. Love is power. But power is not necessarily love.

While Love is You and You are love, you are not indistinguishable from the rest of the universe that is love; you are very much distinguishable, a unique and individual entity. Made of love – yes. But somehow individual and universal at the same time, swimming in a boundless sea of love which is everything? – no.

Love is the power that runs the Universe, which is why we seek it in any form. But don't make the mistake of thinking that it is all the same kind of energy. We don't subscribe to the idea that everything is the same thing, here at the Ecology of the Soul. There isn't some kind of universal energy 'soup', of which all beings and all natural and manufactured phenomena are a part. There is a very definite difference between spiritual and physical energy; and each individual human is an individual human soul, for ever has been and for ever will remain so. We don't come from a universal general miasma, nor shall we return to one.

Our energy (love) powers us through our cycle of births, but becomes depleted – 'running out' – just as any source of power does without replenishment. As the love has been running out, the Ecology of the Soul, our ecosystem of spiritual powers, has become imbalanced, out of whack, corrupted. The effect on the planet, the pain of the Earth and its people, is there for all to see. Souls have lost the connection with their own truth, and see happiness in physical things, the creation and collection of which have ruined both the ecology of the planet and the Ecology of the Soul. Reconnecting to the Seven Powers, rediscovering, recreating, replenishing and nurturing them, is reviving Love.

Love is rooted in the heart, where Anahata, the heart chakra, is located. But if we are non-physical beings made of love, why does it need a specific location in the body? The non-physical owns and drives a body; physical and subtle energy (love) – Prān, Ch'i – flow through the body. This chakra is a center, a pivot, a portal between spiritual and physical. Though it's not in the middle of the body – that's Manipura, the solar plexus chakra, the personal power and endurance one – Anahata is the middle chakra of the main seven.

Anahata honors unconditional love for the Self and others, passion and compassion, devotion and dedication. The word itself is Sanskrit for 'unstruck', 'unhurt' or 'unbeaten'. Not unlike the Zen concept of the sound of one hand clapping, Anahata Nada is the name for the 'unstruck sound', the sound that comes without any two objects being struck together (think about it). It is the Music of the Spheres, the sound, embedded in the heart, that comes from the heart of the Universe, the celestial realm; 'A' for the sattvic principle of subtle purity and spirituality, 'U' for the rajasic principle of activity, and 'M' for the tamsic principle of inertia. A-U-M equals ŌM. Which is to say, ŌM is where the heart is, and your heart is your ŌM. As we said at the beginning, there is pretty much nothing else but Love.

The Power of Love Meditation 1: Commitment

Commitment is an act, not a word.
Jean-Paul Sartre

Until one is committed, there is hesitancy, the chance to draw back, always ineffectiveness… the moment one definitely commits oneself, then Providence moves too. All sorts of things occur to help one that would never otherwise have occurred. A whole stream of events issues from the decision, raising in one's favour all manner of unforeseen incidents and meetings and material assistance, which no man could have dreamt would have come his way. I learned a deep respect for one of Goethe's couplets:

Whatever you can do or dream you can, begin it.
Boldness has genius, power and magic in it!

William Hutchison Murray, The Scottish Himalayan Expedition (1951)

To be free is to be committed to that which is a part of the unbound realm.

Whatever sets your soul to flight is freedom.
C. JoyBell C.

Commitment is a decision. It is a dedication, a devotion. As with passion, commitment is also partly defined by a basic duality. The tension is between the apparent oppression of locking yourself into a course of action, a relationship or a value system, and the actual liberation that comes with making a decision and then making a decision to stick absolutely to that decision. No reservations, no ifs or buts. Conflict, indecision and uncertainty fly away; for better or worse, this is what I'm going to do, and every decision and action that comes after becomes easier.

Not, perhaps, easier all round to put into action in the real world, because you are committing to a difficult and demanding path, but at least now there is no mental or spiritual stress. And as the mountaineer Bill Murray says above, once that decision is made you may find that the phenomena of both the real and the subtle worlds fit in around it, facilitating and supporting your determination and direction. Even if you don't get that wonderful sense of things and events conspiring in your favor and you still have to battle your way upstream against obstacles and barriers, as long as your commitment remains unwavering, you will prevail. Of that there is not an iota of doubt.

Commitment strengthens, deepens your resolve. Resolve and commitment are one and the same thing, actually. It takes courage to do, and gives courage in the doing. And here's another subtle double sense in the idea: if you are committed to improving yourself – your Self – to raising your own consciousness, it's likely that you will be regarded as selfish, because that's your own effort for yourself, and what about the less lucky beings with greater apparent need than you for peace and power? What are you doing for them? For the earth, the environment at large, even?

Well, you're working on the Ecology of your own Soul – You the Soul – because when it comes down to it that's all you can take responsibility for. You may not see it all at once, but your own and others' evolution to a higher, more powerful, more peaceful state of being will have its cumulative beneficial effect on our wounded planet and the suffering souls that inhabit it. Buddhists talk about seeking enlightenment for the sake of all conscient beings. Committing, if you like, to the benefit of all. Your apparent selfishness becomes selflessness, because the physically defined self, the body conscious one that confuses existence with material things, is the one that is breaking down. It takes deep experience and understanding to see that in the spiritual realm, to commit, in one of those *Shorter Oxford English Dictionary* definitions, is to "entrust, give in charge, commend, consign". To commit is to hand over, to renounce, to give oneself up, to let go, to let it flow, in a sense to abandon responsibility. You let a higher power (some call it God) take charge; 'the Lord will provide'. But the Lord helps those, continues the wisdom, that help themselves. Here's that freedom thing again. You're not being irresponsible; you're taking more responsibility for your Self than ever. If commitment is letting go, let go of yourself to find and nurture your true Self.

The Power of Love Meditation 2: Excitement

Get excited and enthusiastic about your own dream. This excitement is like a forest fire – you can smell it, taste it, and see it from a mile away.
Denis Waitley

At the moment you are no longer an observing, reflecting being; you have ceased to be aware of yourself; you exist only in that quiet, steady thrill that is so unlike any excitement that you have ever known.
May Sinclair

Excitement is a component of emotional love. Or it leads to it, or is a result of it. One of the *Shorter Oxford English Dictionary*'s definitions is: "move to strong emotion, stir to passion". This kind of love is in the domain of the mind (though we say we feel it in our heart), the part of the Soul that generates everyday thought, emotion and feeling, and that engages with the physical world through our bodies. We're familiar with its tendency to wander uncontrolled, leading us towards illusory goals and a mistaken, body-conscious sense of Self. But as I've said elsewhere, the mind, as well as being random, undisciplined and playful, is also – when it is under control – extremely powerful. It can hold you down, but it can also propel you up – in fact, it's unavoidably the tool you use to start you off on that trajectory. It's the bridge between physical and spiritual, the launching platform for your higher consciousness, fueling the high-energy, anti-gravity early stages of the spiritual rocket's journey towards inner space.

So the job is to identify and apply the energies of the mind to that launching process. Here we deal with activities and processes of the mind that you wouldn't normally associate with a higher spiritual plane. I already mentioned in the introduction to this chapter that love is seated in the heart, and that the spiritual heart, which we identify with the fourth chakra, Anahata, is a meeting point, the pivotal balance point between upward (spiritual) and downward (physical) energies. The mind is where this duality is played out. We harness love and its 'physical' subsets of commitment and excitement to free us from being stuck in the physical world and let us fly in the spiritual one.

In the straightforwardly physical world, excitement means adrenalin. Theme park thrill seekers, extreme sports fanatics, speed merchants or motorcycle maniacs like me know all about the attractions of that particular little hormone, and some admit to being addicted (or committed) to its charms. The heart rate increases, the blood vessels and air passages constrict or dilate; the net effect is more energy flowing through your physical body, a heightened awareness, faster reactions, enhanced concentration. Just what you need for snowboarding or skydiving – typical fight or flight stuff.

Which leads us to 'spine tingling'. You're in some extreme activity, or you just narrowly caught the train, or the interesting person on the other side of the room whose eye you have been trying to catch suddenly returns your glance, and you get a jolt. It's very much a part of sexual attraction, but it even happens in silly little moments such as dropping a glass and catching it just before it hits the floor. The 'tingle' is your nerve endings feeling the flow of adrenalin, which in this case we can call energy. No great leap of faith or intellect to see and feel that energy as spiritual, to evoke the tingling as you sit in meditation and fire up the Muladhara chakra, at the very root and base of your spine, where the kundalini serpent lives. Even in a small, amateurish and undeveloped way, once you feel him snaking up your spinal column you can easily feel the intimate relationship between excitement and heightened consciousness. It's a balance of power, peace inside energy, the stillness at the eye of the storm. The tingling sensation itself is a trigger for the "still, small voice of calm".

The Power of Love Meditation 3: Ownership

Freeing yourself was one thing; claiming ownership of that freed self was another.
Toni Morrison

Continuing the theme of duality raised in this 'chapter of the mind' where we deal with the pivot points, the balance of power between physical and spiritual, we come to Ownership, and at first glance ask: "Whatever is that idea doing here?" Aren't we supposed to be about giving it all up?

No, we're not, in a word. We're about raising our consciousness, becoming elevated beings, in the world around us and making an impact on that world around us through our spiritual powers, rediscovered and re-created in the 'elevation' process. We're about engaging, not disengaging (although see also Chapter 1: The Power of Nature, Meditation 7, Dispassion – Detachment).

This meditation is about owning that process, a step-by-step journey in real time which automatically also gives you ownership of the final result – your newly created, or re-created, Self. (Not that the result is ever 'final', of course. There's always a higher stage.) Ownership means responsibility (which has a meditation all of its own in this chapter), in the sense of settling on something, then being ready, able and willing to take the consequences. We're in it for the long haul, ladies and gentlemen. If love wasn't driving us, we wouldn't be able to claim ownership.

We are, however, talking about ownership of something subtle, of an idea, an experience, of the Self. Seen in this way, the duality comes up between the self with a small 's' – yourself unenlightened and un-elevated, going about your daily body-conscious business – and the Self with a capital 'S', the Soul. Can't own a Soul, can we? Can we own energy? Can we own our Selves? Isn't the Soul itself the owner?

Duality all the way. It's another yes and no. The non-physical spirit, the Soul, in its pure, powerful, peaceful original state, has no attachments. It is simply the blissful light of a pinpoint of pure consciousness, burning steadily without ever consuming itself. It owns nothing because in that state it just 'is', there is no 'doing' of any kind involved. But when it's working on itself, it's working on owning itself in the sense of controlling itself. And that also goes for the small 's' self and the capital 'S' soul. With ownership comes power, but also duty to the self, the Self and others to administrate that power with grace, harmony and beauty.

Another way of looking at it, couched in yet another duality, is to see ownership as stewardship. This gets round the whole problem of a non-physical Soul owning anything, even an entirely non-physical subtle process and end result. The notion of stewardship celebrates what you have got – the luck, for instance, to be able and willing to follow this high path, the ability to communicate it to others – as a gift. You are looking after your gifts, taking care of them because they have been entrusted to you, but in the end they are not yours to get smug about. Great power comes from this realization that what is yours is not yours. It means you will discharge your duty of care without arrogance and attachment, and will also be better able to meet and combat obstacles on the way because you don't have to defend, explain or apologize. It's a power coming through you. It's You but not yours. If you behave as if the power coming through you is yours, it becomes tainted with possession and fades away.

To own, to truly own the power that is You, is to let go.

The Power of Love Meditation 4: Passion

> Passion is energy. Feel the power that comes from focusing on what excites you.
> *Oprah Winfrey*

> Faith is the highest passion in a human being. Many in every generation may not come that far, but none comes further.
> *Soren Kierkegaard*

> What Reason weaves, by Passion is undone.
> *Alexander Pope, Essay on Man and Other Poems*

> Feel your emotions,
> Live true your passions,
> Keep still your mind.
> *Geoffrey M. Gluckman*

Everyone knows passion. It's the term of choice, much favored by advertising and marketing people talking about car rentals, or coffee, or buses, or software, or anything at all; by creative artists explaining their difficult and often dangerous behavior; and of course by the lover, songwriter, author or poet describing intense and turbulent romantic love. Etymologically, the word has as much root in the idea of suffering as it does joy – more, in fact. The *Shorter Oxford English Dictionary* gives three main areas of meaning, of which the first is suffering or affliction, the second is "being passive" and the third is "an affection of the mind", including… "Any vehement, commanding or overpowering emotion; in psychology or art, any mode in which the mind is affected or acted upon, as ambition, avarice, desire, hope, fear, love, hatred, joy, grief, anger, revenge…" and finally "An overmastering zeal or enthusiasm for some object."

As far as people's common understanding of passion is concerned, there is no doubt that in general it is held to be an uplift, a driving force, and in the case of romantic love, a route to extreme pleasure, to bliss. But passion carries an inbuilt duality. It is both creative and destructive. It is upward and downward looking. It can be heaven or it can be hell.

The intellectual challenge – as distinct from the experiential one – is that passion suggests the opposite of peace. It's more about turbulence, disturbance, emotions out of control, running away with you, leading to actions that you may regret. Things that we associate with the familiar, unruly, chit-chattery, flim-flammery mind. But the mind harbors and nurtures the desire for enlightenment, the energy of 'up' as well as downward-looking flim-flam. Hence passion, dispassion, compassion, passivity and patience (even being a patient) are all part of the same thing. It's a defining principle of being human, a human being; 'human' looks down to the more earthly chakras below the heart, 'being' looks upward to the transcendental ones above it. The heart feels both sorrow and joy, right?

Passion, notionally a force of imbalance, based in the mind, leads the Soul from uncontrolled emotion to a pure, powerful, blissful state of being. A balanced Ecology of the Soul has room for emotion. Your average sadhu, guru or other species of holy man (why are they mostly men?) will tell you that the activity of the mind is a trap, a diversion, an illusion to be conquered, and indeed, in our own meditations we aim to get behind, beyond, over or under the trivial mental chitchat. But make no mistake, the mind and emotions, thoughts and feelings are a massively powerful part of our consciousness and should be understood as our driving force on the upward path. Far better to harness that power and turn it upwards than fight a losing battle.

Let's concentrate on one of the last subsections of the *SOED*'s definition three: "An overmastering zeal or enthusiasm for some object". ("Object" meaning in this case a goal, aim or intention, not yet another piece of consumer trivia.) Your passion to move or improve yourself, to explore spiritual ways of making sense of yourself and the inner and outer worlds you inhabit, to read this book and books like it, to do yoga or sit in meditation and put new and uplifting thought patterns into practice, is all you need. In fact it's crucial, because it's a hard path and without passion you'll lose the impetus. If your passion is truly there, you will truly get what you're aiming at.

The more you sit in meditation, the more blissful and beneficial experience comes to you, the more your passion for it will drive you to do it. You'll become jittery, jumpy and a little grumpy if you haven't done it for a couple of days; your passion, your zeal for the goal – which may or may not yet have made itself absolutely clear to you – is driving you. It's uncomfortable, it won't leave you alone, often you don't want to do it; you'd rather stay in bed. It's passion that gets you up, stands over you while you put your spiritual running shoes on and gets you going. Never say that isn't a good thing.

The Power of Love Meditation 5: Spirit

If you want to accomplish the goals of your life, you have to begin with the spirit.
Oprah Winfrey

In my definition of consciousness, consciousness is the same thing as life. What wisdom traditions also call spirit.
Deepak Chopra

'Spirit' is a word or an idea full of resonance, and not just for the spiritual seeker. It is here in this chapter because it refers to the incorporeal, to a non-physical force which is separate and distinct from, but very much related to, the Soul. It is also very much related to the 'spirit' of other meditations in this chapter, specifically Passion and Energy, and it is best understood through consciousness of the breath.

'Spirit', as opposed to 'Soul', is both an ingredient of love and a way of expressing it. Unlike the Soul, it is not an individual and specific entity. It is a force, a principle of life, but a subtle one, not to be confused with Prān or Ch'i, the physical/subtle energy of life that flows through your body and indeed all living things. It is not consciousness itself, but the mode or mood in which it operates.

We have to be careful with conscious forces or principles of life though, however subtle. The Ecology of the Soul does not admit of a divine omnipresence, either a God that is or is in everything, or a universal consciousness that encompasses all souls, all living beings and probably all the material universe as well. (As I say in the Introduction, where does this omnipresence idea draw the line? Are we supposed to believe that God also exists in cockroaches, oil refineries or radioactive waste?) 'Spirit' is not a general, boundless miasma of consciousness. It is outside the individual Soul, separate and distinct, but guiding, coloring, flavoring – defining the mode or mood of your mental and spiritual activity. Spirit is the subtle bridge, in this chapter of dualities, between physical and spiritual love – physical love meaning the energy that is matter, not the romantic or sexual kind. Like no other attribute, it reveals how physical and spiritual relate to and act on each other.

A bit of etymology, always a help. And very interesting in this particular context. In both Latin and Greek the word goes back to 'breath'. The Latin *spiritus* means breath, but also courage or vigor. Hence 'inspire' and 'inspiration', the giving or absorbing of creative or uplifting energy. It is distinguished from *anima,* the Latin for mind (conscious or unconscious) or soul, but that word too can be traced back to an Indo-European root (where Sanskrit's influence on our modern English can be seen) meaning 'to breathe'. A similar duality – or perhaps we should call it confusion – exists in Greek where pneuma (πνευμα) means 'breath', 'spirit' or 'moving air', and psyche (ψυχη) means 'soul' – yet ψυχη is also from an Indo-European root meaning 'to breathe'.

No surprise, then, that we should pay such attention to our breath and breathing. And illuminating too for our understanding of 'spirit', because it leads us precisely to that bridge, from the physical to the subtle door which opens into the spiritual domain. Breathing is physical, but also very far from it. Here we have the incomprehensible connection, the flow between the outer world and the inner, where energies intermingle and the spiritual seeker can switch from one to the other, like movie cowboys jumping between fast-moving horses – animals. Animal, get it? A being with a vital spark, a non-physical energy. As in *anima,* or even *animus,* the Latin version of psyche (ψυχη), which refers more directly to the mind and its states of being, of intent.

Truth is, both 'psyche' and *anima* have traditionally been used as interchangeable with 'Soul', which confuses things, because Plato and Aristotle had their own theories. Aristotle's hugely influential treatise on the psyche, called in Greek *Περὶ Ψυχῆς* (Perì Psūchês), in Latin *De Anima* and in English *On the Soul*, proposes three souls or psyches – vegetal, animal, and rational. The concepts formed the basis of psychology until the 19th century, but they aren't much help in distinguishing the difference and the beautiful (or dangerous) interaction between physical and spiritual. For that we have to go to meditation, to the experience of and through another part of our consciousness than the rational or intellectual.

Spirit is essence, *Atman*, a word which derives from the Sanskrit *et-men*, which means – guess what – 'breath' (compare with the more recent Hindi *atma*, meaning 'soul'). Spirit is courage, the spark of vitality, an attitude, a way of looking at life, the core truth of an idea or a person. We say "In the spirit of brotherly love", "In the spirit of Abraham Lincoln", meaning following their essential nature. The way it connects the spiritual and physical worlds makes 'spirit' an essential ingredient of Love, which as we know is another word for conscious energy. 100% proof distilled Love, if you will.

The heart is the seat of love, the center of our emotional being which also carries courage, intent and conscience. We speak of "not having the heart" to do something, of "finding it in your heart" to do something else. Spirit is 'outer' heart, still non-physical but not specific to an individual consciousness. A force you can tap into and use. In silence, focus on and listen to your breathing; and feel the Spirit.

The Power of Love Meditation 6: Energy

Love is an energy which exists of itself. It is its own value.
Thornton Wilder

There is a vitality, a life force, an energy, a quickening, that is translated through you into action, and because there is only one of you in all time, this expression is unique.
Martha Graham

The energy of the mind is the essence of life.
Aristotle

When you start to consider a concept like Energy – not exactly tight and tidy, or easily defined – and ponder how it sits in the Ecology of the Soul, you see: a) that it is so intimately bound up in the idea that it practically *is* the idea; and b) that the quest to define and understand it has been undertaken in science as much as in spirituality. More so, in fact, if you choose to define 'modern' science as an exploration of the physical universe. Without engaging in scientific study, to track the 'big picture' of theories and discoveries about the nature of energy and matter is automatically to lead us to that interstitial space where physical and non-physical energies interact.

We're happy with the science that says that matter is energy, right? $E=mc^2$? As Albert Einstein said: "It followed from the special theory of relativity that mass and energy are both but different manifestations of the same thing – a somewhat unfamiliar conception for the average mind."[1] The basic building blocks of matter – protons, electrons, neutrons, quarks, neutrinos

1 https://www.aip.org/history/einstein/sound/voice1.mp3 Retrieved 27/07/15

and their ilk – are infinitesimally small particles whizzing about in what to them is almost unlimited space.

Energy can't be created and it can't be destroyed. As matter, all it does is change. All things are energy, and all thoughts are energy. Matter is energy, and consciousness is energy. Love is energy, light is energy, peace is energy, power is… energy. This is our natural state. We are beings of energy. You are energy, but energy is not necessarily You. You are love, but love is not necessarily you. Spiritual love is Light. You are light, I am light. Not a general, nondescript 'cosmic soup' kind of light; an infinitesimally small – to all intents and purposes so small that it has no size at all – infinitely powerful, eternal, individual pinpoint, an iota of conscient light, with its own unique consciousness and its own unique rôle to play in the eternal human drama. Amazing idea.

There is also 'Glow', which we associate mostly with the chakras. Chakra energy – chakra light – is your energy, not the energy that is You. These are energy nodes in your physical body, portals for Ch'i, Prān, the life force. Focusing on them gives you balance, harmony, stillness: spiritual peace and power. Here's the nub of the physical/spiritual relationship: meditating on the chakras, the light energy that is the conscious and conscient You focuses on the Prān energy that is simply and straightforwardly the glow and go of life itself. The life force. In doing that, the mind becomes still, and the conscious and conscient energy that is You the Soul perceives and experiences both the non-conscient life force, and the conscious and conscient energy that is Your Self – You the Soul.

Anahata, the heart chakra, is the seat of love. As we have discussed, it is the pivot, the balance point, the subtle portal between physical and spiritual. All the chakras, in fact, are steps on the way to our understanding, and experience, of our Selves as non-physical, incorporeal beings. Rather, the chakras themselves are not the steps; our ever-deeper and more intense engagement with them, freeing their energy, the letting go and the letting flow, gives us the steps to tread on the path between physical and spiritual, the rungs of the ladder upon which to climb upwards. Start at the earth level with Muladhara, the root, and end at Sahasrara, the 'connected' one. (We don't end there, actually, but continue on and beyond, entering a state of yoga or union with the Divine.)

A practical exercise

Sit in silence, comfortable and cross-legged, ideally. Focus on your breathing, hearing it resonate in the top back of your nasal airway to quiet your mind, and then focus your awareness (as a start) on Muladhara, the root chakra. This is the energy node centered on the very bottom tip of the spine, round the perineum, that reaches down your legs to the earth as well as forming a 'platform' from which the Prān will flow up your spine towards the top of your head. The awakening or opening process, the 'turning on' of this and all the other chakras, is, not unlike yoga asanas, a trick combination of focusing and letting go at the same time. You have to pinpoint the source, feel it flow and glow, and as soon as the tingle begins, give it up. Let it go. Donate it. Like a fan on flames, the more you release and allow the energy to rise, the more you open your (in this case) hips and groin, the more strongly and perceptibly the energy flows – upwards. Sit on or in the glow, feel it, float on it, love it, enjoy it, feel its color (red) pulsating. You can't own it, you can't keep it. The only way to get more of it is to let it go. This is not the energy that is You, remember; You are the conscient being watching and controlling it. It is leading upwards towards You, and will take You further on up as it passes through the top of your head. That way lies the connection to the energy that is God, the Supreme Soul. But that's for a different chapter (Chapter 7: The Power of Connection, Meditation 7, Home).

The Power of Love Meditation 7: Responsibility

Today, more than ever before, life must be characterized by a sense of Universal responsibility, not only nation to nation and human to human, but also human to other forms of life.
Dalai Lama

Most people do not really want freedom, because freedom involves responsibility, and most people are frightened of responsibility.
Sigmund Freud

You must take personal responsibility. You cannot change the circumstances, the seasons, or the wind, but you can change yourself. That is something you have charge of.
Jim Rohn

With great power comes responsibility, and with great love comes great responsibility. Because great love is great power. And there is no love – and hence no power – greater than the 'atomic' power of the Soul. Or 'atma-ic', perhaps we should say, just to avoid nasty misunderstandings.

'Responsibility' is here at the end of the Love chapter because it's the logical conclusion to all that has gone before. Once we're established in the experience of the ineffable and unstoppable power of love that is our true Self, learning how to enhance and nurture that experience daily, we automatically start having an effect on who and what's around us. As soon as the journey into inner space is under way, not only does our 'vibe' have a subtle effect on people and their immediate mental/emotional atmosphere, we find that we are also motivated to share our experience with others. Whether through simple conversations, teaching, talking, writing, music, art – whatever activity or medium you choose, or chooses you, the beauty that shines in you and out of you must be shared. It's not yours to own, remember; the same paradox that we dealt with in the Ownership meditation of this chapter is at work. The more you give it away, the more you let it go, the more it comes to you and empowers you.

This is the core of the idea. As you take ownership of your newly discovered true powers, you settle into the new sense of yourself – and your Self – generated by the changes and realizations you are going through. Part of this process is understanding your 'stewardship', your responsibility when it comes to managing your powers and their effect on other people. They are in You, they are of You, they are You, but they are not yours. Nurture, cherish and care for them as if you were looking after them for someone else. They are a gift, or at least your new awareness of them is a gift, to be received with love and humility, and to be given with love and humility. You are becoming a powerful Soul, a being more directly in contact with its own conscious energy than most, and people will recognize you as such.

Personal interactions may be full of sweetness and light – if your interlocutor is disposed in favor of spiritual practice and is him or herself some kind of seeker; they may be mildly uncomfortable if the other person is not particularly interested, or indeed is even uneasy about engaging in such topics; and even downright unpleasant, if, as can happen, you find yourself in front of a soul whose awareness is so far from a sense of their own true Self that you become a threat to be combated. Strange and unwelcome, but true; there are souls in this world for whom these messages are anathema. The powers of peace and love shining out of one pair of eyes can make an angry soul angrier, and twist the knife in a tortured soul's heart. All you can do is avoid.

All this connects to another aspect of responsibility for

enlightened beings, perhaps one of the most crucial for your ordinary everyday activity in daily life. Jack Canfield's *The Success Principles* sets it out just as clear as it needs to be said: "Don't blame, don't complain – take responsibility." Anything and everything that happens is ultimately down to you (within reason of course). This is strong meat and takes some deep 'churning' in meditation to figure out exactly how it works. If, for instance, you are a Soul with peace, power and love shining out of your eyes, it's a mistake to put yourself in front of aforesaid tortured souls, and if bad things happen it's as much your responsibility for being there and provoking them as it is the doers' responsibility for doing them. This kind of awareness demands a big heart, a long view and a rock solid confidence in your own power and your own heightened awareness.

It's another perfect duality, a self-contradiction almost, the same one that operates when you let go of your newly discovered powers, or at least you let go of the idea that you own them. Only by letting go can you truly benefit, and bring others benefit, in the knowledge that your power is You but it is not yours. In the same way, the truly enlightened soul who doesn't blame, doesn't complain and accepts responsibility, accepts no blame. He or she does not operate on that lowly level. For us lesser beings it is merely a lesson in living. Of course we accept responsibility for something we have done that may need putting right – a broken window, a broken heart – and in such cases 'blame' is more or less the same thing. The crucial difference is that blame is handed out by others. I accept or reject it – but I take responsibility in the most detached fashion possible. I don't deal in daily tit for tat.

The Power of Love Practice 1: Plant a Power Seed Every Day

Power Seeds are mental devices, thought triggers to generate Soul Consciousness, and hence change your actions. They are a bit like the Zen 'kōan' (for instance the idea of the sound of one hand clapping) that kick your mind out of gear and raise the level of your awareness.

Using Power Seeds, you grow a new garden of consciousness. See your mind as a garden, or at least a patch of fertile soil. Thoughts and feelings grow in it, like plants. Your mind is a riot of tangled and intertwined mental vegetation, much of it good and useful and most of it neither good nor useful. So it's a pleasant surprise that you don't have to struggle with the weeds. All you have to do is plant your mental plot with new seeds – 'Power Seeds' – which grow into thought, attitude, feeling, and action. Which feeds back and creates new thought and feeling. You have created a new mental and spiritual garden – and a new framework for your behavior.

If you really focus all the innate power of your calmed, stilled mind on the Power Seed you choose for 60 full seconds, that thought pattern will repeat and recur throughout the day, accumulating much more than a single minute of your mental activity. It's meditation in action, because the meditation is about action.

Plant one of the mental Power Seeds that appear on the following pages. The Seven Powers, Power Seeds and the Magic Minute section of the book's Introduction gives the full explanation of how to prepare the mental and spiritual ground for your new garden; Part III gives you a whole range of Power Seeds to suit your circumstances. Ultimately, as your Self knowledge increases, you will be creating and planting your own.

Love is the most important thing of all.
The only thing.

Love yourself, but love Your Self more.
Your responsibility is to have unconditional love for Your Self.

Have a heart.
Anahata the heart chakra is at the center of your spiritual and physical being.
The heart is the hub, the portal, for the flow of energy, physical, subtle and spiritual.

Take a breather.
If the heart is the 'hub' for the flow of physical and spiritual energy, the breath is the flow itself. Watch and listen to your breathing and let it carry you into silence. The closer you get to stillness, the quieter becomes your breathing, until you are sitting not in a moving flow, but a floating glow.

God is Love, but Love is not God.

Love is Energy, but Energy is not necessarily Love.

Love is energy, and everything – matter and spirit – is energy.
But every thing is not love.

Energy can't be created and it can't be destroyed. As matter, all it does is change. All things are energy, and all thoughts are energy. Matter is energy, and consciousness is energy. Love is energy, light is energy, peace is energy, power is energy. We are beings of energy. You are energy, but energy is not necessarily You. You are love, but love is not necessarily You.

A balance of power.
The Ecology of the Soul is in balance when our powers are in balance. That balance sets us free and leads us to a place of perfect peace, power and stillness.
Love is the name of that place.
Love is the name of that balance.

Joy. Delight. Fun.
We are beings made of joy, put here to feel delight, to feel high. Fun-damentally, fun is one of the building blocks of our being. Try it; if you go into the still and silent inner space, you come out of it with a grin, feeling mildly euphoric, full of joy.
That joy is Your natural state of being.
Another name for it is Love.

Love is Light, and Light is Love – spiritual light, that is.
The pinpoint of spiritual light that is You the Soul, because it is light, seeks enlightenment.

Commitment strengthens, deepens your resolve. It takes courage to do, and gives courage in the doing.

To commit is to hand over, to renounce, to give oneself up, to let go, to let it flow, in a sense to abandon responsibility. Let go of yourself to find and nurture your true Self.

Love is letting go. Love your Self by letting go of yourself. If you're struggling, let go. If your mind or body is tight, wound up… let go.
Letting go does not mean losing it. Once you have properly let go, you will find 'it' – energy, peace, power, love, stillness – comes to you more abundantly than ever.

The intimate relationship between excitement and heightened

consciousness is a balance of power, peace inside energy, the stillness at the eye of the storm. At the center of the commotion is the "still, small voice of calm".

Stewardship celebrates what you have got as a gift. You take care of your gifts because they have been entrusted to you, but in the end they are not yours.
It's a power coming through you.
It's You but not yours.
To own, to truly own the power that is You, is to let go.

Your passion to move or improve yourself, to explore spiritual ways of making sense of yourself and Your Self, is all you need. If your passion is truly there, you will truly get what you're aiming at.

'Spirit' in ancient languages translates as 'breath'. Hence 'inspire'. The word 'Soul' comes from the same root. 'Spirit' leads to the physical door which opens into the spiritual domain. Your breath is physical, but also very far from it. It is the flow between the outer world and the inner.

Angry, anxious, greedy, fearful, envious, hostile, negative energies are not Me or You. They are subversions of our being, indicators of how far we have strayed from our true Selves.

We are beings of pure conscient energy, which is another way of saying love, which is another way of saying peace.
Our natural, incontrovertible state is peace.

The Power of Love Practice 2: Yoga Seeds – Salute to the Sun (Surya Namaskar)

Position 4: Plank Pose (Chaturanga Dandasana)

The Salute to the Sun, like most things in yoga, has many variations. The one we use here consists of seven 'asanas', to use the Sanskrit name for positions, done in a 12-step sequence. This posture is 'Chaturanga Dandasana' in Sanskrit ('Chatur' means four, 'anga' means limb or part thereof, 'danda' means 'staff' or stave – the four-limbed staff) and 'plank' in English. No prizes for guessing which one we like here at the Ecology of the Soul.

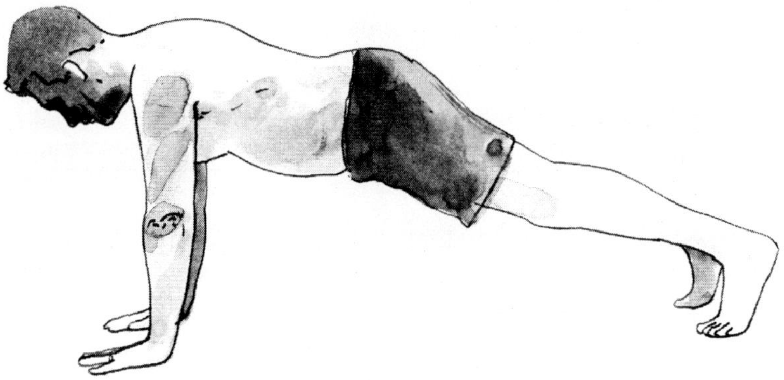

We focus on 'high plank' for this version of Surya Namaskar. It falls naturally into the sequence, whereas 'low plank' is such a trial of strength for the arms that I recommend you learn and practice it individually.

In the sequence, you are between 'lunge' with your right leg forward, and Adho Mukha Svanasana, 'Dog'. Palms flat on the floor, jump your right leg back from the lunge position so that both legs are extending back behind you, your weight resting on your toes, which have flexed to point forward. Your arms are straight up and down from your shoulders, elbows locked. You are turning them into strong structural components, supporting your upper body weight and giving it enough lift to feel light. Those arms have to feel like tree trunks, living but solid.

They need to be, because your aim here is to make a straight line with your body from the top of your spine where it enters your skull right down to your heels. We've talked about opening your channels for the energy to flow; that opening process happens when you make them as straight and unencumbered as you can, and this position concentrates on that straightness. Your head is a natural extension of your spine; you are looking down at the floor in between your hands. As your strong solid arms extend to your shoulders, open your shoulders and chest a little by twisting your arms in their sockets slightly and giving your heart more space. Your lower back must be energized and raised to counter its natural downward curve, but don't raise it by rounding your spine; the lift comes from within the spine itself, and also by tucking your coccyx in.

Remember that you are always feeling and hearing your breathing sound at the top back of your nasal passage, making a hollow echo in your head which in itself is creating your calm, inner focus. Remember also that every move you make is done on an exhalation. Run your attention up and down your body, focusing and feeling the energy in each chakra position, or node. Warmth from red Muladhara, at the base of your spine and flooding both upwards and downwards, connecting you to the earth and the natural world; a tingle from orange Svadhisthana, in the pit of your stomach just above your genitals; steadiness and stability from yellow Manipura at the center of your solar plexus; the opening, pivotal energy of Anahata, the heart chakra, which is green in color, sometimes with pink petals; let go your throat muscles, relaxing your neck and tongue (this is tricky!) so the brain quietens at Vishuddha, the blue throat chakra; you should have no difficulty feeling the energy at Ajna, the indigo 'third eye' chakra, because this is the physical position of the

Soul in the body; and finally, the upward and outward energy of the violet connecting/connected chakra, Sahasrara, carrying the flow out of your system, up and out towards the Divine. The more it flows out, the more there is of it to flow.

Hold the position if you can for seven full in-out breaths, each one focusing on each chakra. Tailbone tucked in, arms locked, chest spread. It's energizing and strengthening; deceptively simple but with a great deal of subtlety. You will enjoy refining Chaturanga Dandasana for the rest of your days. Why not?

Chapter 5

The Power of Communication

Vishuddha, the Throat Chakra

In this chapter:
Introduction
Listening
Speaking
Open mindedness
Seeing others
Seeing your Self
Seeing the Beauty
Vision, Purpose, Goals
Power Seeds for Thought
The Salute to the Sun: Dog Pose (Adho Mukha Svanasana)

To effectively communicate, we must realize that we are all different in the way we perceive the world and use this understanding as a guide to our communication with others.
Tony Robbins

The two words 'information' and 'communication' are often used interchangeably, but they signify quite different things. Information is giving out; communication is getting through.
Sydney J. Harris

The ability to simplify means to eliminate the unnecessary so that the necessary may speak.
Hans Hofmann

Introduction

Why would communication be a part of this journey, which is essentially a journey into inner space? If you're only looking for your Self, what is the need for communication? We aren't talking about talking to ourselves, are we? The first sign of madness, supposedly?

Smart answer, the kind you'd expect; well, of course we are. And it's fairly easy to put all this spiritual seeking, personal development and self improvement stuff down as a kind of madness anyway. If you're squeamish about being written off as a mad person, maybe this book, this path and others like it are not for you just yet. Are you really sure you want to go back to the couch and watch TV? You really are sure that that's the sane path and this is the mad one?

At first sight, communication is an outward-facing activity. You're coming from inside and going outside. Your focus is on others, not yourself. Or your Self. But just as a good deal of the emphasis in the Power of Focus, for instance, is on action and activity, the way in which you manage your relationship with the external, three-dimensional world, so communication is as much about what comes from inside and goes out as it is about a strictly external awareness. You have to know who you are to know what to say and how to say it.

Then again, communication is about far more than just 'saying'. Throughout this chapter, we will explore the idea that in almost every respect communication is not just a two-way but a three-way street, in that you conduct a relationship with yourself, with your Self, and with others around you. And hear – as long as you're listening – what they are saying back to you. Again, inner and outer. Can't have one without the other; as we've said, this is not the book for you if you are determined to sit on top of a mountain or in a darkened room and meditate, untouched by and not touching the world and the people in it. Sorry, people, but as meditators and beings of enhanced consciousness, you have a responsibility. Can't avoid it. Goes with the territory.

One of the most powerful and far-reaching insights into communication as a key contributor to the balanced Ecology of the Soul is the one that says: "Communication is compassion." This just about sums it up. To truly listen, to speak in a way that is heard, to see and understand others and yourself (your Self), to define and cherish your purpose, your vision and your goals, to see the beauty in the people and the environment that surround you, are difficult to the point of impossibility without compassion. It's a major plank of Buddhist philosophy, defining "our Buddha seed or Buddha nature, our potential to become a Buddha... Through meditation we can extend and deepen our compassion until it transforms into the mind of great compassion – the wish to protect all living beings without exception from their suffering."1 Without necessarily being as dedicated as this, at least at this stage, to the enlightenment and liberation of all living beings, the bare fact remains that unless you 'get alongside' others, pay enough attention to their vibe, the subtle wants and needs that they themselves might not be able to articulate, you are not communicating. Same goes for yourself/Self: "If your compassion does not include yourself, it is incomplete," says American Buddhist teacher and psychologist Jack Kornfield[2]

Vishuddha, the throat chakra, where the powers of communication are seated, is associated with the sense of hearing and the action of speaking. It governs a sense of independence, fluent thought and a sense of security, and when open, it is believed it has the power to transform negative experiences into wisdom and learning. It is a purification center, associated with higher discrimination, creativity and self expression. In balance, Vishuddha is the focus of your own internal truth, and hence supports and enhances

---

1 www.aboutdharma.org/what-is-compassion.php/ (Retrieved 28/07/15)

2 *Buddha's Little Instruction Book*, Jack Kornfeld, Bantam, 1994. ISBN-10: 0553373854; ISBN-13: 978-0553373851

your ability to express yourself clearly and honestly with others.

Which puts it all in a nutshell, and neatly and elegantly expresses the inner and outer aspects of communication. You can't do straight talking, or listening without fear or favor, if you don't know who and what you are. You'll get sidetracked into protecting – and projecting – the mistaken, bodily sense of yourself. If you aren't clear with your own internal truth, which is obviously the inexpressible power, peace and beauty of you the conscient Soul, the being of light, then you won't have clear messages for those around you. This is not to say that all your external communications must be confined to promoting and purveying exclusively the eternal truths of Soul, karma and enlightenment; far from it. They're not much use when all you need is to pick up your dry cleaning. Clarity and confidence in all your daily dealings, however mundane, are indicators that you are in touch with your own center, from which and to which the lines of communication are forever open.

Your internal communications network works like this. You, in your consciousness of desire for higher consciousness, send messages to your mind, proposing the need to clarify, to control, to experience, to express. The intellect kicks in as the discriminator, the power of analysis and decision about what to let through and what to discard – both output and input. It feeds back to the mind and enables it to refine and enhance experience, keeping it on the straight and narrow, which is where the power lies. Nothing much narrower than a pinpoint which has location but no size. If it leads to action, you are at least reasonably confident that, as long as this process is conscious and you are Self aware, the action is one that will carry positive consequences, both for you and for those around you. Which leads to karma, which leads to your sanskars (the recorded results of karma, or action, on the Soul), which lead back to the mind and its search for clarity and experience, which goes through the filter of the intellect… and so on. As we said, the power of communication is not just about speaking.

The Power of Communication Meditation 1: Listening

There is only one rule for being a good talker – learn to listen.
Christopher Morley

Hearing is a physiological phenomenon; listening is a psychological act.
Roland Barthes

If we were supposed to talk more than we listen, we would have two tongues and one ear.
Mark Twain

Effective listening requires concentration and the use of your other senses – not just hearing the words spoken.
www.skillsyouneed.com/ips/listening-skills.html#ixzz3ED2Yz21t

This again is an external thing, right? Listening is about communicating, a basic and necessary skill of interpersonal relationships, right?

Well, yes. But nonetheless important for all that. Remember, we're not on the path of spiritual isolation here. If you sit on a mountaintop all the time and only come down once a day to fill your begging bowl, you have no need of interpersonal communication skills, and are trying to do something different from what this book sets out to do. Here we are aiming to balance the Ecology of the Soul, which means a balanced personality, one that engages with his or her fellow men or women, and can effectively communicate the power and attraction of the path we tread – can above all communicate the experience.

But you won't know how to communicate that experience to any such fellow man or woman unless you have listened to them with all your senses and sensitivity, and heard what they want, and want to hear. My father, the Church of England priest you met in the introduction, used to tell me: "Listen. You're in a position of power when the other person is talking. They are telling you things and you are learning."

Listening is also, of course, a matter of the physical senses – like the next meditations in this chapter, the seeing ones – which again might be seen as a diversion from the real business of engaging with the non-physical, the experience beyond the three dimensions. It is the senses, after all, that lead us astray when we are in the grip of body consciousness. In that state, it is only through the senses that we can get even a glimpse of transcendence, which is why we drink, take drugs, have sex, lose ourselves in books, music, movies, art, fishing or baseball, climb mountains, run marathons, or any of the million other things we do to 'get high'. We're seeking an uplifting experience that we think we can find outside ourselves, that transcends the everyday world, and we will indeed get a temporary result. But it will only ever be temporary. There is usually a price of pain to pay, and the result is never entirely satisfactory, which is why we always want more. You break out of the downward spiral of body consciousness by applying your senses to the realm beyond your senses; you listen, quite simply, to your Self.

Not that your Self, the silent, glowing pinpoint, is likely to be saying anything out loud, nor indeed is 'listening' strictly a sense. Hearing is a sense, a physiological phenomenon, as Barthes says in the quote above. He calls listening a psychological act, but in the Ecology of the Soul it is a spiritual one.

Let's come back to communicating with others when we've learned to communicate with our Selves: to listen inside, which is where meditation starts. You listen to your mind, discarding its inconsequential chitchat, settling it and feeling its dormant power. But you are only on the way through. The mind can only help meditation when it is quiet and allows you to fly above or dig below its verbalizations. You listen to your intellect telling your mind to shut down, but be careful that you don't get trapped in thoughts here either. The intellect doesn't work in the same way as the mind; yes, it creates thought, but with aim and intent, and with a self-analytical, self-critical function. Your motivation to meditate comes from all parts of your consciousness, and is refined and directed through the intellect, the controller for that conscious energy. It merely nudges the tiller now and then to keep you on course, and finally lets go when you launch into the Ocean of Peace. And power. And stillness.

Listen to your body. This works for all sorts of meditations, including active ones like running. It is also why yoga plays a supporting but important role in this book; 'physical' yoga demands that you turn your attention inside, listen to parts of your body you never normally communicate with, and understand what's going on there. In that complex territory where physical and spiritual energies interact, you can get a lift in consciousness, a 'buzz' if you like, just by doing something simple like dropping your shoulders and extending your neck. I was recently given a book called *ChiRunning* by Danny Dreyer,[1] which explains techniques to focus on the Ch'i energy at your center and use that to run farther, faster and more injury-free than you thought possible. Your attention is inside, your balance is actively based in your pelvic/solar plexus area (the Manipura chakra, which governs endurance, among other things), your arms, legs, shoulders, knees are relaxed. While running? Is that possible? Indeed it is.

The most important part of listening to your body though is of course the breathing. The breath is right in the center of that

1 *ChiRunning: A Revolutionary Approach to Effortless, Injury-Free Running*, by Danny Dreyer, Pocket Books, 2008. ISBN-10: 1847392784; ISBN-13: 978-1847392787

physical/spiritual territory, the route through which energy flows, exchanging from physical through subtle to spiritual and back. Your breathing determines your state of mind and is determined by it. Move the place where it makes contact with your airways to the upper back of your nasal channels, just before it turns down the throat. The place where snoring, if snoring there is, makes itself heard. You can hear it as it flows, in and out, in and out. I defy you not to find your brain and mind relaxed as your attention turns to your breathing in this way. Now let go your throat, tongue and chin and jaw muscles. Your mind calms. It's a direct link.

Finally – although not actually finally, because there's plenty more – listen to your heart. And listen to the silence. When you come back, you realize that listening is compassion. And that is your single most important tool to communicate with others. If you don't have compassion, you might be hearing; but you're not listening.

The Power of Communication Meditation 2: Speaking

Breathe through the heats of our desire
Thy coolness and thy balm;
Let sense be dumb, let flesh retire;
Speak through the earthquake, wind and fire,
O still, small voice of calm!
John Greenleaf Whittier, from "The Brewing of Soma", 1872, from the King James Bible, 1 Kings 19: 11–13

This is the beginning of any soul conscious meditation, the very heart and nub of it. Speaking, talking or saying to yourself: "I am a Soul. An infinitesimally small pinpoint of light, power and peace, sitting in my enormous body's forehead. Conscious energy, conscient energy." This is the most powerful and significant conversation you will ever have. The more you focus and concentrate on the idea, the more you persuade yourself, the more the meditation experience takes you, the more you are speaking to – and experiencing – your Self, as opposed to yourself. Self hypnosis? Maybe. But what's so bad about that? Plenty of meditations are nothing more nor less. Judge by the results. The quibble always being, of course, that you don't *have* a Self, something spiritual and transcendental that somehow belongs to you. You *are* one. You are It. You *have* a body; you *are* a Soul.

But in this chapter we're expecting to communicate with others, which brings us to the external/internal debate we just had in the 'listening' meditation. We need to be able to persuade others of the truth and benefit of our experience of Soul Consciousness, otherwise it's a strictly selfish project – the mountaintop and begging bowl. That solo route is not the route of the Ecology of the Soul, which by its nature demands that we interact with others, and gently reminds us that part of our job as enlightened beings (or beings on the path of spiritual effort towards enlightenment, anyway) is to bring those others as much benefit as we can give and they can receive. It also equips us to conduct any ordinary, daily interaction with 'added value' power and peace. I'm not suggesting you stand up in the middle of a budget meeting and deliver a full-blown rant about Soul Consciousness, with a guided meditation thrown in; what I am suggesting is that if you are Soul Conscious and 'coming from your center' as it were, by which of course I mean you are seeing yourself as a Soul, your 'vibe', the atmosphere you create around you by your speech and demeanor, will affect those who come into contact with you. "How do you always stay so calm, [insert name]?" is a perfect jumping-off point for an introductory explanation.

It's a place where the message is delivered not just in the words we say, but in the way we say them. But to get there, we need to know how to speak to our Selves. This is also why three of the meditations in this chapter, although 'listening' and 'speaking' indicate a relationship with the external world, actually depend on our ability to hear, to talk to – and to see – our Selves. It's a new relationship. Someone you thought you knew – your Self – turned out to be something entirely different, and you need to redraw your understanding. You can do this by 'persuading yourself to talk to your Self' as above – 'I am a Soul' – and there isn't an enormous amount to learn after that. Simple, really. It's not a mantra; it's an idea you repeat, and ponder, and allow to draw you into a deep experience of peace. And power. And silence.

Which is another key element of this paradoxical process, because silence is exactly where talking to yourself (your Self) in this way leads you. The 'chatter' of your mind has dropped away, and as you the Soul enter your own spiritual dimension, the silence from which you came and to which you will return, so do your other mental activities shut down. No need to steer yourself any more; you have arrived. There will of course be the moments when you drift off and need to bring yourself back into the full-on experience of what we might call active, living silence; but essentially, this is the place where it's all just being. No doing. It's not a space of nothingness. It's beyond sound, a place of pure consciousness, of your light burning steadily in an infinite moment, the glow of bliss, of life itself. You belong there.

But you also, fortunately or unfortunately, belong in your body in the physical world, with your daily part to play in the 'world drama' programmed into your sanskars, subject to the laws of karma and the space/time continuum. You come out of the silence and back into sound, and from here, everyone you meet and speak to in this ordinary everyday world will pick up the pure, peaceful, powerful atmosphere that surrounds you like an invisible cloak. Far better that they notice your inner poise and ask you about it than you deliver an impromptu lecture. You might get a sense of this 'silence within sound' – which only really lasts a short while before you are completely back in the world of sound – by considering the Christian idea of the "still, small voice of calm", taken from the Bible, but more familiar from John Greenleaf Whittier's famous hymn *Dear Lord and Father of Mankind*. His perception is that it is the voice of God, "Speak[ing] through earthquake, wind and fire" to us. "Drop thy still dews of quietness," says Whittier; "let sense be dumb, let flesh retire." It's the same experience, but from a different angle, and for those of us lucky enough to be exposed to Soul Consciousness, it's clear that we too can speak with that 'still small voice'. Nothing more persuasive than the sound that comes from silence, the sound with silence at its heart. Be grateful for the good fortune (that you have made for yourself, karmically speaking) that allows you to speak with this power.

The Power of Communication Meditation 3: Open mindedness

Let yourself be open and life will be easier. A spoon of salt in a glass of water makes the water undrinkable. A spoon of salt in a lake is almost unnoticed.
Buddha Siddhartha Guatama Shakyamuni

Those who cannot change their minds cannot change anything.
George Bernard Shaw

A mind is like a parachute. It doesn't work if it is not open.
Frank Zappa

The mind that opens to a new idea never returns to its original size.
Albert Einstein

Open mindedness is compassion.
Open mindedness is letting go.
Open mindedness is detachment.
Open mindedness is observation.

There is a way in which open mindedness is at the very root – or *is* the very root – of this whole inner-ecological balance project. It's quite simple: this book is for you if you're not only able, but willing to take on, and indeed are actively seeking, change. And that, ladies and gentlemen, if you're stuck in your ideas and in your ways, you don't get. Stuck in your habits, in other words, mental and physical. And spiritual. Or rather, non-spiritual. As in, making the body conscious mistake.

Wake up!

To communicate effectively you need an open mind. Open to ideas, open to change, open to others, open to your Self. Listening and seeing are part of it, but not the whole story. You are without prejudice or preconception, without a set of readymade standards by which you judge someone's speech or actions. Open mindedness is the ability to see and hear people and their issues for what they are, not what they want you to think they are or what you want them to be. It also, crucially, gives you a levelheaded, balanced view of yourself and your actions, leading to a clearer perception of You the Soul, your Self.

Obvious though it may sound, open mindedness comes in two parts: the mind and the openness. The mind is the seeker of experience, the generator of thoughts and feelings. The openness is readiness to experience, a willingness to receive, absorb. But open mindedness doesn't just mean the mind. That is indeed part of it, but it requires a process of opening your whole being, all departments of your consciousness. You are sensitized, aware. Your radar antennae are extended, up and out, receiving. You are seeing the unseen, hearing the unspoken.

What we also learn as we balance the Ecology of the Soul is the value of letting go. It's one of yoga's most fundamental lessons: you can't stretch unless you let go. Pushing or pulling your muscles only pulls muscles. And so it is with the mind and the routes to a higher consciousness. So where and when, in this case, is open mindedness the same as letting go? It certainly is when it's a matter of dismantling your attachment to your own ideas, conceptions and preconceptions, upon which you might have built your coherent sense of yourself. With courage and a rock solid confidence in the spiritual truth of your Self – with self awareness, self consciousness in the best sense – letting go of the top level superficial stuff shouldn't be hard. If it is, meditate on that spiritual truth some more – experience it. Your nature is non-physical, your being is light. How can you be attached to anything, conceptual or practical and physical, if you keep that in mind?

Here's a physical trick to open, relax, or let go of the mind, also important in yoga practice. Let go of your throat, jaw and tongue. We know that Vishuddha, the chakra which 'honors communication', is centered in the throat. It governs a number of other things besides, as we also know: independence, fluent thought and the capacity to transform negative experience into wisdom. (Sounds like open mindedness.) As you sit and settle yourself in meditation, become aware of the muscles around and under your jaw, down your throat, and particularly your tongue, which is itself a muscle. As you identify and consciously let go of the muscles in these areas, your tongue shrinks and occupies far less space in your mouth. Your neck and throat relax, and lo and behold, your mind quietens, slows down, and opens up to the experience of your tiny, powerful, pinpoint Self. That's the first step in open mindedness – opening your mind.

Open mindedness is to do with input from outside, right? External stimuli and how we deal with them. But just as your open mindedness leads you to a non-judgmental acceptance of others and their thoughts, feelings, opinions and ideas, so it should also apply to your own. An open mind, first and foremost, opens itself to the experience, as both the thinking, feeling mind and the analyzing, discriminating intellect recognize, of that which is beyond, above and below the mind. The Self – the Soul – incorporates the mind, but it is not that. Both the mind and intellect are routes to that experience, jumping-off platforms; there is self-management, self control, because you also know with both faculties that only when they are accurately directed will they lead you to the truth of your Self, which is in a place of peace, power and bliss very different from where they operate.

In contrast, you need the sort of commitment to this process that could be called monomanic, or close minded. It's determination, keeping the goal in sight, never allowing yourself to be diverted (or only a little now and then, anyway). It's underlying.

As I say in the previous meditation about speaking, you're not expected to stand up in the middle of a budget meeting and deliver a tirade about Soul Consciousness. As in all things – including the very essence of this book – it's about balance. You conduct your outward daily life in the perfectly normal way, but as soon as you are in a solo space where you don't have to interact, your consciousness of the 'true' consciousness returns.

As this practice develops, wisdom, knowledge and learning develop. But they are only useful, to yourself and others, if they are applied with compassion. In fact open mindedness, like communication itself, is compassion. Which, etymologically, means 'suffering with'. Or call it 'feeling with'. Which you can't do without love. Love of people, love of God, love of yourself and your Self, love of life. You also can't do it without curiosity, the desire to know, to understand – to acquire wisdom. An open mind is a strong mind, able and willing to flex, to absorb, to receive – because it's based on balance, on the confidence and 'centeredness' that goes with Self knowledge.

The Power of Communication Meditation 4: Seeing others

> Our stresses, anxieties, pains, and problems arise because we do not see the world, others, or even ourselves as worthy of love.
> *Prem Prakash, The Yoga of Spiritual Devotion: A Modern Translation of the Narada Bhakti Sutras*

> Because I was more often happy for other people, I got to spend more time being happy. And as I saw more light in everybody else, I seemed to have more myself.
> *Victoria Moran, Lit From Within: Tending Your Soul for Lifelong Beauty*

> One hand I extend into myself, the other toward others.
> *Dejan Stojanovic, The Shape*

This one is definitely focused outwards, and for that reason you may not think of it as a meditation at all. It's about 'reading people', seeing more than you see. Taking the clues, making your observations and conclusions with compassion. It is to be meditated upon, perhaps, rather than being a meditation in its own right.

To speak with a voice that's heard, you have to know who you're talking to. Obviously, you're talking to a Soul. And obviously, you keep that in mind as you talk. Seeing the other person as a Soul is no less a crucial attribute of Soul Consciousness, making up the balanced Ecology of the Soul, than is the ability to focus solely on your own inner awareness. This meditation is also about seeing people as just themselves; understanding and being able to 'get alongside' them at a less rarefied level than the strictly spiritual. Got to make our everyday way in the everyday world, right?

The point being that you can't live in isolation, even if you wanted to, which is not anyway what this book is about. *The Ecology of the Soul* is for people who wish to follow a spiritual path of upliftment and ultimately enlightenment, but who are neither able nor willing to renounce their daily lives, their families, jobs and relationships. You're not doing this just for you; it's inevitable that others will be affected by your state of being, so it might as well be peaceful, powerful and a pleasant experience for them. Clearly we have to find ways of applying the Soul Conscious state of being when we are in action, in conversation, in contact with others, following our ordinary daily routines. It's not right to stay focused inside and let the people you come across through the day go hang; that, for sure, is not a recipe for successful relationships on any level. Neither is it necessary, as we've said in other meditations in this chapter, to put the good word of Soul Consciousness out at every available opportunity, and a good few that you wouldn't call 'available'; you can very easily be counterproductive if you start preaching at people who aren't interested, or who might well be, but not right at this moment, thank you very much. *Be* your message, without having to speak it, and those who are disposed in that direction will pick it up.

All of which amounts to the fact that we need to preserve our own Soul Consciousness when in 'outward looking' mode, and if possible give the people we're interacting with a taste of the peace and power we have been lucky enough to tap into without really appearing to. That has to be done subtly, at the level of the personal atmosphere, or 'vibration', we give out. If you're in the right state of consciousness already, it happens automatically; people notice, though they may not mention it to you directly, that you seem to have something about you that is different from the norm, some sense of unperturbable calm, a 'presence'. (Note how that word carries both the meaning of 'now', as in 'present moment', and also the sense of being, of existence.) It's a question of getting through to the other, to a place where the message – subtle or otherwise – commands attention. It's in your posture, your demeanor, your tone of voice, your vibe. The other will recognize that you are someone to be listened to, remembered – taken notice of.

It's possible – even likely – that while you're doing your daily doings you more or less forget about Soul Consciousness anyway. You won't be surrounded by people with the same sensitivity or sensibility, and you have to deal with them at their own level. But that preservation of the inner awareness I mention above is always in the background, and if you are truly seeing your co-locutor, conversational companion, colleague or kin as a Soul, then the atmosphere will be successfully communicated. You can even make it a sort of harmless game; as he or she speaks, look at their forehead and remind yourself that this is a Soul, an almost inconceivably small pinpoint of conscient energy driving this great big body. What are they getting so het up about?

It's back to two of the main elements of a balanced Ecology of the Soul: compassion, and observation. If you're Soul Conscious, is it really your responsibility to get the message out, subtle or otherwise? Well, yes it is, because of your compassion. You yourself recognized that your own state of being was far from perfect; there are always things blocking your everyday happiness. That's why you're here, that's why you also know that no other soul on the planet is 100 percent happy and content, and that's why you automatically give out that peaceful vibe, in the compassionate understanding that it is what all souls need. Some – most – will not recognize it for what it is; some will do so, but be unsettled by its power and unwilling to make the changes that come with it; some will be seeking change, but this path doesn't suit them.

Which is where observation comes in. If you meditate on this alone, you come to understand that observation is openness.

True, accurate, deep recognition of another person – and this time we're talking about people as people, not as tiny pinpoints of light – can only come when you yourself are as open as you can possibly be to all their signs and signals, most of which they're unaware of themselves. All your antennae are set to 'receive'. Get them talking about themselves – never a hard task with most people. Get them talking about what they really want. If it's just more money or a bigger house or better holidays, keep listening. Where does the root dissatisfaction lie? What is the lack, the void, that the string of complaints and reasons to blame others are there to conceal? Why the aggression, or nervousness, or apparent cynicism? Remain open to their vibe. Yours is stronger. When all's said and done, it comes down to love, of which both compassion and observation are components. Your love for God (for that's what it is) leads to your love for people, your fellow human beings. You're interested in people, which is why you want to see them clearly. And this brings you to the double whammy that you carry with you through all your dealings, on a soul conscious or ordinary everyday level: observation *is* compassion. Try it. It's already there, inside.

The Power of Communication Meditation 5: Seeing your Self

This is at the heart of the whole thing, the whole Ecology of the Soul project. It's the meditation where Soul Consciousness starts. So we'll do this one differently. Break off for a minute, relax and put your spiritual feet up for a thousand words or so. Here's a little story.

A hill station called Mount Abu in Rajasthan, November 1975. (Hill stations are villages or towns in the mountains all over India, the name a legacy from 'British Raj' days when the sahibs sent their memsahibs and families from the plains to live in higher, cooler, healthier climates during the fierce summer heat. The towns still thrive, usually as resorts.) A young man is visiting on his way to Pune, where he has arranged to study hatha yoga with the Master, BKS Iyengar. He has come overland from the UK, in an assortment of dirty trains and ramshackle buses, including a memorable journey over the Khyber Pass from Afghanistan into Pakistan on top of a 1947 Dodge station wagon carrying 23 people and all their worldly goods, including livestock. He is in Mount Abu for no other reason than he has a week to spare before his course starts in Pune, and, significantly, he feels, he was given a 'sign' in the Second Class Dining Room in the New Delhi railway station. Tucking into his two thin-shelled white boiled eggs and anemic white toast, he has been surprised by an old man sitting opposite him, who without introduction or preamble, leans across the table, fixes him with a luminous stare, wags an admonitory finger and says: "You must go to Mount Abu." No rhyme or reason. Just that. "OK," thinks I – for it is indeed me – "it's on the route, and I've got a week. Plus there's a lake. Maybe I can do a little swimming and sunbathing."

I stumble off the bus in the cooling evening, find a room on the very rooftop of one of the many cheap hotels (Veg or Non-

Veg), and go for a walk to explore and find something to eat. Nailed to a tree is a moth-eaten metal sign indicating the presence of the 'Raja Yoga World Spiritual Museum' down the street. "Aha," thinks I, "I'll check that out." Raja Yoga, to me the non-academic hatha yoga student (ie I haven't read Patanjali), is the top rung of the ladder of yoga, the one you get to after many lives of spiritual effort. This has to be interesting, in that quaint, naïve Indian way of theirs.

The 'Museum' is a low bungalow with a wide verandah, spotlessly clean red-painted floors and a succession of rooms in which glass display cases hold sets of scale model figures in tableaux of – for example – 'The World in Grip of Five Vices'. Five dastardly dacoits (bandits), armed to the teeth, ugly as sin (which is what they are), with red demonic eyes and in sore need of a dentist, tug on ropes which have ensnared the poor world, a model globe with an alarmed facial expression, as if they have just lassoed it. One of the guides working there, an old man with a ramrod-straight drill sergeant's back, eerily powerful blue eyes and (I swear) an apparent aura of silver light, steps up and starts explaining. The five vices are Anger, Ego, Greed, Attachment and Sex Lust. He has already nailed me as a good prospect for his hard sell, which starts out, astonishingly, with an admonitory finger and the earnest instruction: "You musht give up thish shexh lusht. It is the shword which killsh the shoul." (His teeth are a bit loose.) Whoa there, Grandpa, I'm not here to completely explode my life, I just want to know where the Raja Yoga bit comes in amongst all this, OK?

I have a week. There is nothing else to do; sunbathing is not an option in 100 degree heat (pushing 40, for Celsius people), and there is boating on the lake but no swimming. I'm in India on my spiritual journey to study yoga, so why not keep going back to this museum place and interrogate these people? They're quite clearly bonkers, and their glass cases, art directed in the same popular culture graphic style as dishcloths illustrated with

Aesop's Fables or Bollywood film posters, are so far from my vision of what Raja Yoga should look like – if it looks like anything – that I just have to get to the bottom of it. Besides, that man's eyes… and I swear I could see his aura. Must be something there.

It's the Raja Yoga Seven Day course in three dimensions. Each one of the glass cases shows one of the lessons. The one I'd missed on my first day, drawn on by the comedy world-with-a-face in the grip of his comedy bandits, is the simple 'You Are a Soul'. Body is car, soul is driver (they're not strong on the use of the definite article). But I'm more interested in talking to these people than I am in their tableaux, which are clearly designed for the standard, Bollywood-fed Indian holidaymaker audience. It's a real intellectual struggle, because the clever Cambridge-educated Westerner can find no purchase in his normal adversarial style of proposition and response, analysis, inquiry and debate. It just doesn't work here. It's what in ripe language one would call a head-f**k. The Raja Yogis seem to think that it's impertinent to question their teachings. Accept and get on with it, or move on.

Finally, after about five days of frustrating exchanges, it is judged that I am ready for the meditation experience. I'm shown into a darkened room with an entirely cushioned floor and an egg-shaped red plastic light on the wall, a pinhole in the middle and the edges cut so the light radiates out around it in a rough representation of an aura. "Focus on the center of your forehead. Tell yourself: 'I am a Soul, not a body. I live in the center of this body's forehead. I am a tiny pinpoint of light. I am peaceful. I am a peaceful soul.' Just keep telling yourself that."

The rest, as they say, is history. I emerge from the meditation room dazed and buzzing, flying. This is it. This is the truth, the power, the peace that I have been looking for, dressed in the most unlikely clothing imaginable. I have been lifted, carried on an ocean of peace, to a place of eternal silence where I know I belong. I came from here and I will return here. My mind is quiet. The power is peace, and the peace is power. After all's said and done, all the argument and debate, all I had to do was let go. It's not an intellectual process; it's the experience of my Self. Let myself go, and find my Self. It's all there, in that tiny pinpoint, which I will see and surely know is the true Me for the rest of my life. Of this life, rather, because there have been many, and there are many more to come. I am truly seeing my Self as my Self. A Soul.

That was 40 years ago. I'm still working on it.

I never got to Pune.

The Power of Communication Meditation 6: Seeing the Beauty

Everything has beauty, but not everyone sees it.
Confucius

Anyone who keeps the ability to see beauty never grows old.
Franz Kafka

The highest and most beautiful things in life are not to be heard about, nor read about, nor seen but, if one will, are to be lived.
Soren Kierkegaard

Seeing the beauty in yourself, your Self, and your surroundings is not only seeing it, but showing it. Communicating it. You are getting used to living with eternal, infinite beauty; the beauty of power, the beauty of peace are inside you – they *are* You. Communicating this beauty is giving it as a gift, often automatically and always without that attitude of ownership that destroys the very thing itself. This is not the beauty you can hoard and keep as a secret stash. It is You, but it is not yours. The more you give it, the more you have it, or indeed are it. And you give just by being. As your consciousness of your Self develops, as the extraordinary contrast between your infinitesimally small Self and your infinitely large supply of peace and power comes ever clearer, you recognize that You are not just a light burning in a void. You are living light, which is to say you can't exist without giving off your light, your atmosphere, your vibration. Seeing – and being – the beauty of your Self automatically communicates it. Output is inevitable.

The beauty is also to be seen in moments of time, and of course in the external world, which is admittedly a challenge, because our Ecology of the Soul project focuses on the inner Self. See the beauty in the moment, the circumstance, the coincidence, the here and now; remain amazed by the beauty of existence, of awareness, of consciousness; of the physical and the spiritual; of transformation, regeneration and renewal; of creation and re-creation (or just recreation). Let it catch you at any random time; stop you so you take notice.

When you notice it, see it, grasp it, bring it inside, absorb it. Breathe it in. Which gives us a clue to help with the external/internal debate, the way we deal with the physical world and how that can contribute to our spiritual progress. Let's imagine a sunset, or a sunrise. Observe. Do so minutely, carefully, wholly, giving your complete attention, in a way your whole being, to the phenomenon. Drink it in. This is the physical world: how does it impact on the spiritual? We're working on the non-physical, right? Seeing the beauty in your surroundings sets the tone for your relationship with the physical world, but also, automatically, your relationship with your Self. If you are turning your face to the beauty at every opportunity, having made that conscious choice, you are reinforcing your own natural beauty. It's at the shoreline, the undefinable, changing territory between the ocean of spirituality and the land of physicality – one affects the other, actually helps change its nature. Seeing one makes you see the other, strengthening your Self at the intellectual 'knowledge' level but also at the level of experience. Beauty and peace are your natural state, not ugliness, aggression and depression. Carry that knowledge – that experience – within you and it will shine out.

"Giving your complete attention," I said above. Observe. Let's mine that idea a little, because its influence and impact spread out into all areas of the process of balancing the Ecology of the Soul. Observation is concentration, paying attention. But wholly, one hundred percent. It's crucial because observation is also compassion. You look with love. Anything that will exercise that power of compassion within you is worth having and worth doing, because compassion is the single, overarching principle which drives all your relationships with the external world – and indeed, as the Buddha says, with yourself. There is the beauty of your Self, the *jyoti bindu*, the pinpoint of light, the never-ending flame; and there is the beauty of your own consciousness of your Self.

If you are Soul Conscious enough to see others as Souls, then you are seeing their beauty – which they probably don't see themselves – and they cannot help but respond. That's if they are Souls in search of peace and power, or at least aren't heavily disposed against it, recognizing the 'vibe' when it comes through. They're interested, they're receptive, they're listening. You will also come across Souls for whom this vibe is not just uninteresting or irrelevant, but actively inimical. For the people – Souls – who respond nastily, aggressively or destructively, it is somehow a threat. It makes them uncomfortable, or worse. Here, the usual best policy is to move swiftly on. Look them in the eye, see the Soul; and move on. Don't, whatever you do, allow yourself to engage so far that it gives them the chance to attack or disrespect the peace, power and beauty that you are seeing, absorbing and just plain being. It is bad karma for the soul in question, and also for you, because it is your responsibility to protect this consciousness, to look after it as an act of stewardship.

This leads to the question: how do we cope with ugliness in general? There's unlimited beauty in the world (and in the world inside You), but there's also an abundance of ugliness. Endless stretches of polluted industrial wasteland, rubbish tips as big as cities that are home to thousands of people, poisoned rivers, ravaged rainforests; inner city poverty, deprivation and degradation; war, famine, natural disaster, cruelty, pain, disease and despair. For many of us there isn't much beauty in our daily lives; for many more, there is worse than none. Life, quite simply, is hell. If you are confronted with this ugliness, if it feels overpowering, the only thing you can do is refer to your inner landscape. Close your (notional) eyes and concentrate on the beauty within. Know that the root cause of this ugliness (apart from the natural disasters) is human souls who have strayed far from their true nature.

Keep your compassion up to the mark, but there is a point at which you have to avoid, simply to protect your own state of mind and stop yourself being dragged down. No one is served if you lose your level of consciousness as well. As for natural disasters, if you're there on the spot your compassion will drive you. It might also drive you if you're not there in person, leading to donations and contributions or other charitable work. But if you feel powerless, remember that you are made of power and peace, and just by remaining in that consciousness you are bringing beauty to the world. Communicate it by being it.

The Power of Communication Meditation 7: Vision, Purpose, Goals

> Vision is the art of seeing what is invisible to others.
> *Jonathan Swift*

> You are here in order to enable the world to live more amply, with greater vision, with a finer spirit of hope and achievement. You are here to enrich the world, and you impoverish yourself if you forget the errand.
> *Woodrow Wilson*

> Your vision will become clear only when you look into your heart. Who looks outside, dreams. Who looks inside awakens.
> *Carl Jung*

This meditation is to help you define and cherish your vision – your purpose, your goals. And to communicate them, which in itself is a crucial part of the process of definition. Vision comes first, and vision of your Self comes first inside that. It's like creativity. A balanced Ecology of the Soul enhances creativity, but you are actually not making your Self, only discovering or rediscovering your powers. In the same way, your vision of your Self is already inside you, because it is You. It just got obscured, is all. Once that vision is clear, your purpose and your goals become clear. And clearly, even automatically, communicable.

That's at a transcendent level, but you've got to get there first, and have a map so you know the route. Do we have any misgivings? Too goal-oriented, are we? It seems that goal orientation isn't a popular idea in some quarters. It pays to remember, since we're deep into a project that is entirely devoted to the goal of achieving (returning to) a higher state of consciousness and the mental and spiritual benefits that go with it, that many – most? –

people don't set themselves goals, personal ones, anyway. Motivation is often a problem, particularly if it depends entirely on the self. Athletes and sportspeople spend their whole time moving from one goal to the next, and of course politicians, business and salespeople, military commanders and many other professionals are equally dedicated to achieving an outcome that they have set themselves or that has been set for them. Here and now, we know what our goal is: that higher state of being. But every single soul that commits him or herself to this clear and simple aim comes to it with his or her own specific, individual motivations, needs and desires. One goal for many, many paths in one path.

Desire. The target for disapprobation, especially from the teachings of Buddha. But our desire is ultimately for enlightenment, or at least a state of consciousness nearer that state of bliss than we are now. What is it you really want, top of the list? It's important to be honest with yourself. Peace of mind? The power to change? Understanding? Bliss? Happiness? Freedom from worry? Better sleep? More energy? More creativity? Better sex? More self control? If you're in the "I want to earn $250,000 a year by December" camp, you're in the wrong place. The Ecology of the Soul doesn't deal with material desire, or at least, it doesn't make any promises of material abundance. You might well find yourself working better and earning better and more able to take advantage of the opportunities that come your way – you will definitely have a more positive attitude, which is about 90 percent of the battle – but we're not here to make you rich, and if that's why you're here, you need to look elsewhere. This project is strictly about returning to your natural, higher state of peace, power and love. As I say, other things may well come to those who are achieving this higher consciousness, but your focus is on your Self and your beneficial effect on others, and indeed the world at large.

Self-improvement gurus and teachers like Jack Canfield are

very insistent on this idea of goals. It's the key element to their whole process; you can't move forward unless you have somewhere or something to move forward to. Break it down into the different areas of your life, decide what you want and when you want it by. This 'deadline' is very important. But this approach also creates stress, especially if you miss your 'targets'. Canfield and others like him provide a whole system of safety nets to prevent you feeling a failure, and love and compassion for yourself is the first and foremost of these. You'll never get anywhere if you're beating yourself up the whole time. But a balanced Ecology of the Soul avoids that tension in the first place: a) because we're not setting our goals in the physical world – "I will be earning $250,000 a year by December" makes it very easy to fail; and b) because all our goals, our true purpose, are already inside us. We just need the vision to identify them and align them with our understanding of what we're doing here in the first place.

There is your goal, your vision for yourself – your Self – and your vision of the world you'd like to create, to inhabit. Both require self discipline, which is the thing a lot of people have a problem with. In the final instance, no one is going to tell you to get up that extra minute (or 5, or 10, or 15, or 30) earlier, or run that extra mile. It's you, and only you, that is ultimately responsible for yourself and your Self. And self discipline is the key. Sorry, I know this is unpopular in a world whose every effort, it seems, is to remove the need to make effort – everything has to be easy. But there's no way round this one. You are taking hold of yourself, making yourself think and act in a particular way, and stopping yourself thinking and acting in other ways.

How does this click with communication? Why is it here, part of the Power of Communication? Because once you're on this path, your vision clear and your goals set, communication is automatic, inevitable. It goes back to clarity. Understand and express your vision clearly and you take others with you –

because you can't, however hard you try, remain isolated. You have a responsibility towards this chosen path of yours. Even if you don't set yourself up to teach, people will ask you questions: "How do you stay so calm all the time?" etc, etc. The reason why your vision, purpose and goals take the top spot among the meditations in the Power of Communication is that here is where you discover that you're not just doing this for yourself (your Self). Inherent in the effort is the expression of the effort, be it overt or covert. Enlightenment, or at least the experience of the path to it, is a gift of unimaginable power and beauty with which we have been blessed. If we didn't share and spread it where it falls on fertile ground, it would crumble to dust. It's that simple. Give it away, or you'll end up with nothing.

The Power of Communication Practice 1: Plant a Power Seed Every Day

Power Seeds are mental devices, thought triggers to generate Soul Consciousness, and hence change your actions. They are a bit like the Zen 'kōan' (for instance the idea of the sound of one hand clapping) that kick your mind out of gear and raise the level of your awareness.

Using Power Seeds, you grow a new garden of consciousness. See your mind as a garden, or at least a patch of fertile soil. Thoughts and feelings grow in it, like plants. Your mind is a riot of tangled and intertwined mental vegetation, much of it good and useful and most of it neither good nor useful. So it's a pleasant surprise that you don't have to struggle with the weeds. All you have to do is plant your mental plot with new seeds – 'Power Seeds' – which grow into thought, attitude, feeling, and action. Which feeds back and creates new thought and feeling. You have created a new mental and spiritual garden – and a new framework for your behavior.

If you really focus all the innate power of your calmed, stilled mind on the Power Seed you choose for 60 full seconds, that thought pattern will repeat and recur throughout the day, accumulating much more than a single minute of your mental activity. It's meditation in action, because the meditation is about action.

Plant one of the mental Power Seeds that appear on the following pages. The Seven Powers, Power Seeds and the Magic Minute section of Part I, the book's Introduction, gives the full explanation of how to prepare the mental and spiritual ground for your new garden; Part III gives you a whole range of Power Seeds to suit your circumstances. Ultimately, as your Self knowledge increases, you will be creating and planting your own.

If you're only looking for your Self, what is the need for communication?
You have to know who you are to know what to say and how to say it.

Communication is not a two-way but a three-way street.
You conduct a relationship with yourself, with your Self, and with others around you.

Communication is compassion.

"If your compassion does not include yourself, it is incomplete."
Jack Kornfield

You break out of the downward spiral of body consciousness by applying your senses to the realm beyond your senses. You listen, quite simply, to your Self.

Your motivation to meditate is refined and directed through the intellect. It nudges the tiller now and then to keep you on course, and finally lets go when you launch into the Ocean of Peace. And Power. And Stillness.

If you don't have compassion, you might be hearing, but you're not listening.

This is the most powerful and significant conversation you will ever have: "I am a Soul. An infinitesimally small pinpoint of light, power and peace, sitting in my enormous body's forehead. Conscious energy, conscient energy."

Part of our job as enlightened beings (or beings on the path of enlightenment, anyway) is to bring others as much benefit as we can give and they can receive.

Your own spiritual dimension is Silence, but it's not a space of nothingness. It's beyond sound, a place of pure consciousness, of your light burning steadily in an infinite moment, the glow of bliss, of life itself.
You belong here.

Nothing is more persuasive than the sound that comes from silence, the sound with silence at its heart. Be grateful for the good fortune that allows you to speak with this power.

Open mindedness is compassion.
Open mindedness is letting go.
Open mindedness is detachment.
Open mindedness is observation.

Open mindedness requires a process of opening your whole being, all departments of your consciousness.
You are seeing the unseen, hearing the unspoken.

An open mind opens itself to the experience of that which is beyond, above and below the mind.

Seeing the other person as a Soul is no less a crucial attribute of Soul Consciousness than is the ability to focus on your own inner awareness.

When all's said and done, it comes down to love, of which both compassion and observation are components. Observation *is* compassion.

The beauty of power, the beauty of peace are inside you – they *are* You. Communicating this beauty is giving it as a gift. It is

You, but it is not yours. The more you give it, the more you have it – or *are* it.

See the beauty in the moment, the circumstance, the coincidence, the here and now; remain amazed by the beauty of existence, of awareness, of consciousness; of the physical and the spiritual; of transformation, regeneration and renewal; of creation and re-creation (or just recreation). Let it catch you at any random time.

Observation is concentration, paying attention. But observation is also compassion. You look with love. Compassion is the single, overarching principle which drives all your relationships with the external world – and with your Self.

Vision, Purpose, Goals: Desire.
What is it you really want?

Enlightenment, or the path to it, is a gift of unimaginable power and beauty. If we didn't share and spread it, it would crumble to dust. Give it away, or you'll end up with nothing.

The Power of Communication Practice 2: Yoga Seeds – Salute to the Sun (Surya Namaskar)

Position 5: Dog Pose (Adho Mukha Svanasana)

The Salute to the Sun, like most things in Yoga, has many variations. The one we use here consists of seven 'asanas', to use the Sanskrit name for positions, done in a 12-step sequence: Prayer, Mountain, Forward Bend, Forward Lunge (one leg forward), Plank, Dog, Cobra, Child, Forward Lunge (the other leg forward), Forward Bend, Mountain, Prayer. Aim to hold each pose for seven in-out breaths. You can do less if it hurts!

'Adho' is Sanskrit for 'down'. 'Mukha' is 'face'. 'Svana' is 'dog'. The pose obviously resembles the way a dog stretches as it gets up and prepares for action – front legs stretched away as far as they can go, rear end as far in the air as it can go, back in a concave stretch. The difference is they put their head up, while we let it hang down on a loose and relaxed neck, letting it lengthen between our shoulders. Dogs also usually do their 'get up and go' routine the other way as well, stretching up and forward on their front legs and giving the old rear quarters a serious pull, but that counts as another asana for us humans.

Benefits claimed for this asana include calming the brain, and helping relieve stress, mild depression, the symptoms of menopause and menstrual discomfort. It improves digestion, relieves headache, insomnia, back pain, and fatigue, and is therapeutic for high blood pressure, asthma, flat feet, sciatica, and sinusitis. Not much it can't do, it looks like.

In this version of Surya Namaskar, you're coming from Chaturanga Dandasana, the Plank. You're supporting yourself on your hands and arms, straight up and down in line with your shoulders. Your back and legs are in as straight a line as you can make them, all the way down to your stretched-away heels, set the same distance apart as your hips. Your feet turn the corner and go straight down to your toes on the mat. Everything is energized.

From this position, all you have to do is on the outbreath raise your behind in the air to make the characteristic inverted 'V' shape. Push your heels away – practitioners who have been doing this for years can get their feet flat on the floor, depending on the length of their hamstrings – settle your hands into the floor, fingers spread slightly apart. Now you can feel the route of the energy through your hands, up your arms, transferring through your shoulders into your spine, which is as long, elongated and, as it stretches, slightly concave as it can get, up to the peak where the base of your spine is highest, then over the top and down your legs to your heels. Your feet are energized.

The stretches are in your arms and the backs of your legs. This asana is probably the one in which the strange and counter-intuitive trick of relaxing, letting go into the stretch and thus allowing you to stretch, is most important and its effect most noticeable. Essentially, by making space between each of your vertebrae, you are lengthening your back, which pushes your behind farther up in the air, stretches the backs of your legs more, and extends your arms. At each outbreath you are opening all the way up and down the spine, searching for and feeling each separate vertebra, and separating it further. Keep letting your heels move towards the floor.

This is a dynamic pose, and what you will find is that pressure builds in the channel between your shoulder blades, because as you stretch your arms, you are actually pushing down and compressing on that point. What you have to do is let go between the shoulder blades, let it 'go soft', as one of my teachers used to say. It demands a precise locational awareness of exactly what is happening in specific muscle groups and the ability to control, or let go, at that particular point. If you manage to let this softness come between your shoulder blades you will be astonished at how much extra length it will allow your spine to grow. It's probably barely a few millimeters in actual measurement, but from the inside it feels as if you're really getting 'big air' between each of your vertebrae. To take advantage of this looseness and get that extra length, you need to extend your arms more, which at the same time stretches them and puts more compression into that channel between the shoulder blades again. So it's a pushme-pullyou effect: let go, stretch, compress, let go, stretch. And don't forget to let your neck muscles go so your neck lengthens and your head droops towards the floor.

It's unlikely, especially if you're a man, that you'll readily get that characteristic slightly concave curve into the spine which makes it easier to push your behind ever farther up into the air and push your heels down towards the floor. For the first few years of practice, anyway. (Ha ha, only joking, but with serious intent.) It's often quite easy for me to forget that the sensations I feel during practice are the result of 40 years' work, but it does mean that I can try and describe the essential 'end experience' of an asana. Men, because we are already more muscular than women – and more 'outward' with it – tend to adopt the physical culture of strength, endurance, the 'hard man' thing. It militates against this subtle combination of pushing but finding the softness inside the push, and if you have done any sports-related training at all or do a physically demanding job, you will have become more muscle bound anyway. I'm not talking Mr. Universe here; it's a normal everyday phenomenon for most guys. Muscular development is all very well, but if you are to make sense of hatha yoga you need to create a route around that solid strength, let it go soft. Open up, and let go.

Chapter 6

The Power of Focus

Ajna, the Brow Chakra

In this chapter:
Introduction
Accuracy
Compartmentalization
Concentration
Craftsmanship
Determination
Clarity
Mindfulness
Power Seeds for Thought
The Salute to the Sun: Cobra Pose (Bhujangasana)

> The moment my intellect realizes I am non-physical, not a body but a focus of powerful energy within a body, I am able to use this power.
> Raja Yoga 7-Day Correspondence Course: *http://brahmakumaris.info/download/BK%207%20Days%20Course/7-Days-Correspondence-Course.pdf*

> One reason so few of us achieve what we truly want is that we never direct our focus; we never concentrate our power. Most people dabble their way through life, never deciding to master anything in particular.
> *Tony Robbins*

> The ego is nothing other than the focus of conscious attention.
> *Alan Watts*

Introduction

Focus is extreme concentration.
Focus is power.
Focus is space.
Focus is empty.
Focus is a pinpoint.
Focus is the infinite void inside the pinpoint.

The narrower focus gets, the more powerful it gets. Focus your mind like a magnifying glass concentrating the sun's rays, gathering them into an ever smaller and ever hotter pinpoint. At which hot point the light burns through the surface on which it is falling, peeling away the layers of mental chitter chatter and exposing a still, small point of light, of fire, of power. Of peace.

Ajna, the brow Chakra, or 'third eye', is the chakra connected to the Power of Focus. It 'honors the psychic'. It governs the balance of the higher and lower selves, trusting inner guidance, intuition, visual consciousness and clarity. The awakening or opening process, the 'turning on' of this and all the other chakras, is, not unlike yoga asanas, a trick combination of focusing and letting go at the same time.

The key paradox of focus is the tension between a force so constantly refined and refining that it becomes smaller and ever smaller, more and more powerful, and the infinite space inside it, which becomes larger and ever larger, more silent and more peaceful. As you devote your whole mind – for it does start in the mind – to the idea, which leads rapidly to the experience, there is a sense of 'breaking through', but it isn't quite like that; the mental process is, like many meditation techniques, a sort of trick of perception you play on yourself. It's another way of making your mind grapple directly with the astonishing fact that you Your Self, You the Soul, are at the same time as powerful and as peaceful as you could possibly be, both experiences but two sides of the same coin, and all enshrined in this inexpressibly small pinpoint of conscience – in the sense of awareness or 'conscient-ness'. We distinguish it from plain and simple consciousness by calling it Soul Consciousness, in other words an enlightened awareness and experience of the being that You are. Not just aware, but Self aware.

Another way of understanding it, and we do need the understanding to lead us to the experience, is to think of the idea of 'infinite'. You the Soul are infinitesimally small, but at the same time within that tiny infinity is the boundlessly vast infinity of consciousness, thoughts, feelings, experiences, memories, actions, lived through many years of many lives. They're not infinite of course, unless you accept the idea that your lives are lived out in a never-ending cycle, but count your thoughts in a single day? No way. Count them not just in one life but many? Even less likely. And that's just thoughts, the very top layer of the Soul's activity, at the level where most of the process is disposable. You have yet to delve into emotions, memories, learnings, analysis, judgements, dreams, habits, personality traits. (See Chapter 2: The Power of Creativity, Meditation 6, Self Creation for the 'anatomy' of the Soul, which is basically made up of the mind for thoughts and feelings, the intellect for understanding, analysis and judgements, and the sanskars for personality traits and behaviors.)

Like each one of the seven powers that make up the living Ecology of the Soul, the Power of Focus interconnects and intertwines with all the other powers. It is a gateway through which you learn, understand and experience all your seven powers and the balance between them, simply because it is the first and foremost mental process of meditation, the starting blocks if you like. As you can see, this book's chapters and sections all begin with a quote or quotes taken from the wisest people on the planet (and sometimes the silliest) which are supposed to kick your mind into the right gear for contemplation and meditation. The interesting thing about focus, I found as I was nosing round looking for the right quotes, is that it comes up in many a quote but almost never refers to or defines itself. They're all about what you can achieve with focus and rarely if ever are they about focus itself.

The energy drink Red Bull appears to be adopting focus as its brand mantra (http://focus.redbull.com/, retrieved 28/07/15), and claims to have worked with neuroscientists to identify the seven elements of focus, but illuminating and helpful though the project is, one can't help but think that neuroscientists aren't going to tap into the elements of consciousness at the deep levels that we need to get a grip on this power.

What those seven elements – 'Solve', 'React', 'Endure', 'Juggle', 'Adapt', 'Filter' and 'Control' – do do, however, is point at the 'open' element of focus, the counterpoint of the narrowed-down pinpoint idea. The sort of focus you get when you have all your chakras humming at once, or a successful yoga session with your awareness spread throughout your body. It's spread out and activated in a number of places, but because it's all working so well together the experience is of all your nodes of energy or awareness being heightened as one, at one and the same time. 'Uber-focus', perhaps.

It's all in the mind – or at least, it all starts in the mind. Well, that's hardly original, and indeed such an idea appears in more than one other place in the book. Which is no bad thing, considering that the seven powers and their seven meditations are essentially seven sides of the same seven-sided coin. Or 49-sided, if you like. It's the mind, the faculty of thought, feeling and unruly chitchat that gets such a bad press from all the gurus and enlightenment pundits, upon which you are depending for your kick-start into the clarity and singularity of purpose that expresses focus. You must determine in your mind that that's where you want to go, and lead it with its own self-controlling and self-directing abilities to tell yourself (it might seem like self hypnosis, but if it works, so what?) what You are. Go over the idea, using proper verbal (though silent) expression: "I am a Soul, an infinitesimally small pinpoint of light sitting in this forehead. I am light. I am silence. I am stillness. I am peace. I am power. I am in this body but not of it, detached."

This kind of self-training leads rapidly to the genuine experience, and as the genuine experience repeats and grows, you cease to need the initial mental kick-starting. The more time you spend in Soul Consciousness, the more centered and balanced you find yourself, able to apply and benefit from this consciousness, and this growing ability to focus, in daily life. The trick, of course, is being able to maintain that equilibrium when things, circumstances and people are conspiring against it. That needs a lot of practice.

The Power of Focus Meditation 1: Accuracy

> Fast is fine, but accuracy is everything.
> *Xenophon*

> Accuracy is the twin brother of honesty; inaccuracy, of dishonesty.
> *Nathaniel Hawthorne*

> Accuracy of language is one of the bulwarks of truth.
> *Anna Jameson*

When you know who and what you are and have some kind of rudimentary understanding of your 'thought process' – in which a thought starts then carries through, leading you to judgement, analysis and experience – you begin to realize and appreciate the value of accuracy.

There are some who would say that a consistent and determined commitment to accuracy in thought, word and deed is: a) unrealistic given the world we live in and the kind of beings we are; and b) a sort of pathology whose description is more or less insulting, ranging from 'anally retentive' to 'obsessive compulsive'. People who strive for accuracy, they say, get hung up on getting every small thing absolutely right, lose sight of the main goal, get lost in the detail, miss the point, fail to see the 'big picture'. But I say, perhaps because throughout my life a great many of my own ordinary 'daily activities', as well as the meditative ones that depend on and generate the Power of Focus, are intimately associated with accuracy, that those 'some' who say such things are themselves missing the point.

The point, of course, being the point. Or, in this case, the pinpoint. Which is a way of describing, understanding and experiencing who and what You are, the unique conscient being that has some understanding of your own thought process. As soon as you engage with the idea, and willy-nilly thence the experience, of Your Self as a Soul, an infinitesimally small pinpoint of con-science (forgive the clumsy coinage, we need a word here that expresses not only consciousness, but *knowledge* of consciousness), you are bang smack up against the need for accuracy. Not so much a need as a *sine qua non*, a starting requirement. To train your mind, refine it so that it leads you to confront your own infinitesimally small, peaceful and powerful self, is to embrace accuracy, to dive deep into it, to live and breathe it. Accuracy of aim, accuracy of intention, accuracy of execution.

Which is all in the mind, which as we said in the introduction to this chapter is the first tool that you use on your way to focus, and which in and of itself is a tool of focus. We'll get on to tools when we get on to craftsmanship, which is another meditation in this Focus chapter, but right now all you need to focus on is focus. Which is another way of saying accuracy. They are pretty much the same thing.

As for thought, word and deed – the mind leading you outside instead of inside your Self, to external matters of perception, analysis, judgement and action – accuracy becomes the pivot of yet another of those paradoxes that we keep coming across in our journey of re-creation, the restoration of the balanced Ecology of the Soul. Commitment is another one (Chapter 4: The Power of Love, Meditation 1, Commitment); it sets you free. Similarly, accuracy, far from leading you into the blinkered dead-ends of your detractors, sets you free. It liberates you from unnecessary effort, unnecessary thought and indeed unnecessary – and hence, potentially destructive – action.

Those who are not on the journey to Self discovery, Self empowerment and Self re-creation have little patience with the idea of unnecessary thought or action. They don't see any benefit in monitoring and refining their thought process, seeing where the energy is going, how it could be better used. They 'just get on with it'. But 'just getting on with it' can be messy, and worse, it can waste energy. And wasted mental energy leads directly to wasted spiritual energy. Something we certainly can't afford if we are to make any headway on the journey, which is after all not exactly an easy one.

The real, deep reason why waste of mental and spiritual energy is so important to avoid is rooted in that wonderful, beautiful, terrifying, apparently simple but endlessly complex, Law of Karma. It works at ordinary, everyday, on-the-face-of-it superficial levels, as well as profound, universal, consciousness-enhancing (or diminishing) ones; and if you want an example, what could be more mundane than doing the dishes? Imagine a household with no dishwasher. Yes, there's a mind-boggler for a start. It so happens that my household hasn't had one for two years, and we have never missed it. All the malarkey about saved time is a myth, in my opinion – but that's not the point. The point is that now we do the dishes by hand; if we put the forks, knives and spoons in the drainer basket in exactly the same order as they go in to the cutlery drawer – forks far left, knives in the middle, spoons on the right – then when it comes to take the basket to the cutlery drawer your cutlery is already sorted and you save some seconds not having to re-sort as you go.

Save some seconds? Big deal. No wonder those accusations of 'anal retentive' and 'obsessive compulsive' fly about in our house, just like anywhere else. But think about it for a second (using your intellect, as well as your mind). With the pre-sort, you have saved yourself not only a few seconds of time, but a good deal of mental energy. Without that pre-sort, now something like 20 decisions have to be made as you fill the cutlery drawer, some of which may go wrong simply because you're trying to do it too fast. And – which is where the law of karma comes in – if you haven't pre-sorted, you're risking someone else wasting their mental energy on you by letting their mind stray with negative thoughts towards whoever just put the knives, forks and spoons in the drainer randomly, willy-nilly. That's where accuracy counts; you don't draw other people's negative attention. Which, karmically speaking, is bad for you and bad for them.

Accuracy is freedom. Depend on it. Just don't go over the top and become that true obsessive compulsive. Control, of course, those negative thoughts if you are a 'pre-sorter' and your companions are not; but experience the elation and lightness of doing it as efficiently – as accurately – as possible. Zen thinking is full of the idea of meditation in action, complete mindfulness (the final and all-encompassing meditation of this chapter); accuracy leads to the pinpoint that is You, and from that pinpoint to action. And back again.

The Power of Focus Meditation 2: Compartmentalization

> I claim that human mind or human society is not divided into watertight compartments called social, political and religious. All act and react upon one another.
> *Mahatma Gandhi*

> One's life has many compartments.
> *Harold Pinter*

> Alas, everything that men say to one another is alike; the ideas they exchange are almost always the same, in their conversation. But inside all those isolated machines, what hidden recesses, what secret compartments!
> *Alfred de Musset, Fantasio*

Compartmentalization, like focus itself, is stripping right down to the point. And finding the paradoxical space inside the tiny narrowness. Deciding what's important and ignoring the rest. A willful act of ignoring, sometimes, which can be as destructive as it is constructive. So – treat compartmentalization with caution. It's a crucial tool in your mental toolbox, but remember it is only that – a mental tool. The mind itself is not where the true You resides. It just helps (or hinders) on the route.

Another thing. Compartmentalization, judging by the quotes about it to be found on the world wide web, is not by and large a popular idea. In fact there were no quotes at all about 'compartmentalization', and only a few about compartments. Most of them are about secret compartments, an idea that brings with it all the resonances of subterfuge and deception: "I will love you as a drawer loves a secret compartment, and as a secret compartment loves a secret, and as a secret loves to make a person gasp…" says Lemony Snicket in *The Beatrice Letters*.

It's also true that people practice compartmentalization as a way of hiding things from themselves, and, of course, others. Things that you might be ashamed of, things that you keep separate because they don't fit with your idea of yourself; things that you certainly don't want others to know about you, particularly your nearest and dearest, whose opinion of you would be much changed if they knew the truth. It's always a matter of secrets and subterfuge when it's like that: you are concealing who you really are and what you are really doing, both from yourself and those others; concealing the truth.

The compartmentalization that we are meditating on here, however, though it uses a similar mental process to the one that creates and contains awkward secrets, is the one that leads you directly to the truth of your Self rather than away from it. Or rather, it allows you to maintain the knowledge and experience of the truth of your Self, in the face of the daily grind. This kind of compartmentalization is crucial, in fact, for a life of meditation and a journey of inner discovery, simply because you have to deal with daily life on a daily life level, and can't go through your days insisting to your colleagues, boss, friends and family that you are a Soul, not a body, and they should only engage with you as such. When you are very successfully entrenched in the deep experience of Soul Consciousness, perhaps after a particularly rich and focused meditation, it's easy to see others in this way, but it's not going to work if you demand that they see you likewise. So: compartmentalize. It's your secret, if you like. Be the Soul in the body, doing its daily things; soul is driver, as they say in Raja Yoga, body is car.

There is a word for this kind of mental behavior, much more familiar to the followers of meditative and monastic disciplines such as Zen, and indeed to Raja Yogis, whose practice is in a way monastic, but whose 'daily life' focus is very much about operating effectively – and Soul Consciously – in the real world.

The word is 'detachment', an idea that also brings with it a host of possibly negative connotations, because to be detached is somehow not to care, to be disengaged, to be callous (see Chapter 1: The Power of Nature, Meditation 7, Dispassion – Detachment). Which of course it is not; your yogi would argue that only by achieving a very high state of detachment from the body and body consciousness can he or she bring spiritual benefit to many, at an unlimited level.

You compartmentalize the experience of being a Soul. You are on the bus or train, at your desk or at the beach, driving or working, talking or walking, playing or paying. You are a Soul doing these things, through your body. You are detached from your body, you have compartmentalized so that you can make it do the things that need to be done while you look on, an observer. No one knows that you have or are seeking this enlightened state of mind, this sense of being 'above the action', but they might well recognize how focused and effective you are, because here's the irony, and that paradox that seems to keep popping up: as you detach, compartmentalize your consciousness, your ability to focus and be effective increases because somehow, right inside the very experience of being detached, you find a space. A space that allows you a view. A feel for the rhythm, the pace, the balance of things. Some call it 'in the zone'. And it is your engagement with things and people we're talking about. This is a spiritual path, but right now we're dead physical. Why not do it the best you can? Be more complete (a paradox in itself). No one is pretending it's easy; but it works.

The Power of Focus Meditation 3: Concentration

> Elegance is achieved when all that is superfluous has been discarded and the human being discovers simplicity and concentration: the simpler and more sober the posture, the more beautiful it will be.
> *Paulo Coelho*

> The degree of freedom from unwanted thoughts and the degree of concentration on a single thought are the measures to gauge spiritual progress.
> *Ramana Maharshi*

> We apply our effort to be mindful, to be aware in this very moment, right here and now, and we bring a very whole-hearted effort to it. This brings concentration. It is this power of concentration that we use to cut through the world of surface appearances to get to a much deeper reality.
> *Sharon Salzberg*

Well, this is the big one, isn't it? Because without concentration there is no meditation. True or false?

But what is concentration if not letting go?

Here's what hatha yoga has taught me: you can only stretch if you let go. The more you stretch, the more you feel the Prān, the Ch'i, the subtle/physical energy. But pushing yourself to stretch only breaks you. You have to learn how to selectively let yourself go, so you can use your weight and some muscles, while the others are in relaxation – so they can stretch.

Same with the mind. It's an organ. If you force it, it won't let go. It's amazingly powerful, the mind, a huge store of creative energy, but: a) it's a tricky customer; and b) it isn't You. It's a part of You. It can lead you up, up and away, or it can take you down, down, down. The true You can learn your own mind's games, learn how to 'deal with' yourself. Control your mind, in other words. And unleash its power to rocket you into a further consciousness. No talk of bending spoons or charming snakes; this is mind over mind, not just mind over matter.

I'm trying to find a way to take you into the quietness that is true concentration. I think it's best understood in stages, but it's not something ultimately that you get through the intellectual 'understanding' process. It has to be experienced. Luckily, the understanding leads you to the experience.

The first stage is where you bring yourself to concentrate, get ready for it, prepare. The next is, committing to the project (anything from 20 minutes in a corner on a blanket to doing a lap of a racing circuit). The third is, whatever you are doing, you enter a space ('the zone'?) which is somehow inside the focus, at its heart, at its eye. The eye of the mental storm. Calm, quiet and still. You're at your best, no doubt of it.

Riding motorcycles really, really fast is not something a lot of people do, so forgive the references if you're not interested. Just bear with me, and come with me inside my helmet for a really good lap. I can't think of a better way to express it than the familiar 'zone', and I know that athletes, sportspeople and performers, traders and dealers, business and pleasure people, a myriad of roles, activities and behaviors, all have this experience of riding, perfectly balanced, on the wave of the moment. It's a quietness. Still, but in intense motion. On this fast lap, there's an astonishing amount of input/output mental processing going on. A million minute decisions and adjustments a minute. Grip, angle of lean, acceleration, line, braking, momentum, gyroscopic forces… but right there inside my helmet, I'm just. Thinking. One. Thought. At. A. Time. (And it's not going to be about the laundry, the weekend, work or whatever.) It's total focus, total concentration, so much that you lose yourself. From inside that quietness, I get the best lap times. You can't follow it. You have to be it.

Further on, leaving motorbikes behind and entering the strictly meditative arena, while all that processing is going on in your mind, or more, between your mind and your intellect, the very pure spiritual energy that neither thinks, nor decides, nor feels – and that is indeed You – has been waiting to take over. And when concentration hits this level, there is no question of letting go. You're not even there if you haven't already let go. It's as celebrated jazz and rock drummer Ginger Baker said about his interminable drum solos: "You're playing the drums, giving it everything. And then after a while you realize, it's the drums playing you."

The 'I am a Soul' state of no-thought is as wide and as vast and as deep and as high as any thought can think – in fact, thinking thoughts is useless. This is just being, as infinite as it gets. It opens right out and takes you with its own power, willy-nilly. In my bike helmet, I lose myself, but I don't find my Self. When the power of concentration has taken you this far in meditation, it takes over, almost as if you're not doing anything at all except floating in the combined beauty of bliss, power and peace. And definitely finding your Self in the middle of that. Not only finding, but realizing the indescribable phenomenon that you are. Infinite, but advisedly so. Infinitely small, infinitely powerful, infinitely existent (ie eternal), but not infinitely spread out all over the Universe. Infinitely unique, if you can bear that rude assault on the English language.

And you got here by concentrating. Narrowing it down. Refining. Stripping out the crap. But you never forced it, because when you force it, crap has a way of coming back at you. You politely but firmly, gently but strongly, steer yourself (your mind) away from the crap until it becomes easier to turn off, and later, a disused mental habit. That's the way our minds change, and that's the way we change ourselves into the sort of people the new world needs.

Concentrate. But with kindness. Kindness to yourself brings you face to face with your Self.

The Power of Focus Meditation 4: Craftsmanship

> Without craftsmanship, inspiration is a mere reed shaken in the wind.
> *Johannes Brahms*

> Craftsmanship names an enduring, basic human impulse, the desire to do a job well for its own sake.
> *Richard Sennett, The Craftsman*

> The Christian shoemaker does his duty not by putting little crosses on the shoes, but by making good shoes, because God is interested in good craftsmanship.
> *Martin Luther*

This is a great one for me because I spent ten years as a carpenter, joiner and cabinetmaker, and learnt many things during that time. I had just recently taken my history degree from the University of Cambridge and was determined to use my hands to learn, not go the book-learning route. Which meant, idiot that I was, that I taught myself my skills exclusively by working with others and making mistakes. If I'd picked up a book I could have learnt in two years what it took me ten to absorb. So you could say that the most important thing I learnt in that ten years was how to learn.

Craftsmanship, like almost every meditation in this chapter, is another way of saying 'mindfulness'. When I give lectures on design and craft to design students, I start with this proposition to get them thinking: "Design is an activity. Craft is a state of mind." And that idea abides, and runs through all our meditation and spiritual practice, because as we go about our daily lives in the world, we need tools to apply what we are learning about

Soul Consciousness. The Zen principle of meditation in action is another way of looking at it, and indeed the meditation we have just done on concentration comes at the same thing from a different angle. All mental ingredients in the same recipe.

There's nothing in life that you can't make a meditation, and to which you can't apply a principle of craftsmanship. There's nothing you do in life that can't be done better if you approach it with total attention, total commitment, total absorption. Total love, in other words. All these things go to make up craftsmanship, a craftsmanlike attitude to the task at hand, a devotion to that task that comes from the conviction that within this task lies power, beauty, peace and freedom. No accomplished craftsperson will deny that the key ingredient is love. You apply love, approach the task with it; and then the task itself, and the end result, show it back to you and to others who enjoy it.

I'm tempted to describe craftsmanship as the search for perfection. And if it is indeed that, then it links directly to the task of balancing the Ecology of the Soul, because what we are after here is nothing more nor less than perfect balance. But of course we all know that in a necessarily imperfect world – it can't be anything else, because it's physical – perfection is impossible. If you become a perfect human being, you're likely to leave the body, because you can't be perfect in an imperfect body.

But hey, the search is the thing. And the dedication to the idea. Much of the success in practice comes from the mental focus that is the overriding power of this chapter; elimination of unnecessary or superfluous thinking, total concentration on what's in front of you and the resulting liberation that we have already talked about in other meditations. Absorption. Losing yourself and finding your Self in that loss, that gap, that void.

Again as we have said, much of the focus of this chapter – it is about focus, after all – is on outward activity, how we deal with daily life. Focus and concentration are of course the primary activators of meditation, and without them we won't even make a start on the inner journey, never mind get anywhere; these are mental processes, and when we're in the region of the mind we're in the frontier regions, the parts that lead to the higher, deeper and wider enlightenment that leaves the mind behind. The intellect is involved of course, because self criticism, editing and deciding if you're satisfied – and if you're not, going back and doing it again – are all part of the process.

There is craftsmanship we can apply to activities that apparently admit of that kind of approach; without thinking of yourself as a craftsperson, you might cook a wonderful meal with all the love and attention and skill you can muster, or you might stitch a repair in your kid's jeans, or even apply your makeup with particular panache for a special evening out. But if that seems credible for the sort of activity where you would expect to find craft, what about all the other dull and boring bits of life? I challenge you to look at all aspects of your life and fail to find a single example, somewhere, somehow, that enshrines these principles and shows that you have this craftspersonlike motivation. Even the dishes can be done with an attitude of craftsmanship, accuracy, devotion, complete attention.

Much of the power and effectiveness of this meditation comes from the 'now', the 'presence', the enlightened place in the void of the moment that is familiar territory if you follow, as do I, the work of Eckhart Tolle. Focus, accuracy, concentration, craftsmanship all require complete attention in and to the moment. But, as I learned to my (and often my employer's) cost in my cabinetmaking days, that same complete attention has an awareness within it of sequence and consequence. If I do this, that will happen. This can't be done before I do that. If I do that in this way, the next part of the task will be more difficult/easier/quicker/slower/less effective/more effective. Assembly, disassembly, tinkering with engines, making beds, stitching curtains, cutting the grass in the yard: that element of space/time continuum is there, already rooted inside your craftspersonlike attitude. If you are doing something you have never done before, said attitude causes you to tread carefully and contemplate sequences and consequences as you go. So you hold the now and the immediate future in your consciousness at the same time. If it is a familiar task, you see it unfolding in front of yourself, knowing that what comes next is part of the now.

Another paradox for your mind to chew on. And like most paradoxes, useful to flip your mind over on its back with all four legs waggling in the air. We'll come to mindfulness, but there's something here about accuracy, achievement, concentration, and as near to perfection as we can get – by overriding the mind. Mindfully.

A final thought: do we apply craftsmanship to meditation itself? What about controlling the mind? Is that the task of a craftsperson?

The Power of Focus Meditation 5: Determination

The truest wisdom is a resolute determination.
Napoleon Bonaparte

At the core of life is a hard purposefulness, a determination to live.
Howard Thurman

And so you touch this limit, something happens and you suddenly can go a little bit further. With your mind power, your determination, your instinct, and the experience as well, you can fly very high.
Ayrton Senna

There are two determinations: the intellectual process of discrimination – deciding, distinguishing, choosing between one thing and another – usually right and wrong, or which route to follow; and the 'gut feel', more a state of mind and heart than an intellectual process (some call it an emotion), in which you are committed, focused, dedicated, motivated, persevering, coping with setbacks, pushing forward single-mindedly to your goal.

As far as determination in the sense of deciding is concerned, it's usually understood as a scientific process which includes calculation, testing and analysis. At a more general level, the one which is more use to us, it can be seen as a kind of precursor of the 'committed, focused, dedicated' sense, because it's obviously not worth committing to, focusing on or dedicating yourself to a path of action that isn't going to bring you to your goal. You have to discriminate.

But we all know the goal, here and now, right? We're committed to, focused on and dedicated to a path of increased self knowledge, greater spiritual power and peace, and a truly balanced Ecology of the Soul, which is made up of the seven spiritual powers. Once we've determined that (and you wouldn't be here if you hadn't), the 'deciding' sense of determination fades away, right?

Well, no, it doesn't. Guess what. You have to use your power of discrimination – determination – at almost every turn, every step you take, because your determination/discrimination process is hard at work choosing exactly which step it is that you do take. Thinking and feeling is one thing (or two things); acting is another thing entirely. 'Coming into action' brings you into direct contact with the Law of Karma (the word itself means 'action'); and inexpressibly complex and profound though that law is, you can be sure of one thing: every action has an equal and opposite reaction. Consequences. As in the physical realm, so the mental, emotional and spiritual. So you'd better get that decision right, right?

This understanding relates both to your choice of a particular spiritual path, and to your own ability to judge whether a word or deed that you are about to say or do is useful, productive and germane to your goal, your progress on that path, or counterproductive. It's not often a conscious process, given that words and deeds flow and don't normally go through this refined filter; but when it comes to the Big Things, you do pause, consider and decide, one way or the other. It's also true to say that the huge majority of your words and deeds in any given day aren't remotely connected to your spiritual path anyway. Missed the turning? Go on down the next block and turn right and right again (or left, of course), come back the other way. No connection to Soul Consciousness there, it's straightforward wayfinding. (You can, however, deal with frustration or disappointment in a Soul Conscious way.) But if you have a problem with someone or something, or if there's an opportunity to do the 'right thing' that you know in your heart is in line with the principles of life set out in this and many other books, then you are determining. And the more Soul Conscious you get, the easier that determination becomes.

As far as the choice of path itself is concerned, we all also know that the most common behavior in this respect is 'pick'n'flit'. It's comparatively rare for people like us, aware and committed to spiritual progress, to dedicate ourselves exclusively to one specific path or set of teachings. We take what we find to be of benefit from a range of ideas and practices, using a meditation technique we learnt here that goes with a philosophy or insight that we came across there, plus the bits and bobs of yoga, Tai Ch'i, Pilates or other discipline from somewhere else that we know suits us best. There's determination in that, too; take the best bits and leave the rest.

As for determination in the committed, focused, dedicated sense, this is where you get down to the work. Make no mistake, however it's packaged as the Ecology of the Soul, Buddhism, Mindfulness or anything else, this path of self-awareness and self-enhancement is not an easy one, and anyone who tells you otherwise is lying. It's called self-discipline. You have to make room in your life not only for creation of new ordinary day-to-day habits and elimination of the old ones, but also for new mental habits. It means a constant watchfulness over the mind, a refusal to let it run away with you under any circumstances, not just meditation. You have to keep that naughty pup on a leash, and that's tiring.

But there are ways and means you can use to help yourself become your Self; determination isn't just a matter of brute force. It's also self management. Are you determined to achieve the power and peace that comes with greater self knowledge and a higher consciousness? You are? Really? Really really *really*? Well, if old habits die hard and you wake up feeling annoyed with yourself, you need some methods, tricks and devices to help you get back on your horse again. No one's out there judging you, by the way. You are who you are, ever were and ever shall be so, so there's no point begging, praying, blaming or lamenting. You just pick yourself up, dust yourself off, and get on with it. Again. That's determination.

Here are some pointers:

1. Love yourself. Which, of course, leads to Love Your Self. Don't get annoyed with yourself when your mind wanders; be patient. Don't start mentally kicking yourself when you fail to do something you know you should, or do something you know you shouldn't. Two steps forward, one back. Or two forward, three back. Once you're on the path, you're on it. This book is not for people who choose to dedicate themselves 100 percent to the path of renunciation and the search for enlightenment, begging bowl in hand; it's for people who live ordinary everyday lives, with all the distractions and material matters that that entails. Be kind to yourself.

2. Create a habit. Habits come and go. If there's one you know you need to conquer, instead of trying desperately to eliminate it while not being sure what's going to go in its place, create the new one and let the old one wither and fade away. Create a mental device that kicks in when your nasty old habit rears its head; not a straightforward roadblock, which is very difficult to maintain, but a diversion. Drink too much coffee? Bring it down gradually to one or two cups at specific times, and add in some nice tea perhaps, a bit of a treat. Enjoy the coffee, but don't be its slave.

3. Find tricks to play on yourself. This is another way of saying remove old habits by creating new ones. I'm no expert at conquering addictions, but for the less vicious habits you can

> manage yourself very effectively with simple tricks and devices. Got up from your desk to get yet another cup of coffee? Walk back and forth the whole length of the office. Twice. Get involved in a conversation. Think: "I'll make one after the meeting." When the meeting's over, go back to your desk via another route, not past the coffee machine. You got to 4pm and you still haven't had that coffee. Might as well see it through to the end of the day. And you get a hit of self satisfaction: yes, I succeeded there. Next time it will be easier.

These sound like ordinary everyday things, not spiritual efforts. But it's all relevant; it's all mind control. Because mind, as we very well know, is the last port of call for thoughts before they tip over into action. It's your actions that count; mental habits are different again of course, and much more difficult. Take it easy, a step at a time. Love yourself.

The Power of Focus Meditation 6: Clarity

Clarity affords focus.
Thomas Leonard

The more of me I be,
The clearer I can see.
Rachel Archelaus

For me the greatest beauty always lies in the greatest clarity.
Gotthold Ephraim Lessing

There are so many meanings and resonances for this idea that we begin to wonder if we've hit on the one single word that expresses everything we need to know about the Ecology of the Soul. At such times we turn to our friend the *Shorter Oxford English Dictionary* (I love how language and ideas shape each other), and discover that in straightforward dictionary definition terms, Clarity just gets a one-liner: Brightness, Glory, Clearness.

In themselves, that Big Three would keep us chewing a while – although using 'clearness' as a definition of 'clarity' is a bit of a cop-out in my opinion. But it does lead us to Clear, for which there is a whole column and a half of definitions, subtleties of meaning, and references. It comes from the Latin *clarus*, which translates as bright, clear. The Old French *clair* is also mentioned; *éclairage* in modern French means lighting, illumination.

Out of the many meanings for clear and hence clarity, we can choose from: Brightly shining, fully light, bright, serene; transparent, translucent, lustrous; clearly seen, distinct; easy to understand; free from confusion; subjectively free from doubt, certain, positive, determined; pure, unsophisticated; unencumbered; free from contact; to make or become clear or bright; to make pure from stain, to purify, clarify; to remove, so as to leave the place or way clear; to set free from debt; to leap clear over, pass over; to clear up; to make or become clear, orderly or perspicuous.

Don't need much more than that, do we. Then there are the multiple associations of clarity with our mental, intellectual and spiritual processes:

Clarity of mind;
Clarity of thinking (are they the same thing?);
Clarity of purpose;
Clarity of vision – again, the same but different;
Clarity of communication;
Clarity of judgement (right from wrong, good from bad – a whole world of moral and ethical complexity);
Clarity of perception, both inner and outer.

Clarity is what you get when you break through. Confusion and struggle, uncertainty and imbalance are behind you – they have led you here by a roundabout route, but now they're over. If clarity is a place, it's a profoundly quiet and welcoming one, somewhere you emerge into, looking round and realizing you have arrived. Clarity has stillness, silence, focus, 'centeredness'; you know where you are, where you're going, where you fit and where do others. (Arrived or still going? See below.)

Like every other mental and spiritual attribute or condition with peace and stillness at its heart, clarity also carries great power. Focus itself is a power; clarity is a product of focus, the two inextricably intertwined. This is where you begin to experience what the mind can really do when it's fine-tuned and working for you at peak efficiency. The unnecessary drops away, all you are left with is the way forward, and in this particular respect that clarity of direction is what gives you power and peace. Which is to say that clarity gives you the sense of the way forward simultaneously with the sense of having arrived. It's your destination and your direction at one and the same time.

Like focus itself, 'all you are left with' implies a stripping down, a refinement, a reduction of activity down to where, since we are so focused and pinpointed, there is nothing much going on in the mind at all. Does a silent mind mean nothingness? No. You could almost say a silent mind means 'everythingness'. It's one of the crucial paradoxes that underpin many, if not most, of the processes of consciousness dealt with in this book and ones like it. It's the breakthrough we talked about at the beginning of this meditation, the same phenomenon which simultaneously encompasses going forward with clarity of purpose and having arrived with clarity of vision. Pinning down and opening out. Within the heart of the stillness and silence that is true focus, or in this case true clarity, is the expanse of consciousness, an infinite breadth and depth of awareness, a warm, glowing, beautiful, blissful state of being that is true 'aliveness'.

The Raja Yogis describe this state of being – they also use the phrase to describe God – as an "Ocean of Bliss". An ocean in a pinpoint. Ocean of Peace, Ocean of Power will do just as well. Bliss doesn't mean just floating, with all awareness switched off; it means intensely, powerfully aware, because it's just the static that has been switched off. Now you're dealing in pure consciousness, because the intense, powerful awareness, the 'true aliveness' of bliss is strictly consciousness being conscious of itself. Consciousness feeding on consciousness, experiencing simply the pure bliss of pure being. From this pinpoint of infinity, everything else flows. Clarity of perception, of mind, of thought, of judgement, of purpose, of direction, of vision, of communication; everything is enshrined in this one single experience, the experience of Your Self. However many multiple meanings and resonances there are in the idea, it boils down to one thing and one thing only: knowing, and experiencing, your Self as a non-physical Soul. That's all you need.

The Power of Focus Meditation 7: Mindfulness

The best way to capture moments is to pay attention. This is how we cultivate mindfulness. Mindfulness means being awake. It means knowing what you are doing.
Jon Kabat-Zinn

If you clean the floor with love, you have given the world an invisible painting.
Osho

Walk as if you are kissing the Earth with your feet.
Thích Nhất Hạnh

Do every act of your life as though it were the very last act of your life.
Marcus Aurelius

Mindfulness, which seems to have taken off as a favorite topic amongst the global personal growth community, is nothing more nor less than paying attention. Whole philosophies, books, teachings and teachers are now explaining, promoting and purveying mindfulness, which is no bad thing of course – but it is a means, not an end. Far from it being some exotic new break-through idea, I have always understood it as a generally accepted standard, a basic building block of the contemplative, meditative life, and one you can stitch into your daily life to transform any given moment.

Not to say 'no big deal', because it is a very big deal, but it is an idea as ancient as meditation itself, and one that pops up in a variety of religious practice. I first came across it in my scanty reading round Zen Buddhism (consisting almost entirely of Paul

Reps' *Zen Flesh, Zen Bones1*), but the sense, at least, of paying complete attention to the here and now is not the exclusive domain of any named or recognized religion.

Mindfulness is meditation in action, is what it is – except for when it's meditation in meditation. It's absorption, losing yourself in the moment so that all that exists is that moment and what's in that moment. One of our paradoxes again: static and moving at the same time. This is very close to the teachings of Eckhart Tolle, who gets a lot of namechecks in this book, and whose main message is in the title of his first book, *The Power of Now*.[2] Essentially he's saying that we need to wrestle our mind away from past and future (which is where, if we clearly and honestly look at our own thinking, we realize we spend most of our time: "I wonder what he meant?" – "Did you see that goal?" – "What train shall I get?" – "What shall I feed the kids tonight?" etc, etc, etc) and exist in the Now.

What Eckhart doesn't have, with the greatest of respect, is the understanding of the Soul and its component parts, its anatomy if you like. This is important because 'mindfulness', which as we say above really means nothing more nor less than paying attention, is not exclusively a matter for the mind. The mind, again as we continue to emphasize throughout this book, is a much maligned department of consciousness, generally held to be a flippertigibbet, the source of unruly chitchat that needs to be tamed – but it is also a faculty of great power, capable of surprising feats.

If we keep to our understanding of the mind as that faculty we use to think, feel, 'emote' and respond to external and internal stimuli (such as memories), we realize that the practice

---

1 *Zen Flesh, Zen Bones* compiled by Paul Reps and Nyogen Senzaki, Tuttle Publishing, 1998. ISBN-10: 0804831866; ISBN-13: 978-0804831864

2 *The Power of Now* by Eckhart Tolle, Yellow Kite, 2001. ISBN-10: 0340733500; ISBN-13: 978-0340733509

of mindfulness demands processes of the intellect as well. It goes to the heart of the process of controlling our own minds, begging the question: am I controlling my mind with my mind, or my intellect? The intellect is the rational part, remember, the information gathering, analyzing, judging, discriminatory part. The part from which you're much more likely to get discipline than the undisciplined mind. The part that says: "I, a soul in a body, am performing actions with my body, and the more complete my attention to and experience of those actions can be, the more Soul Conscious – and, perversely, detached from those very actions – I can be." It's that detachment that we are seeking, the experience (through the mind) of a state of inner peace and power that, yet again paradoxically, exists inside the action. Or, more accurately, that state exists inside our perception of the action.

But best not to get too complicated here. While you're doing your daily things you don't really have to figure out if your mind is in a higher gear than your intellect, or where your sanskars kick in. It's just a matter of you, the Soul, monitoring your own consciousness. And, just as meditation can be sitting in a quiet place and meeting the mind's vagaries head on to break through to the blissful experience of your Self as a pure source of living peace, so it can also be achieving a quietness of mind through action itself.

Some Zen ideas help pinpoint this paradox and underline the perception that mindfulness is about much more than the mind – or, you could say, much less, because here you are, in action, turning your mind off. Zen kōans, for instance, are designed to trick the mind, to obfuscate it in such a way that it blows a fuse and stops getting in the way of experience. Zen is paradoxical, or nonsensical, because 'sense', or intellectual process, is also not the route to the center, to the still, small voice of calm. Mind is attracted, intellect receives and analyzes stimuli and decides how to deal with the attraction. But neither delivers the whole story. I have always loved the response of Don Van Vliet, aka Captain

Beefheart, to a *Rolling Stone* interviewer who asked if he was "into Zen": "No thanks, I prefer an overcoat." We're in the territory of the sound of one hand clapping, the tricks and turns that open the door into infinite space, infinite light, infinite peace.

If we expand mindfulness into as much of our daily life as possible, it's clear that some of our activities lend themselves better than others. Sitting in a meeting, you can practice as much clarity of perception as you can achieve, but there's too much going on for you to reach silence. And silence isn't where you want to be anyway, if you have to make your pitch. My favorite example is doing the dishes, which isn't perhaps such a universal experience as it was since pretty much everyone (except us) has a dishwasher these days. You can still do it filling and emptying the dishwasher, but the sense of craft (see Meditation 4 in this chapter, Craftsmanship) isn't as developed.

Doing the dishes is a deadly dull humdrum chore, boring but demanding attention so you can't 'switch off' while you're doing it. Instead of racing through it to get on to something more inherently worthwhile, you stop yourself, come into the Now, as Eckhart would say, and give all your mental and intellectual power to the action(s). It becomes a launching platform. Do it with intent, do it with care, do it with complete attention, focus entirely on the task at hand. Do it, most importantly, with love. There is no task that is not done better with love. Meditation in action makes beautiful action. Don't let your mind go elsewhere while you cope with the chore on sufferance, as it were. Engage. Engage completely. And lo and behold, come out of that state with a perfectly clean and tidy draining board – and an (almost) perfectly clean and tidy mind.

Last Zen-ish quote on this particular example, which I might have read somewhere, or I might have made up:

Student: "Oh, I see, so you meditate while you're doing the dishes?"

Master: "No. I do the dishes."

The Power of Focus Practice 1: Plant a Power Seed Every Day

Power Seeds are mental devices, thought triggers to generate Soul Consciousness, and hence change your actions. They are a bit like the Zen 'kōan' (for instance the idea of the sound of one hand clapping) that kick your mind out of gear and raise the level of your awareness.

Using Power Seeds, you grow a new garden of consciousness. See your mind as a garden, or at least a patch of fertile soil. Thoughts and feelings grow in it, like plants. Your mind is a riot of tangled and intertwined mental vegetation, much of it good and useful and most of it neither good nor useful. So it's a pleasant surprise that you don't have to struggle with the weeds. All you have to do is plant your mental plot with new seeds – 'Power Seeds' – which grow into thought, attitude, feeling, and action. Which feeds back and creates new thought and feeling. You have created a new mental and spiritual garden – and a new framework for your behavior.

If you really focus all the innate power of your calmed, stilled mind on the Power Seed you choose for 60 full seconds, that thought pattern will repeat and recur throughout the day, accumulating much more than a single minute of your mental activity. It's meditation in action, because the meditation is about action.

Plant one of the mental Power Seeds that appear on the following pages. The Seven Powers, Power Seeds and the Magic Minute section of Part I, the Introduction, gives the full explanation of how to prepare the mental and spiritual ground for your new garden; Part III gives you a whole range of Power Seeds to suit your circumstances. Ultimately, as your Self knowledge increases, you will be creating and planting your own.

Focus is power. Focus is a power.
The narrower focus gets, the more powerful it gets.

Focus is a pinpoint. Focus is space, focus is empty.
Focus is the infinite void inside the pinpoint.

Focus your mind like a magnifying glass concentrating the sun's rays, gathering them into an ever smaller and ever hotter pinpoint.

You the Soul are infinitesimally small, but at the same time within that tiny infinity is the boundlessly vast infinity of consciousness, thoughts, feelings, experiences, memories, actions, lived through many years of many lives.

Never mind mind over matter. This is mind over mind.

Accuracy of aim.
Accuracy of intention.
Accuracy of execution.

Accuracy frees the mind, liberates. Precision eliminates confusion and indecision.

You are an infinitesimally small, infinitely powerful, infinitely peaceful Soul. Infinitely existent (ie eternal), but not infinitely spread out all over the Universe. Unique.
Without accuracy, you'd never find your Self.

Compartmentalize the experience of being a Soul. You are on the bus or train, driving or working, talking or walking, playing or paying. You are a Soul doing these things, through your body.
"Soul is driver, body is car."

The mind is the first tool on the way to focus –
And also a tool of focus.

Concentrate. But with kindness.
Kindness to yourself brings you face to face with your Self.

There's nothing in life that you can't make a meditation.

Do we apply craftsmanship to meditation itself? What about controlling the mind? Is that the task of a craftsperson?

Override the mind.
Mindfully.

Love yourself.
Which, of course, leads to
Love Your Self.
Don't get annoyed with yourself when your mind wanders.
Be patient.

Go for
Clarity of mind
Clarity of thinking (are they the same thing?)
Clarity of purpose
Clarity of vision
Clarity of communication
Clarity of judgement
Clarity of perception.

An ocean in a pinpoint.
Within the heart of the stillness and silence that is true clarity is the expanse of consciousness, an infinite breadth and depth of awareness, a warm, glowing, beautiful, blissful state of being that is true 'aliveness'.

Mindfulness is meditation in action – except for when it's meditation in meditation.

Mindfulness is not exclusively a matter for the mind.

"I, a soul in a body, am performing actions with my body, and the more complete my attention to and experience of those actions can be, the more Soul Conscious – and, perversely, detached from those very actions – I can be."

Do it with intent,
Do it with care,
Do it with complete attention.
Focus entirely on the task at hand.
Do it with love.
There is no task that is not done better with love.

Meditation in action makes beautiful actions.

The Power of Focus Practice 2: Yoga Seeds – Salute to the Sun (Surya Namaskar)

Position 6: Cobra Pose (Bhujangasana)

Focus is our sixth power and rests in the sixth chakra, bringing us in the seven-power sequence to Cobra position – Bhujangasana. You are working more directly on your spine than in most of the other Surya Namaskar positions. Saluting the Sun, Asanas and Chakras in Part I, the introduction section, explains why we are matching a yoga position from Surya Namaskar (the Salute to the Sun) to each chapter, gives a general look at the ways in which adoption of a mild yoga habit underpins and strengthens your awakening of the Ecology of the Soul, and goes into the techniques in more detail.

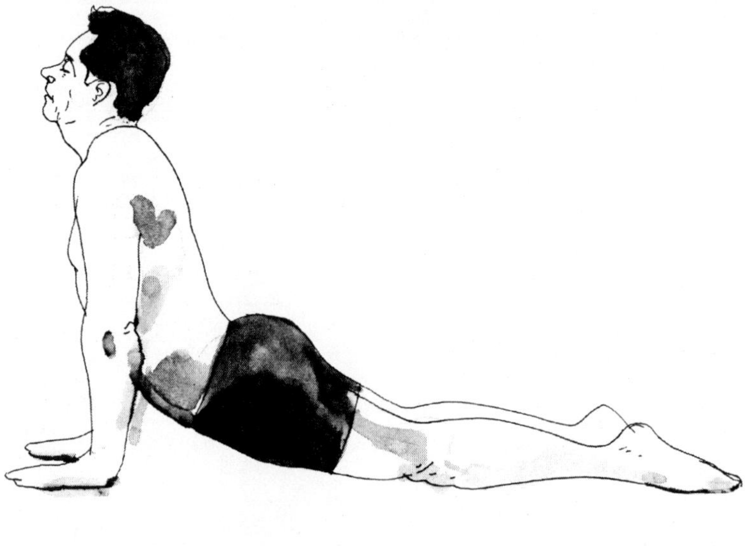

Remember that you are always feeling and hearing your breathing sound at the top back of your nasal passage, making a hollow echo in your head which in itself is creating your calm, inner focus. Remember also that every move you make is done on an exhalation.

'Success' in yoga asanas – feeling the benefit, feeling you are making some progress – depends on being able to create a strong, muscular framework with some parts of your body so that you can let go other parts (usually the spine) and open them to the flow of Prān, Ch'i, the life force. The trick is to be conscious of those parts enough to separate them out. You put your awareness into different parts of your body, like a conductor telling the violins to go fortissimo and the woodwind to rest. In Cobra/Bhujangasana, your arms are locked solid and you're pushing through your spine hard down at the coccyx, and then forward and up from there in a kind of dynamic curve. Within that strong frame, you're letting your spine go, making space between each vertebra and allowing your spine to lengthen, extending its curve in radius and height so your head goes further and further up and back.

You've come from Adho Mukha Svanasana, Dog pose. Move from the 'behind in the air' position to lie on the floor face down, legs stretched out behind you, toes extended, and arms bent so your hands are flat on the floor directly under your shoulders. Come up onto your straight arms so that your hands are positioned flat on the floor the same width apart as your shoulders but a little forward of them. Stretch your legs out behind you, keeping your elbows locked and your arms rock solid and straight. As your body straightens out as if you were going to Plank (Chaturanga Dandasana), relax and let go in your sacral area so that your hips and lower abdomen rest their weight on the floor. Your feet point and stretch out backwards. Let your weight sink down onto your pelvic area and start the push through your coccyx, which since your spine is already curved follows through from down to forward to up. Your arms are still straight as a die, and they will be beginning to feel the strain. Lock them and push down harder, making them longer to accommodate your lengthening spine. Shuffle your shoulders back a little so that your chest opens, and as you keep your arms locked, rotate them outwards slightly in their sockets to allow your chest to open more.

It doesn't look like it from outside, but this is a dynamic position. As your spine lengthens, it will knot up here and there because the opening process, like a creaky door, goes easier in some parts than others. Identify the spots where it's knotting up, and with a combination of push from your coccyx and 'let go' from your mind, find the space between those vertebrae. You will also quite likely come up against compression of vertebrae and muscles just between the tops of your shoulders, where your thoracic (chest) vertebrae turn into your cervical (neck and head) ones. The curve can kink here and restrict the flow. Reestablish the strength in those arms and widen your shoulders at the base of your neck. Open it out some more. Feel the flow up into your head, find more space between those vertebrae, and let your head fall farther back.

And here's the really tricky part. While you're doing all this, see if you can let go in your neck and throat. Relax those muscles and the tension will also go out of your tongue, which itself is no more or less than a muscle. I'm not pretending this is easy, but you will find as your practice develops that letting go of your throat and tongue automatically quietens the mind. You cannot think chattery thoughts when your tongue is relaxed. As it relaxes it shrinks, so you feel more space inside your mouth and throat. Start thinking again, the tongue swells up, the saliva glands kick in and you're back to the chatter.

How long should you hold it? Don't overdo it; be gentle with yourself. And most importantly, don't count seconds while you hold a pose, count breaths. It keeps your attention on your breathing, and allows you to let go a little more on each outbreath. If you're at beginner level, five complete in-outs, as long as they are slow and contemplative and felt in that top back of your nasal passage, will be enough. Maybe more than enough, if you're stiff. As you gain flexibility you can lengthen your practice, but don't paint yourself into a corner where you now can't afford the time for a Salute to the Sun in your busy morning schedule. If it's the weekend or you're on holiday, perhaps you can make a bit more time. Or, perhaps you can just give yourself a rest day.

Now. Tell me you don't feel centered, energized, vitalized, strengthened, and good and ready for anything the day can throw at you. Did you plant your Power Seed yet?

Chapter 7

The Power of Connection

Sahasrara, the Crown Chakra

In this chapter:

> Only Connect.
> *EM Forster, Howard's End*

Introduction

This is the chapter that carries, notionally at least, the culmination of the effort in all the others. The book is designed to be dipped into at any point, however, so you could have come straight here without following the upward path of the chakras, and now find yourself right at the very top of the human energy tree, in amongst the 1000 petals of Sahasrara. To paraphrase kundalini philosophy, the Crown chakra, number seven, is the one through which your subtle energy, having refined and raised itself through the previous six chakra nodes – base of spine, gut, solar plexus, heart, throat, forehead – arrives at pure consciousness, a state of liberating 'samadhi' or enlightenment. "The mind is still, one-pointed or concentrated, but individual awareness remains present."[1] There is also the sense – and this is far more important for the Ecology of the Soul, which finds the chakras useful as a route to understanding our Selves, but doesn't subscribe to full-blown kundalini – that the energy rises right through Sahasrara, and keeps on going. Up. To a union, a connection, a communion, a conjoining, with the Supreme Soul, otherwise known as God. You may not have a topknot, but if you did, that's why it would be there – so God can pull you up, out of your body consciousness.

Union, connection, communion, conjoining: they all mean yoga. Yoga is union; yoga is communion. Yoga is communication; yoga is connection. The common use of the Sanskrit word 'yoga', from 'yujir yoga' (to yoke) is 'to add', 'to join', 'to unite' or 'to attach', but there is another strand of meaning, from 'yuj samadhau', which signifies 'to concentrate'. Commentators on the Yoga Sutras of Patanjali seem to consider the latter meaning as more correct,[2] but for our purposes the distinction is academic only, because the concentration of meditation leads us to the experience of connection, of union with a Soul whose powers are supreme, and at the heart of this experience is the bliss of samadhi in its generally accepted sense of enlightenment.

All the other chapters are about your Self, the Soul, and how to regain the true consciousness of your Self as a Soul – Soul Consciousness. This one is about what you do with your Self once you've reached a stage that you can genuinely experience and feel as Soul Consciousness. It's also about what you do with your fellow travelers on this path, how you interact with them

---

1 http://en.wikipedia.org/wiki/Samadhi

2 Bryant, Edwin (2009) *The Yoga Sutras of Patañjali: A New Edition, Translation, and Commentary*. New York, USA: North Point Press. ISBN-13: 978-0865477360

and how you connect; how you listen and learn, give and take. It's even about your connection with those who are not on the path, but who might be interested, or indifferent, or even downright hostile.

Connection with the limitless, inexhaustible, infinite source of peace and power is all we seek. This whole book is focused on you focusing on your Self and discovering the amazing, infinite reserves of power and peace inside your Self – but what's inside your Self is not the full story. Why do we continue to strive, to plumb ever-greater depths of peace, bliss and silence? Because our sanskars, the recorded results of our actions – our karma – over thousands of years of birth and rebirth tell us that there is more, a greater power than our own that we can tap into. One that is outside our Selves, not omnipresent, and one into which we do not merge and lose our own individual identity. At the heart of the yoga experience is the loss of the sense of individuality, yes; we are subsumed in a glow of rosy fire, the mind still, basking in the light of peace, floating on the Ocean of Bliss. But when we come back to our bodies, we are still unique individual Souls, and so is the Supreme Soul. No merging, no disappearance into a general overall miasma of consciousness which somehow includes all living things and even matter.

Although we are flying high on our newfound, rediscovered spiritual energy of Soul Consciousness, as this very consciousness grows it becomes clearer and clearer that the truly inexhaustible source is outside us. Our project has been rediscovering and reinvigorating our natural, innate power and peace, because we have dropped away from that awareness of Self and got lost and weakened in body consciousness. As we re-focus our true Soul Consciousness, it awakens our desire – and our inherent, soul-remembered experience – for connection to the Source that never falters, tires, loses its way or its energy, because it never does actions driven by a mistaken sense of itself. It's ultimately all-powerful, all the time. It was for ever thus and for ever will be.

We call it God, and yoga is the union, the communion, the connection that we seek with Him/Her/It – however you want to characterize a Soul who has no body, is therefore without gender and, more importantly, has no karmic relationship with a body, or indeed with anything in the physical world, come to that. (For ease of reading and to try and keep the language unclunky, I'm just going to use the pronoun 'He'.) God is not your Self, and your Self is not God. As Souls, we are alike, but the key difference is that He is karmateet – beyond karma. Beyond action, in other words, and certainly beyond the results of action.

It's a lifetime's work – many lifetimes – to understand and fully experience your relationship with the Supreme Soul, which is why in this book I'm not going into great detail. We've got ourselves here, and now it's more a matter of pointing the way for our own personal study, practice and progress. As you will know if you've read any other part of the book, the essential teaching, the basic knowledge of Soul we are dealing with, comes from the Brahma Kumaris' teachings of Raja Yoga, so when you're ready that's where I recommend you go. But you do need to be ready, and by that I mean have a good grip on Soul Consciousness. This is strong stuff – too strong for some.

The Power of Connection Meditation 1: Giving

Kindness in words creates confidence. Kindness in thinking creates profoundness. Kindness in giving creates love.
Lao Tzu

For it is in giving that we receive.
Francis of Assisi

You can give without loving, but you can never love without giving.
Robert Louis Stevenson

This chapter is about the Power of Connection, connectedness – and hence, relationships. Because part and parcel of connection, communion or union, is community, commonality. If you're filled with uplifting spiritual energy, the automatic response is to give it – share it (see the Sharing meditation in this chapter). In fact it's so automatic you can find yourself giving without even being aware of the response. The higher you become, the more your very existence becomes a gift.

Traditionally, the wisdom has been that it is more blessed to give than to receive. "It is in giving that we receive," says St. Francis above. Are giving and receiving therefore one and the same thing? They are consequent upon each other, but not the same thing, surely? One is inward bound; one is outward. And what is it we're giving, exactly? Straightforward, 100 percent proof love, power and peace? Can we manage that? Can we manage to give it to anyone and everyone, whoever they may be and whatever their attitude towards us? Or is it only possible for us to give at that level to people close to us, in other words souls to whom we have some attachment, some karmic account?

Meditation releases us from karmic debt and credit, which keep us back, hold the Soul down from regaining its natural high consciousness. Karma simply means action, remember, and every action has an equal and opposite reaction, in the moral and spiritual sphere as much as the physical. Over many births, your actions and their reactions have intertwined your fate or destiny (the more commonly understood sense of 'karma') with that of other Souls. Check to see how many other people – Souls – occupy your mind and consciousness. From your mother, father, wife, husband, lover, children, boss, colleagues, down to the guy who trod on your toe in the street, there's always karma involved. The more people – Souls – you are in karmic connection with, the more difficult it is to rise.

See people as Souls, each living in their own body's forehead, and each with their own karma. This kind of vision is Soul Consciousness, which helps you detach and arrive at that place where, although there is detachment there is also love (see Chapter 1: Nature, Meditation 7, Dispassion – Detachment) – and giving is automatic, because the Soul who reaches very high is giving just by being. Others are receiving subtle benefit from you, while you may not yourself be aware of actually giving. Your consciousness is creating an atmosphere, a vibration, to which other Souls respond in an exchange, a communality or commonality, that is karma free because there is no action involved. Which, if you're really serious about this path to a higher consciousness – to regain the balance of all your powers in a restored spiritual ecology – has to be a good thing.

So we're giving without engaging. Heading that way at least, and I'm certainly not proposing that you just walk away from your family. Being a part of it without committing your consciousness in attachment, ego and anger – detached but loveful – is the way to go. Which leads us to the insight that all giving is loving, and that since, as we know, we can't give love outside ourselves before we have learned to love ourselves, we have to learn to give to ourselves in the same way. And then to give ***of*** ourselves, and then to give ourselves entirely.

Somewhere in that process, ourself becomes our Self – the real Me, I the Soul. Personal pronouns get a bit mixed, but you get the idea. Giving to yourself is allowing your Self to breathe, but it doesn't feel as if you're pampering the infinitesimally small pinpoint of eternal, inextinguishable conscient light that is You. It's much more a matter of making time and space for yourself in your ordinary everyday life, giving yourself enough quietude and solitude to refresh, refuel and reinvigorate.

You're already giving your Self meditation time, and ideally some yoga as well, or other similar physical/subtle/spiritual activity. The kind of giving we're talking about here can happen at any moment, in amongst the hustle and bustle. Crowded train, busy street, stressful office, noisy bar: close your eyes a moment – if it won't get you into trouble – and go inside. Breathe at the back of your nasal passage, yoga style. If you're standing, tuck in your tailbone and straighten and extend your spine and neck. Relax your tongue. Just. Let. Your. Mind. Go. Quiet. And as you kick back into activity, track the benefit back to you the Soul, your Soul Consciousness. You're empowered, ready, more able and more willing to give.

This is where consciousness of your gifts and gratitude for them rise to the surface. A great deal is being written and spoken about gratitude at the moment; it's being commandeered by the Law of Attraction brigade as a key state of mind to deliver what you want. I'm uneasy about using it as a device to get that new car you're hankering after, but I do recommend it as a contemplative mode in which you consider your gifts. Your luck, if you like – which we know is another way of saying karma. And it's not a matter of thanking God, who, as an all-powerful, all-knowledgeable Soul without a body, is hardly likely to be organizing the physical world in your favor. It's not a matter of thanking anyone, in fact; more a matter of respecting your own luck.

For your gifts are not yours. They are yours to do good with, to act in stewardship. If you don't give them or give with them, they will fade. And the more you give them and give with them, the more powerful and abundant they will be. Which leads to the enormous idea of giving yourself – your Self. It's an act of love. When we fall in love, one of our deepest, most basic desires or impulses is to give ourselves completely to our beloved. It's (supposedly) what marriage is about. But when it comes to giving yourself – your Self – to God, you yourself become the gift. And that takes some doing, because as soon as you have reached one level of renunciation – giving yourself means giving up pretty much everything, or at least giving up your attachment to it – you realize there's a multitude of levels more. Such an extreme path is by no means for everyone, but we can all experience the essence of it in meditation. I am a Soul, You are the Supreme Soul. Connect. No wires, cables or Wi-Fi protocols required. Go on, give yourself. Get lost.

The Power of Connection Meditation 2: Receiving

> The only gift I have to give, is the ability to receive. If giving is a gift, and it surely is, then my gift to you is to allow you to give to me.
> *Jarod Kintz*

> In ordinary life we hardly realize that we receive a great deal more than we give, and that it is only with gratitude that life becomes rich.
> *Dietrich Bonhoeffer*

> Neither give nor take sorrow.
> *Dadi Janki,* Brahma Kumaris World Spiritual University

> It was still – and always – safe to give since there was a certain deal of control to be exerted over giving. Taking, or allowing oneself to receive, was an altogether more risky business. For receiving meant opening up the heart again.
> *Mary Balogh*

> Are you receiving me?
> *XTC*

Giving is the subject of much talk, meditation and discussion – we've just come from there. But people seem to pay far less attention to the art and science of receiving. The 'more blessed to give than to receive' idea takes a beating here; obviously, giving is crucial in so many ways, one of the foundations of your new Soul Consciousness. But just giving, always in 'output' mode, can lead to a false arrogance of humility, and become in itself a step to body consciousness. You're proud of your giving, of yourself as a giver, but you don't have the humility to be able to receive.

Receiving = gratitude. To receive is to be open to transmissions. There is a sense that receiving makes you bigger, you have more, you are expanded, enlarged. (As long as it is your consciousness that is enlarged, rather than your pockets or your belly.)

Give and take; give and receive. Give and take may or may not be the same thing, but receive and take certainly aren't. Take is active, receive is passive. There is also 'passive mode' take, as in 'take it lying down', but of course in any give or take transaction with another human soul, karma is surely involved.

So here, let's focus on receiving, on acceptance of that which is given. Acceptance also comes up as a way of dealing with circumstances (Chapter 3: The Power of Endurance, Meditation 1, Acceptance), but here the key experience is allowing input; taking on board. Receiving requires you to open up. It needs an openness and open mindedness that implies vulnerability and the taking of risk. It's often a stretch for the Soul, a healthy exercise, because ego gets in the way of receiving from other people – Souls. You feel you will be obliged, beholden, somehow in their power. A debt has been created. It's safer to give. But either way, inevitably karma is already at work, and such feelings (apart from your own personal relationship issues) demonstrate your inbuilt karmic consciousness.

But are we going to allow this karmic bond, this account, to abide? What is there that we can give or receive which won't tie us down in karmic entanglements? Nothing physical, obviously, and clearly on an emotional level the entanglements are deeper and stronger. All human relationships are governed by karma, so there is little point in attempting to go through life breaking all karmic bonds, unless you're ready for the mountaintop, the loincloth and the begging bowl. It must be a matter of consciousness, which, perversely, you can neither give nor receive; you can just point the way, or have it pointed for you.

So we're going through life giving, taking and receiving. In the Giving meditation in this chapter we touched on giving to yourself, or your Self, which not only begs the question who exactly is giving to whom, but which also leads directly to the one about receiving from yourself. Or your Self. How humble do you have to be? Are you giving yourself tough advice, or giving your Self unconditional love, or giving yourself forgiveness for transgressions, or giving your Self the opportunity to thrive, to climb a high spiritual peak? Are you telling yourself to do things you're not doing, or not to do things you are doing? Are you ignoring yourself, or your Self? Even in the closed circuit of your own consciousness, the giving and receiving is going on.

But the process isn't entirely circular. This chapter is about connection, which presupposes an external being or agency. And the input/output of giving, taking and receiving automatically presupposes connection, which then leads to communication. It's the 'are you receiving me' part of this meditation which is the real nub; how is your reception? Are you truly receiving? How tuned are your antennae to subtle atmospheres and vibrations – from other Souls, or indeed, and most importantly, to the Supreme Soul, whose transmitter is always on? We are attuning ourselves, fine-tuning ourselves, focusing. We make the connection, the communication begins; that's yoga, the union, the yoke.

It's simple to describe, but you can bet on spending the rest of your life – in fact all the rest of all your lives – working on it. The receptivity is in the pinpoint, shining ever more intensely and receiving ever more clearly as your Soul Consciousness grows. The key paradox, the Zen kōan, is that the smaller the pinpoint, the more powerful it is. You are receiving, and Super Soul, Paramatma, out there is transmitting. Experience an unlimited ocean of peace, love, bliss and power, all contained within a living point of consciousness of no size. By focusing on your Self, you generate your own spiritual charge and take power from that. But as an eternal human Soul, your charge is depleted by the ravages of action, of karma. The thing about the superhuman Supreme Soul, God, however you want to call Him, is that He does no action and thus has no karma to deplete His own power. The ocean remains eternally unlimited. Plugging into that pinpoint, to coin a fairly awkward phrase, will give you all the power you'll ever need. And that, ladies and gentlemen, is what we call yoga.

The Power of Connection Meditation 3: Sharing

Share your knowledge. It is a way to achieve immortality.
Dalai Lama XIV

When you're surrounded by people who share a passionate commitment around a common purpose, anything is possible.
Howard Schultz

Happiness quite unshared can scarcely be called happiness; it has no taste.
Charlotte Brontë

Love only grows by sharing. You can only have more for yourself by giving it away to others.
Brian Tracy

Sharing the burden
Sharing the news
Sharing the joy
Sharing the pain
Sharing the blues
Sharing the experience
Sharing the moment
Equal shares
Share and share alike
I want my share

Sharing is held to be the sort of thing that people/Souls of good heart and mind, a certain elevated consciousness, do. A child doesn't want to share his sweets. Share is give and share is take (receive). It's both. What's the difference between sharing and giving? In sharing you expect something back. You've given out, now you are expecting a return. Or if you've received, you know you're expected to give. That's the deal. All give or all take (receive) is not sharing.

You can share one to one, but the impulse to share also makes it a communal transaction and creates community, commonality, which is an aspect of union/communion. You're lucky to find a bunch of people (Souls) who know the same things as you do, understand what you're trying to do, do the same things, share the same beliefs. You're building a community, sharing a goal, a common vision. An understanding. A set of shared values. This is the main focus for this meditation.

The relationships with one's Self and with the Supreme Soul are very much individual, contained and private. But hosts of Souls are plugged into the Supreme Soul at any given moment. Are we sharing the ocean of peace? Not really. We're not sharing the experience, anyway, in the sense of being aware of each other in the midst of said ocean – only of the Self and the Supreme Soul. But we are sharing the knowledge and the happiness of it, and the knowledge, happiness, strength and courage that come from being a member of a community with shared goals and shared values.

Sharing makes more. It's the perfect paradox. Share your knowledge, gain more knowledge. Share your love, gain more love. Share your peace, gain more peace. Does that work with shared power? Yes, of course, if it's spiritual power we're talking about. Not in politics, perhaps. The Brian Tracy quote about love above says: "You can only have more for yourself by giving it away to others", which is more about output than input, not so much the harder receiving part as the easier giving. "You can only have more for yourself…" suggests it's already there and it increases by giving, somehow enlarging your stock already laid in. I think the more important understanding to work on is the openness, the ability and willingness to receive, which we talked about in the last meditation. You have to be able to accept and absorb what's coming back at you as part of this two-way process, otherwise it's not really two-way.

You need humility to receive and confidence to give, security in the knowledge that what you're giving is worth having. If we are concentrating in this context on sharing spiritual love, energy and insight into Soul Consciousness rather than the risky and needy give-and-take of love in human relationships, then we can put our minds at rest as far as confidence in the value of what we have to give is concerned – because what we have to give isn't our own property in the first place. You only have more, to extend Brian Tracy somewhat, when you're giving what you've already received. It's a gift, and it will atrophy if you don't respect its nature and give it. There's some subtle circular paradox at work here which starts before "have more": it's only by giving that you receive, or indeed have, at all. Two sides of the same coin, part and parcel of the same thing, as we have suggested, but at one level discounted. Yes they are different, but they are so intertwined that you can count them as one and the same – and experience them as such by sharing.

The overall theme of this chapter – Connection – carries Community at its heart. Community is built out of the 'other' sharing, neither give nor take, but 'we're all in it together'. This is the one that creates the bonds (they don't have to be karmic ones) in which people – Souls – work together to achieve a shared goal. It may be to re-create the sense of heavenly bliss they have all individually been given; it may be to work in common cause to eradicate a single great evil from the face of the earth. The heart of it isn't anything to do with give or take, but with shared experience, over which we have varying degrees of control. We might have been meditating, mountaintop yogis together, in this or another life; we might have been in a concentration camp. Either way, we have a unique commonality and communality, a shared culture, which is power-giving, but exclusive. (We had better be careful not to be considered a cult.) You only have to sit in meditation with a handful, or better still a hall-full, of people (Souls), all thinking the same thing, all at once, all in the same place, to experience and understand the power of this communality. It's 'unknowing sharing'. The effect is palpable; you are helped, raised higher.

Another quick autobiographical picture of a young man on a mountaintop (Mount Abu, actually – spiritual backpacker in a small hill resort, not Loincloth Man in the wilderness) who has been attending the meditation classes of the Brahma Kumaris World Spiritual University for some weeks now, having abandoned his hatha yoga destination in Pune and set up in a cheap rooftop hotel room. Hearing that some young Australians who had got interested in, then heavily committed to, this knowledge and way of life in London and were now on their way out to Mount Abu, where I had landed by sheer chance (oops, karma?), of course I had to stay and meet them. My type of guys. Hearing Anand Kishore Bhai's lilting tones abjuring me daily against the dangers of sex lust was charming, but there was a great gulf in attitudes and intellectual process. So when Chris and Stephen appeared, boom. There was a light in each other's eyes we recognized. We were same age, similar education, same (international) culture, same values. And that was the moment I realized that with this kind of sharing, yes we could change the world. Or better still, make a new one. Because God knows, we need to.

The Power of Connection Meditation 4: Trust

He who does not trust enough, Will not be trusted.
Lao Tzu

As soon as you trust yourself, you will know how to live.
Johann Wolfgang von Goethe

Trust is the glue of life. It's the most essential ingredient in effective communication. It's the foundational principle that holds all relationships.
Stephen Covey

Trusting your individual uniqueness challenges you to lay yourself open.
James Broughton

It is better to suffer wrong than to do it, and happier to be sometimes cheated than not to trust.
Samuel Johnson

Trust is faith.
Trust is belief.
Trust is confidence.
Trust is a guarantee.

What has trust got to do with the Power of Connection? Because connection presupposes relationship and all relationships are built on trust. The idyllic romantic relationship, or the long-term one, bruised and battered but still precious, where trust might be broken but can be rebuilt, or the more or less fulfilling and trusting relationships with your kids, your parents, your friends, your boss: at the human level, trust doesn't have to be absolute and always 100 percent reliable. You can trust someone to deliver so far but no further, or at the far end of the scale, even to lie, cheat or screw you over, right?

If connection is a power, it is also a state of being where power is flowing. It's an ability we all should have, to connect not only on the human plane but at a higher level; and plugging in at that higher level – to your Self, and to the Supreme Soul as time goes on – you feel the power flooding in. It's OK for it to be one-way; if you can open your Self enough to receive from your Self then you can open to God, who trusts you to receive.

Because to connect you need to open, to receive, to accept; and to do all those things you need to trust. Each one of our three foregoing meditations in this chapter – Giving, Receiving, Sharing – depend on trust as their key ingredient. Opening, receiving, accepting, is an act of faith. Trust is belief, belief is faith. Why do we need this, when this beautiful knowledge is laid out so clear before us? Because we're suspicious, frightened, untrusting. On our journey to become elevated, to reach a higher level of consciousness, it can get scary. We're taking on new ideas, abandoning old ones, treading unfamiliar and what can seem like precarious territory. The higher we go, the scarier it gets, because we're afraid of falling. Can you trust yourself to go this high? Do you feel balanced, safe? Trust your Self, rather than yourself.

Trust is a state of mind, an attitude to life. You're trusting or you're suspicious. It seems the whole world is suspicious, expecting to be cheated or outmaneuvered; it's a standard requirement in business, that's how it works. Yes, if you trust you will almost certainly be exploited. But if you remain suspicious you will remain closed, cut off, unable to receive, unable to grow. You might end up with more money, but you certainly won't end up with more love, peace, power and balance.

Is 'trust yourself' the same as 'believe in yourself'? What

exactly is it you're believing, when you believe in yourself – your Self? (Two different things.) 'Belief in yourself' is usually associated with the Positive Mental Attitude that is a staple of any sports, business or 'life coach'-type training, as in: "You can do it, you know you can". You trust yourself, you have faith in yourself, to succeed. As in so many other instances in the self-help, self-enhancement, self-improvement arena, the fine line between positive thinking and self hypnosis is very fine indeed. Belief in your Self, however, is not only the absorption and acceptance of the fact that you are a single, solitary, eternal, non-physical being, an infinitesimal pinpoint of living light; it is faith in the process on which you have embarked, faith that you will make progress in that process, faith that you will arrive. Faith that You Will Be Fine, that everything will be all right. It starts and ends with faith – trust – in your Self.

As far as others' trust in you is concerned, it's a given that people (Souls) who go high have higher responsibilities. We have to show the world the way, by communication and by action. How successful we are in bringing these ideas to life in our own lives – how much we actually live it – is the key point on the path of effort, and indeed is a question I lay at my own door, if I'm honest. Do I trust myself to carry this message? Yes, unequivocally. Am I without 'sin', a living exemplar of said message? – No. Not by a long chalk. But I'm working on it. Aren't we all?

The Crown chakra, Sahasrara, 'honoring spiritual connectedness' – the Power of Connection – is at the top of the head, or indeed just above. It is also traditionally associated with detachment from illusion, referring to pure consciousness. It is where the subtle energy you have raised through the chakras exits the body and keeps on going – up. But the Ecology of the Soul (from Raja Yoga, as taught by the BKWSU) focuses self-awareness on the Soul's position in the center of the forehead, which is Ajna in chakra-land. And it is Soul Consciousness we seek, and Soul Consciousness through which we gain awareness of and connection to the Supreme Soul. We're not raising the Kundalini here, although we have worked up through the chakras as centers of subtle energy.

Sahasrara is where, traditionally, the subtle transcends into the non-physical, but we have already identified and established the location of our non-physical Self – the center of the forehead. Not to say we have no need of Sahasrara; once we have released it down below, the subtle energy needs to flow outwards and upwards, otherwise we'll have a blockage. It serves to illustrate the difference, and the relationship, between physical, subtle and spiritual, but the traditional understanding is that the connection arising from Sahasrara is the connection to the 'universal miasma', the formless, shapeless, infinite sea of nameless energy that is somehow everything at the same time as it is one thing, and that people (Souls) think of as God, or the Divine. Thankfully, the Ecology of the Soul bases its understanding on the Brahma Kumaris' teaching of Raja Yoga, which identifies, in the clearest possible terms, the specific, unique, individual, eternal human Soul that is You, and the Unique, Individual, Eternal, Karmateet Soul that is God. No miasma involved. That's the connection, chakra or no chakra, between two Souls. Much easier to trust than connecting to a miasma.

The Power of Connection Meditation 5: Grace and Gratitude

Grace – II Favour. 6. Theol., etc. **a.** The free and unmerited favour of God. Hence, the source of grace, God. **b.** The divine influence which operates in men to regenerate and sanctify, and to impart strength to endure trial and resist temptation. **c.** The condition of one who is under such influence.
Shorter Oxford English Dictionary

Gratitude is not so much thanking someone or something; more a matter of respecting your own luck.
The Ecology of the Soul, 2015

Grace is not part of consciousness; it is the amount of light in our souls, not knowledge nor reason.
Pope Francis

This is the meditation where you don't have to do the work. Not entirely true of course, you always have to do the work. But the concept of Grace, God's "unmerited favour" or gift, is key to the early stages of making the connection with the Supreme Soul, because you're surprised to discover that the work is being done for you. Or at least, it goes both ways. It's not just you trying to plug in to a remote, impersonal and distant source of divine energy. He too, amazingly, is engaged in the effort to connect, and can and will lift you up and plug you in in the most astonishingly palpable way. You are literally plucked from your body conscious, tentative, faltering meditation and plunged deep into the ocean of peace, flown high on wings of light. I have personal experience of this phenomenon (see Chapter 3: Endurance, Meditation 3, Faith), and for that, like the many others who have experienced it, I feel blessed. Which is how Grace rolls.

"Unmerited" is the interesting part. We don't deserve it, nor have we worked for it. What, all your hard work, your reading, studying, meditating don't count for anything? If God is to give His "favour", isn't it a matter of merit – you've deserved this, surely? Well, no, because if you worked for it and it was given to you as a reward or because you somehow deserved it, it wouldn't be Grace, would it. It would just be a return on your investment of effort. The whole point about God's Grace is that it is given freely – almost, you could say, indiscriminately. No strings attached. Which doesn't, in turn, mean that when it comes, it comes at a time when you don't need it. It's appropriate all right, it fits. But there's no way you can earn it; you just have – to continue the overall theme of this chapter – to be open and ready to receive.

Gratia Dei, the Grace of God, has a direct link to gratitude, the consciousness that you are receiving gifts. At one level, 'Grace' is an attitude, a way of seeing life with powerful beauty at its heart and soul, and acting on that perception. It's to some extent a choice. A 'state of grace' is somehow different, an elevated consciousness that may be too super-refined to last in the everyday. To Christians it means 'free from mortal sin', and hence joined to God or at one with God as a consequence. Grace as attitude is also a subset of *Gratia Dei*, which comes to you without rhyme or reason, but which you can choose to nurture, to adopt. It doesn't tend to come to those who don't care for it or who don't put at least some work into it, but it has been known. Mostly, it's available to those who see and appreciate the beauty in their own life, who can communicate it to others, and who are acutely conscious that this beauty is a gift. It's not yours to own; you haven't made it. You simply enjoy, and get high on the experience and the knowledge of the gift, look after it, appreciate it.

Paramount in creating and maintaining the open state of mind that allows you to receive is gratitude. So, perversely, it can be seen as the wrong way round; gratitude first, receive after. This is how the Law of Attraction (supposedly) works: create the mindset of abundance, and abundance comes to you – though there are many dangers here, especially when the idea is compromised by applying it to material abundance. It's the same as the feeling of being blessed I describe above: accept with humility. It connects directly to the experience of receiving grace, of benefiting from God's free favor, but as a general rule gratitude is worth practicing on a daily, even hourly basis, simply because it brings contentment, inner peace and joy.

A friend of my father's, a priest like him, used to have a favorite sermon. It was called "Count Your Blessings", and in it he exhorted his congregation to… well, to count their blessings. To go over all the things in your life that you feel blessed with. Make a list. Health, all your limbs, education, an adequacy of material things (not necessarily wealth), family, friends, the kids, music, food, drink, sport, movies, holidays, the dog, the cat, the car, the TV. Love. People to love and be loved by; landscapes, seascapes, sun, wind and rain, natural beauty to enjoy. Life itself.

Constant gratitude in the ordinary everyday context is just a simple extra mental move. Look at something or someone that makes you smile, that makes you feel good; and as the thought "How beautiful" or "How great" flows through, add on the gratitude, like the tail of a comet. Remember that this beauty in front of your eyes or mind or heart is a blessing. Don't know who to thank? Obviously not God, because He doesn't create beauty or happenstance; but as long as your gratitude is genuine, it's OK to say, "Thank you, Lord!" meaning circumstances generally. Or your own karma.

There's a list of gratitude-related words. Grateful. Gratify. Gratuity. Gratuitous. Gratis. Congratulation. They all signify, with one emphasis or another, a gift that is free, that you don't have to pay for. Gratitude and Grace are, in a way, the same thing, revolving and feeding each other. It's back to that Law of

Attraction trick: the more gratitude you feel, the more you are given.

The Power of Connection Meditation 6: Ecology and Ecosystems

> An ecosystem is a community of living organisms in conjunction with the nonliving components of their environment (things like air, water and mineral soil), interacting as a system.
> *http://en.wikipedia.org/wiki/Ecosystem*

The 1983 edition of the *Shorter Oxford English Dictionary* doesn't have the word 'ecosystem'. But its definition of 'ecology' is: "[from the Greek όίκος house (used for 'habitat'): see –LOGY.] The science of the economy of animals and plants; that branch of biology that deals with the relations of living organisms to their surroundings, their habits and modes of life, etc." The separate suffix '-logy' is dealt with in truly obscure etymological fashion, but suffice it to say it is also from the Greek and signifies 'word', 'discourse', or 'to speak', and from there, wisdom and knowledge.

Enough with the definitions already. But as you've probably noticed if you've read anywhere else in this book, we do tend habitually to turn to definitions simply because of the amazing truth that language shapes ideas just as much as ideas shape language. If we've got a (comparatively) new coinage, just such a one as 'ecosystem', which didn't make it into a 1983 edition of one of the world's most authoritative dictionaries, we've already worked out what words we will use to describe what we're thinking about. We'll take 'eco' because that goes with 'ecology' and all things green and environmental and of course we'll tack it on to the word 'system', which expresses order, organization and 'component interdependence' – everything working in harmony with everything else, and everything working dependent on everything else working. The knee bone, as the song goes, is connected to the thigh bone. And hear the word of the Lord.

So. The 'ecosystem' definition's key ideas are interaction; a community; living and nonliving. And if we follow 'ecology' through from the Greek, we end up with something like 'the wisdom (or knowledge) of home' (see Part I: Introduction, Why Ecology?). Which is to say, the idea and the reality of Home in many senses – including our natural habitat and also that of community – are at the heart of these powerful concepts. I think it's a coincidence that ŌM or A-U-M, the foremost Hindu mantra sound, taken traditionally to be the sound of the first ever vibration emanating from the 'divine, all-encompassing consciousness', sounds just like 'home'; it is held to be the name of God, the vibration of the Supreme, but as 'home' it is the non-physical dimension we came from and to which we will return.

We discuss the Soul World, also known as Paramdham, in Chapter 3: The Power of Endurance, Meditation 7, Stillness; and Chapter 1: The Power of Nature, Meditation 1, Silence. The point to remember at this point is that Home, the Soul World, has many properties and qualities exactly the same as those of You the Soul your Self. You are made of light, your home is made of light. You are silent, your home is silent. You are the essence of peace, your home is the essence of peace. But what our Soul World home is not is conscious, or conscient, in the sense of being aware of itself. It accommodates a vast number of individual units of consciousness – Souls – and in that sense is a community, but being 'incorporeal', ie without a body, the Souls there can't interact, give and take, even be aware of one another.

Our own internal spiritual ecosystem is made up of spiritual powers, not organisms. The forces, the abilities, the functions, of the Soul – some of which you may have in more abundance than others – are the matter at hand. We rediscover, regenerate and re-create them, bring them to a fine pitch of harmonious effectiveness. We bring them into balance.

Given the minimum undeniable benefits of being able to (even notionally) control your mind and gain at least some embryonic sense of your Self, I'd say you were doing pretty well, wouldn't you? But the next step is, once you've got the internal ecosystem more or less in shape – or at least, you know what you've got to do to get it in shape – you automatically start applying yourself to the external ecosystems. Your own fellow human beings, and what sort of shape they're in; and the world we live in, and what sort of shape that's in. Pretty dire, on both counts, no one would deny. (Except the deniers.)

As we near the end of the book it will pay us to remind ourselves why we're here. We've spent 40-odd meditations focusing on our inner Selves and the powers that make up our internal ecology and ecosystems, and how to rediscover and revive them. The point of all this effort is to change ourselves – change our Selves. To eliminate the old bad habits of thought and action and create a new consciousness – and new forms of action – which will lay the behavioral foundations for the new world which is definitely coming, willy-nilly, whether we like it or not. That's why we have Power Seeds and Magic Minutes, so that the inner transformation is carried from thought through to action, and we start to look, feel and behave like enlightened beings.

No one knows better than I do how truly, deeply difficult it is to eliminate habit; even as we plant new mental seeds, our set mental processes and the cumulative effect of repeated actions combine to exert undue power over the weak flesh, and we – I – find myself doing yet again that thing or things which I know are A. Very. Bad. Idea. This is because our actions have made our sanskars, which in turn are the drivers for thought and action. We have to go very deep to eliminate old and create new sanskars, but the first step is just about as simple as it gets: it's all about action. Do it. Or don't do it. Don't let yourself come into action when it's the wrong one; don't let yourself fail to act when it's the right one. And you know which is which.

That's the only way we'll change the world, or failing a radical overhaul, create a completely new one. Meditation is all very well, but it's action that counts. An easy synonym for 'ecosystem' is 'habitat'. It doesn't cover the whole sense of the idea, but it does a pretty good job, and I like it because it chimes with 'habit', and brings us to the memorable mantra: "changing your habits changes your habitat". And that is why your Ecology of the Soul is an ecology of powers. Because we need strength not only to cope with the daily grind, but to re-create our habits, ourselves, our Selves, and our habitat. The physical world, that is, not the Soul one. Can't have habits when you've got no body to act them out with, can you? (Apologies for ugly grammar.)

The Power of Connection Meditation 7: Home

At the hearth of the Almighty, basking in His glow.
The Ecology of the Soul, 2015

Seven powers, seven meditations each. That makes 49, 48 of which are meditations in the sense of 'guided ponderings'. This one is a proper guided meditation, a journey to take your mind on. Self hypnosis? Maybe. Maybe not. Most meditations are. Who really cares, when it engenders the consciousness you're looking for, gets you on the road to the state of being that you think will fix things, yourself – your Self – included?

Just follow the thought lines. Say them out loud if you like. It's based on the very first lesson of 'The Seven Day Course' that was being taught in Raja Yoga Centers round the world when I was a practicing member. Listen to or download the recording at www.theEcologyoftheSoul.com, and there are many more at www.brahmakumaris.org.

Physical preparation

This is not physical yoga, but being comfortable in the right position and paying attention to your breathing and muscle relaxation is a very good way to go. Your back should be as straight as possible, propped up against a wall or low chair if cross-legged doesn't suit. Tip your chin slightly down, move the sound your breath makes to the top back of your nasal passage, let it echo in your head… then – relax your tongue. A great big muscle all the way down to the bottom of your mouth. Let it go, feel it shrink, feel your mind go quiet. It stops making saliva, so you won't need to break into the quietness of your mind to swallow.

The Lines of Thought

Take as long as you like considering, delving into, plumbing the depths of, tasting, experiencing, each line.

Don't try for too long at a time when you start. Concentration fails after about 20 minutes for the new meditator, and spending longer when your mind isn't in it is counterproductive.

"I

am a Soul. An infinitesimally small pinpoint of shining, conscient light right here in the center of my forehead. This is me, sitting up here commanding this body. This body is not me. I am consciousness, but I am individual.

The smaller I can see my Self and understand my Self, the more powerful I can be. Intense. Minuscule – so small that I really have no size at all – but magically powerful.

I think.

I feel.

I calculate.

I decide.

I shine.

I am aware of my Self, able to say: this is Me.

I am also Peace.

My Peace is in my Power, and my Power is in my Peace.

But I don't own Peace, I don't own Power.

I am Peace. I am Power.

In the physical world, I drive my body in my daily doings. The Spiritual World or Soul World is the dimension from which we come and to which we return, and where there are still unborn Souls. I shift my imagination, my mental picture, and visualize Me suspended in the deepest Silence imaginable, an Ocean of Peace. I am light, I am made of light, I am in a dimension of light. It has its own unearthly gold-pink glow, but it is also suffused with the light of millions of Souls like me, suspended in their own Ocean of Peace. Or of Bliss. Or of Power.

I am Still.
I am Silent.
I am floating in an Ocean of Peace.
I am floating in an Ocean of Bliss.
I am floating in an Ocean of Power.
I am floating in an Ocean of Love.

This is a non-physical dimension, but I am aware the light, and even the light of the millions of Souls here, is somehow emanating from one particular place. I draw near, in consciousness only. Just knowing and wanting to connect draws me nearer.

This is the eternal, immortal, incorporeal, karmateet Supreme Soul. God, Shiva, Baba, the Lord, whichever of the many multiples of names you have for Him. He is a Soul. Incredibly, He has no size either, like us. But His light, His power, His bliss, His very force of being are of a different order of magnitude from us 'ordinary' human Souls. In this Soul is the knowledge of every human Soul's karma. He knows your story better than you do, thousands of years either side of your current birth in the cycle. Nothing surprises Him; He does not judge. Karma is enough when it comes to getting your just desserts. This is God the Father, God the Mother, God the Holy Ghost. Connect. Merge (you will come out again). Link. Yoke. Make the connection just by thinking about it. Simply plug in. Feel His power, love, peace, bliss, flowing into and through your being."

Take a while coming back. If you've had a good one, you'll probably find you sort of croak when you 'come into sound' again. It makes you realize how far away from the physical you have been. Congratulations. You've just had Yoga – of the Raja kind.

The Power of Connection Practice 1: Plant a Power Seed Every Day

Power Seeds are mental devices, thought triggers to generate Soul Consciousness, and hence change your actions. They are a bit like the Zen 'kōan' (for instance the idea of the sound of one hand clapping) that kick your mind out of gear and raise the level of your awareness.

Using Power Seeds, you grow a new garden of consciousness. See your mind as a garden, or at least a patch of fertile soil. Thoughts and feelings grow in it, like plants. Your mind is a riot of tangled and intertwined mental vegetation, much of it good and useful and most of it neither good nor useful. So it's a pleasant surprise that you don't have to struggle with the weeds. All you have to do is plant your mental plot with new seeds – 'Power Seeds' – which grow into thought, attitude, feeling, and action. Which feeds back and creates new thought and feeling. You have created a new mental and spiritual garden – and a new framework for your behavior.

If you really focus all the innate power of your calmed, stilled mind on the Power Seed you choose for 60 full seconds, that thought pattern will repeat and recur throughout the day, accumulating much more than a single minute of your mental activity. It's meditation in action, because the meditation is about action.

Plant one of the mental Power Seeds that appear on the following pages. The Seven Powers, Power Seeds and the Magic Minute section of Part I, the Introduction gives the full explanation of how to prepare the mental and spiritual ground for your new garden; Part III gives you a whole range of Power Seeds to suit your circumstances. Ultimately, as your Self knowledge increases, you will be creating and planting your own.

The mind is still, one-pointed or concentrated, but individual awareness remains present.

Yoga is union.
Yoga is communion.
Yoga is communication.
Yoga is connection.
Yoga is concentration.

What's inside your Self is not the full story. Why do we continue to strive, to plumb ever-greater depths of peace, bliss and silence? There is more, a greater power than our own that we can tap into. One that is outside our Selves, not omnipresent.

Our desire – and our inherent, soul-remembered experience – is for connection to the Source that never falters, tires, loses its way or its energy.

If you're filled with uplifting spiritual energy, the automatic response is to give it – share it. The higher you become, the more your very existence becomes a gift.

See people as Souls, each living in their own body's forehead, and each with their own karma.

Your consciousness is creating an atmosphere, a vibration, to which other Souls respond.

Gratitude is not so much a matter of thanking something or someone, more a matter of respecting your own luck.

Your gifts are not yours. If you don't give them or give with them, they will fade. And the more you give them and give with them, the more powerful and abundant they will be.

"I am a Soul, You are the Supreme Soul."
Connect.
Give yourself.
Get lost.

Neither give nor take sorrow.

Receiving = gratitude. To receive is to be open to transmissions.

How tuned are your antennae to subtle atmospheres and vibrations – from other Souls, and most importantly, the Supreme Soul, whose transmitter is always on?

Experience an unlimited ocean of peace, love, bliss and power, all contained within a living point of consciousness of no size.

Share your knowledge.
Gain more knowledge.
Share your love.
Gain more love.
Share your peace.
Gain more peace.

If you can open your Self enough to receive from your Self then you can open to God, who trusts you to receive.

Can you trust yourself to go this high? Do you feel balanced, safe?
Trust your Self, rather than yourself.

Paramount in creating and maintaining the open state of mind that allows you to receive is gratitude. Gratitude first, receive after.

Count your blessings.

You are made of light.
Your Home is made of light.
You are silent.
Your Home is silent.
You are the essence of peace.
Your Home is the essence of peace.

Change your habits; change your Habitat.

I am a Soul. An infinitesimally small pinpoint of shining, conscient light right here in the center of my forehead. This is me, sitting up here commanding this body. This body is not me. I am consciousness, but I am individual.

I am Peace.
I am Power.
I am Light.
I am Love.

The Power of Connection Practice 2: Yoga Seeds – Salute to the Sun (Surya Namaskar)

Position 7: Child Pose (Balasana)

The Salute to the Sun, like most things in Yoga, has many variations. The one we use here consists of seven 'asanas', to use the Sanskrit name for positions, done in a 12-step sequence: Prayer, Mountain, Forward Bend, Forward Lunge (one leg forward), Plank, Dog, Cobra, Child, Forward Lunge (the other leg forward), Forward Bend, Mountain, Prayer.

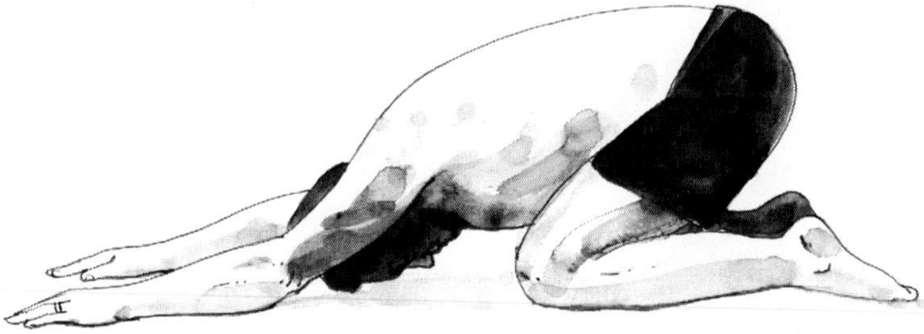

The main function of Child pose, Balasana, is rest and relaxation. It's an intermediary pose, with its own technique and benefits, but usually used, like Uttanasana, the forward bend, to refresh and retrench after some strenuous poses and before the next batch. You've just come from Plank (Chaturanga Dandasana), Dog (Adho Mukha Svanasana) and Cobra (Bhujangasana), which have held your back as straight and as firm as a girder, and then stretched, curved and elongated it in both directions. So it needs a bit of a rest, as do you.

From Bhujangasana, on the outbreath pull up to your knees and raise your buttocks and push them up and back, then subside, letting your chest and front portion relax down on to your upper thighs. It pays to suck your stomach in, then sort of settle your behind as far back towards your heels as it will go.

Your ideal is for it to be resting on your heels. (Let your stomach go once you have made this adjustment.) Keep your hands where they are, so your arms remain stretched out in front of you. Adjust yourself so your breathing is regular and unhindered and you feel comfortable laid along your upper thighs. If your tummy and front parts bulge in inconvenient places, set your thighs apart somewhat so the bulging bits can settle in. As you get comfortable, remember the breathing in the top back part of your nasal passage. Your toes are pointing backwards, your feet resting on their tops.

Because you're sort of scrunched up like this, getting a stretch seems much further away than it does in pretty much any of the other positions. Your arms, laid out in front of you as they are, will keep your upper body open; let go your spine in the neck, and particularly the area at the top of your back between your shoulder blades. Your forehead is resting on the mat. Because most of your weight is supported, you'll only feel a stretch or relaxation coming through if you really let go. You feel your body slumping down further on to your thighs, but don't tip forward or back; remain with your weight balanced in the center.

Focus on your spine, and on each outbreath let it elongate in two directions, towards your arms at the front and your feet at the back. Your neck stretches forward; your behind drops back. You can't push to make this happen; it will only happen as you let go. Your body goes soft and allows this stretch. When a teacher helps with this pose, the usual trick is to place one hand on the student's upper spine near the neck and the other on the lower back near the buttocks, and gently press both ways to elongate the spine in opposite directions. You really feel it when it's done this way, and it gives you a sense of what you're trying to achieve.

The variation of this pose is to bring the hands up alongside the body, laying them on the mat with palms up and fingers pointing backwards. But not until you've done the stretch with arms out in front. Arms to the side increase the sensation of elongation and relaxation, but you have to be soft and relaxed first, otherwise your head will be uncomfortable and possibly restrict your neck and thus your breathing. The main thing, as in all yoga positions, is to open out and let go as a way of getting the stretch.

Part III

Power Seeds

More mini-meditations for daily action

Plant one a day, give it the Magic Minute of 60 seconds of deep thought – more if you can manage – then let it repeat on you through the day.

Power Seeds are mental devices, thought triggers to create, enhance or encourage Soul Consciousness, and hence change your actions. See The Seven Powers, Power Seeds and the Magic Minute in Part I, the Introduction for a general explanation, and specific examples related to specific powers at the end of each power chapter. Here is a random collection to get you going. Create your own and if you feel generous, contribute to our community by uploading them to www.theEcologyoftheSoul.com.

Give it a minute, or better, two. Use one-half of the time to contemplate the idea. Use the other half (30 seconds or 1 minute) to visualize today's action. When the time comes, that pre-programming will kick in.

Ecology = The Wisdom of Home
The Ecology of the Soul.
The Ecology of Behavior.
The Inner Balance.

Accuracy. Painstaking accuracy frees, relieves. 'Just do it any old how' leads to bondage, condemning you and others to waste time and energy dealing with it or fixing it.

Acquire: Decquire.

Ask for help. Offer help.

Attention. Pay attention. Observe accurately, painstakingly, intelligently. Immerse yourself in the task at hand. The more focused you are, the more free you are. With complete attention comes complete liberation.

Balance. A good meditation is a perfect balance. You sit on a wellspring, a source of power. You balance on top of it, like a ping pong ball on a jet of water. Only not like a ping pong ball, because in that balance is stillness, silence, peace. You aren't bobbing about like the ping pong ball; you are floating on a cushion of glow. Perfect balance.

Be angry. Be kind.

Be bothered. Don't bother.

Be greedy. Be abstemious.

Be grounded. Be light on your feet.

Be mean. Be generous.

Be polite. Be blunt.

Be unselfish. Be selfish.

Beauty: Bring beauty to your practice. Practice beauty.

Behavior: Habit is involuntary action. Mental habits create physical habit. To rid yourself of habits you don't want, don't struggle to delete them. Just create new ones.

Behavior: Your Habits create your Habitat.

Behavior: In a state of calm receptivity, ponder your day; upcoming or finished. "Show me where I will need to be..." Or, "Show me where I could have been..." Create a positive frame of mind around behavior that you may be or have been dissatisfied with; swapping out the negative for the positive. Positive creates positive, negative creates negative; as your mind changes, so does your behavior. Reinforce.

Breathe. Listen to your breath. It's your own energy. It's not You; You are the one listening, the one with awareness.

Build a fire inside. Increase your own energy-generating capacity.

Care about the surface, the way it looks. Care about what's inside, underneath.

Care. Be free of care.

Commitment strengthens, deepens your resolve. It takes courage to do, and gives courage in the doing.

Committed: Be committed, attached, free. Be uncommitted, detached, free.

Conscient beings have Conscience. And **a** Conscience. And

Con-science, and Consciousness. Even Conscience-ness?

Conscient. It's a tricky word. Dictionaries don't tend to have it. It's You the Soul, having knowledge – being aware – of your Self. Consciousness, with knowledge of itself.

Conscious, subconscious, unconscious.

Conscious, subconscious, superconscious.

Consciousness. Conscience. Conscient-ness.

Create a beautiful mind.

Create colloquy, or co-loquy.

Creation/Inspiration. Where did that come from? Was it deep down inside you already, or is it a gift from outside?

Creation is re-creation. Creation of the Self is re-creation. And recreational.

Creativity: Everyone is creative. Everyone has creativity. What's yours?

Creativity: What is your strong suit? Which private part of your world holds your true creativity?

Creativity: You the Soul, being no more nor less than energy, are incapable of being destroyed and therefore of being created. But self exploration, acquiring self knowledge, is the ultimate creative act. You create your Self.

Cut it like a surgeon.

Design yourself. Redesign yourself.

Destiny: 1) You can make it because the only one responsible for your fortune is you. 2) You can't make it because it is already made.

Do it now. Don't do it now. Do it in the here and now.

Do it slowly. Do it fast.

Do it watchfully.

Eating makes you. You are what you eat. Eat how you want to be.

Energy is matter and matter is energy, but right deep down at the heart of it, matter is nothing. Matter is no matter, in other words. When you go subatomic, down among the charm quarks and the neutrinos, there is much more nothing than something. Just a few very very ***very*** tiny bits of energy fizzing round in some very very large (relatively) spaces. Inner space, in fact.

Energy is power. You are energy, but energy is not you. Are you breathing? Then you are making and using energy. Are you thinking? Feeling? Dreaming? It's energy. Our personal energy crisis is that we are disconnected from our internal power. To connect, go inside.

Energy is power. Your body is physical energy, 'You' are the soul, non-physical energy, controlling both. They are inter-twined and mixed, influencing each other.

Energy: Everything material is always energy, always in

movement. The natural state of you the Soul, the single infinitesimal pinpoint of light, of conscient energy, is stillness. Still energy, but giving off vibrations.

Energy: It's the energy conservation/generation thing. Mental energy. Which is after all another way of describing thought. Create and conserve energy; reduce, dissipate or block it. It's up to You.

Energy: A double whammy. At the same time as your new awareness allows you to connect to the 'dumb life' flow of subtle energy, you are fully experiencing the unique, individual node of 'smart consciousness' energy that is You.

Focus on focus. Bring the lens of self awareness to bear to concentrate your power.

Forgive yourself. Push yourself.

Hang on. Let go.

Hang on to it tight. Let it go loose.

Have a heart. Love is at your center, just as Anahata the heart chakra is at the center of your spiritual and physical being. It is not You – You are sitting in the center of your body's forehead. The heart is the hub, the portal, for the flow of energy, both spiritual and physical.

Joy. Delight. Fun. We are beings made of joy, put here to feel delight, to feel high. Fun-damentally, fun is one of the building blocks of our being. Try it; if you go into the still and silent inner space, you come out of it with a grin, feeling euphoric, full of joy. That joy is the energy that is You.

Another name for it is Love.

Light: You are light. To feel light is to feel carefree. When you feel yourself as light, you are enlightened. You enter delight. This is enlightenment.

Listen inside. Listen outside.

Listen to yourself. Listen to others.

Listen while you do it. Watch while you do it.

Love: Another name for energy.

Love your Self. You are a pinpoint of conscient energy driving a mass of material energy. You are a miracle. Enjoy it. Love it.

Love yourself. Not with arrogance or ego, but with quiet understanding. Know your strengths and your weaknesses, but be gentle to yourself. Hate the sin, love the sinner, in this case your Self. You're on a journey, it isn't going to happen overnight. Know the difference between loving yourself and loving your Self.

Male female: Think masculine, think feminine. Father Time, Mother Nature.

Matter is energy, and energy vibrates. It fizzes, it hums, though not necessarily in a sonic sense. Like it or not, you – in both your non-physical, soul energy sense, and in your material sense – are vibrating, and you are giving off vibrations. So why not vibrate at as high a frequency as possible?

Mind creates action: Action creates mind.

Mind: 0% mental waste = 100% mental power. Go to 100% mental efficiency in one fell swoop for your Magic Minute, or two minutes. Then increase the number.

Mind: A training program. Train your mind, train your eye. Acquire a good eye for beauty. Transfer it to your mind's eye. Just look for the beauty.

Mind: Emotions happen in the mind. Thoughts happen in the mind. Apparently you are able to know what you are thinking by checking out how you are feeling. Or is it to know what you are feeling by checking out what you are thinking? Thoughts create emotions. But emotions also create thoughts. When it comes down to it, the place you want to get to is a place where neither thoughts nor emotions are active or engaged. Then when you come back, see what it has done to your thinking and feeling.

Mind: Focus. Focus the power of the mind. Redefine the mind to yourself, your Self; instead of viewing it as the wayward nuisance it usually is, see it now as a source of strength, a great untapped wellspring of energy. Thoughts, feelings and actions all spring from the mind. Focus it, and it – and you – become powerful.

Mind. Mine diamonds, dive for pearls. Mind the diamonds, mind the pearls.

Mind. My mind is not my Self? How can that be? Aha. It is one PART of Me. OK. So what is the whole Me, the absolutely, totally, definitive Me? The Me with all its parts included? And what are those parts?

Mindfulness: Make it with craft.

Mindfulness: 'God is in the detail', duh. The point being that deepest attention on the smallest thing carries you directly to the transcendental. What are you transcending? The world of physical matter, of detail. By using detail you transcend detail and break through to a world of being, of pure consciousness, of pure energy.

Mindfulness: Detail. God is in the detail, we heard that already. Detail vs the big picture. What is the value of detail? What is the value of being pin sharp about every tiny little thing? It's mindfulness again. Paying attention in the here and now, because wherever our minds want to take us, we only ever are in the here and now.

Mindfulness: A sailor reads the sea, no picture bigger. The wind, the weather, the waves, the currents, where we're going and where we're being taken. But on and below deck, detail rules. The right knot for the right rope for the right task; the specific tool for the specific job, the specific place it's kept. Is your detail as important as your big picture? Do they balance out? Are they part of the same awareness, or do they fight?

Mindfulness: Craft is care. Do it mindfully. Do it with mindedness.

Mindfulness: What is the danger of detail? Failing to see the big picture. What is seeing the big picture? Seeing how what you're doing fits into other big stuff – heaven and earth, the clouds, the sun, the moon, the sea and the stars; the fate of humanity; the meaning of love.

Mindfulness/Mindlessness: Completely mindful attention on

the present, the here and now, can lead to the desired and desirable state of mindlessness. When thoughts slow down and even stop, interference in your process of becoming conscious of your consciousness stops. You break through into 'conscious consciousness'. Soul consciousness.

The Natural World: Reconnect with the natural world, right? Desirable. How are we all going to do that, living in megacities? Simple. As a physical/spiritual organism, you are part of the natural world. An organism with consciousness, which makes you: a) incredibly powerful; and b) equally responsible. You're sitting on top of it. You are it.

Nature: We are Nature but Nature is not Us.

Originality: Origin. Where did that original idea come from? Is it the sudden flowering of a completely random inspiration, a bolt from the blue straight into your consciousness, or is it the culmination and distillation of an array of thoughts, observations and experiences, some of them yours, some of them from others? Is it a breakthrough in something you've been working on, or did it just flow in unannounced? There is no such thing as unconnected originality. It all comes from your own origin. In silence, track back to that.

Pain: What can we learn from it?

Passion and dispassion: Passionate and dispassionate. Connected and detached. Which is when? Can they be at the same time? Do they feed or fight each other?

Passion means transcendence, but it also means pain. Suffering. It means the height of delight and torment at the same time. It means committing yourself to something that somewhere deep down you know is going to hurt. Pain can sharpen your awareness but it can also lock it out and demand attention only on itself. Be careful to make pain your teacher, not your keeper.

Passion: Everyone is passionate. Everyone has a passion. What's yours?

Peace of mind: The peace of God which passeth all understanding. I'll give you a piece of my mind. Is it the peaceful piece? I'll give you a peace of my mind.

Peace versus power: Are they two sides of the same coin? Surely they're inimical? How is it that a peaceful state is a powerful state? Or, more to the point, how is a powerful state a peaceful one?

Peace: 'Hold your peace.' 'Say your piece.'

Person and personality: With a quiet mind, the person is quiet. 'Person' and personality are chatter, the product of a busy mind. When the mind is quiet, 'personality' disappears and the floating glow takes over. The glowing float. The person that is you is dormant, in favor of the consciousness that is You. Underneath the chatter, the True You abides. In silence.

Play it like a pianist. Play it like a pro. With precision.

Prān is flow and Atma is glow. Physical/subtle energy, the life force, the Ch'i or the Prān, is always moving, always flowing, which implies going from one place to another. The energy of the pure, peaceful, powerful, silent Soul is still. It is not only still, it is stillness. Silence doesn't just mean beyond sound, it means beyond the multifarious inner mental activity of the mind. The more of that chatter you shut down, the more you let go, the more you connect to the pure spiritual energy that is You.

Prān: What can we learn from it? It flows in your veins, your internal ecosystem, your brain, your mind, your heart. Not 'Your soul' because: a) *You* are the Soul, it isn't 'yours'; and b) it's the spiritual energy observing the subtle/physical.

Problems: Identify a 'problem'. Without being cast into a mold of negativity, focus on a specific issue – with yourself and your own state of being, your own behavior, your own thoughts or habits, or with how you are responding to what the world is giving you – and generate a Power Seed that fits. Push out the old thought pattern by planting a new one.

Procreation, reproduction: What powerful process is that? We know how the physical part works; what about the Soul part, the mental and spiritual?

Pull hard. Let go. Pull hard here, let go there. To stretch in mind or body, you must let go.

Responsibility: Whatever it is, take it. "Don't blame, don't complain. Take responsibility." (Jack Canfield)

Root your Self. Be the root, be the branch. Even be the leaf. But not until you're sure you have rooted your Self.

Silence: Are you 'on' all the time? Do you fear silence? Do you fear solitude?

Silence is a live state. Having the power of silence creates power. Living in silence, even for a tiny time, regenerates the

Soul, because that's where You come from. Go deep into silence, as deep as you can in 60 seconds. It may take longer.

Silence: Death. Of course it's death. Look at the Soul World. There we all are in our non-dimensional dimension, non-physical, incorporeal beings. No body. Soul without body = dead body, right? Yep, but not dead Soul. No such thing. Can't happen. You are eternal, indestructible.

Silence: Death. You seek the silence, the stillness of mind that, from the inside at any rate, looks and feels like death. Is 'mindlessness' death, or real life, pure life? Can you get 'mindless', anyway? If you reduce thought to a minimum, the goldfish slowly circling the bowl – one small thought every few breaths – is that mind ceasing to function, or is it functioning better than usual? Not wasting its power on trivia. More powerful, more focused.

Silence: Solitude. Your Magic Minute is a minute of solitude, of your journey alone into your own inner space. Not the solitude of loneliness, but the solitude of aloneness, of solo awareness. Often people are afraid of silence and of solitude because there are no supports, no distractions. It's true. You are alone with Your Self, and this can be scary. Mostly because Your Self is someone you haven't met before.

Sin: Sit down and think about Sin for a minute. Only 60 seconds, it won't hurt. What does it really mean? It means being untrue to your Self and to nature, and to the nature of your Self. Your Self-Nature. All the pain, harm and suffering in the world's history, spinning down to the present moment, arises from people getting themselves wrong. Their Selves wrong. And misunderstanding their place in nature. Because nature is after all bigger than us, right? If it wanted, it could wipe us out in a trice. But it doesn't need to. We are doing that to ourselves.

Soul Consciousness: Focus on the spot in the center of your forehead that ancient wisdom calls the seat of the Soul. It's why Indian traditions, both religious and material, put a mark in the center of the forehead. Create the image of You, the pinpoint of light, sitting there in your forehead controlling this vast, enormous, gargantuan physical body. Separate your Self from your physical self. Become aware of your Self as a being of light, power and peace. You are light. Shine.

Soul: The Soul is light. It glows but it is still.

Soul: You the Soul are conscient, self aware. You are an indivisible, unique unit of consciousness. You are a pinpoint of light.

State of mind: A state of mind is only ever a moment. It's momentary.

Switch on: Switch off.

Take a lesson from the world's poor. Are you throwing away something that those with nothing would kill for?

Take care of yourself: Take care of others.

Take time. Make time. Lose time. Lose your sense of time.

Talk: Don't talk to the trees. Talk to your Self.

The power to change. The power to accept what can't be changed. The wisdom to know which to use when.

Things relax, people fidget. Money talks, people mumble.

Thoughts and feelings: Thought creates feeling creates action. Emotions are seated in the mind. What are you feeling? If you know what you're feeling, you know what you're thinking. Change your thinking, your feelings change, your actions change.

Thoughts control/affect the body – temperature, heart rate, blood pressure, breathing rate, muscle tension, sweat.

Thoughts control behavior. Negative thoughts about yourself create negative – or at least, undesirable – behavior.

Thoughts, like magazines and newspapers, come in words and pictures. You can't have thought without words and pictures in your mind, or words and pictures without thought. Your Magic Minute is the time you give yourself to jump over the fence and play in the field without words and pictures, without thoughts. First the words, then the pictures, slow down and finally stop. Amazing how refreshing it is.

Thoughts: You think thoughts. But you can also listen to or watch the thinker, as Eckhart Tolle says. Thoughts are chatter. Listen to yourself chattering, and then shut up a minute. Now listen to yourself being silent. And then realize that it's not the true You that's thinking, because You are the one that is watching or listening, right? Of course you can't stop thought without a lot of practice. Don't force it, never force it, because forcing it is thinking it. You can slow it right down, still it. And then find you have distilled it.

Thoughts: Do you think your thoughts, or do your thoughts think you? "I can't help thinking"... but you can. Your thoughts are in control of you? That's madness. You are thinking those thoughts, right? So what is this, a runaway train? The thoughts control the thinker? The most difficult thing about controlling your own thoughts – deciding which ones to have and which ones to reject, to 'unthink' – is realizing and deciding you can do it. Once you are over that hurdle, the task is clear. And this in itself is a Power Seed you have just planted.

Thoughts. You create them. And they create you. Thankfully, the top level, everyday, exterior, 'normal' you. Control them by working from the deep down level of the true You. They are not You, but they can work for you. Or against You.

Tread lightly. Lighten up.

Vision: Visualize. Take vivid pictures of your powerful Self and project them on your own mental screen.

Walk like a cat.

Walk like a dancer.

Walk like a lion.

Walk slowly.

War is nature: Nature is war.

www.theEcologyoftheSoul.com

BOOKS

O is a symbol of the world, of oneness and unity; this eye represents knowledge and insight. We publish titles on general spirituality and living a spiritual life. We aim to inform and help you on your own journey in this life.